THE SIXTH *TIMES*
BOOK OF BEST SERMONS

The Sixth *Times*
Book of Best Sermons

Edited and Introduced by
RUTH GLEDHILL

Foreword by
CANON MICHAEL SAWARD

CONTINUUM
London and New York

Continuum

The Tower Building
11 York Road
London SE1 7NX

370 Lexington Avenue
New York
NY 10017-6503

www.continuumbooks.com

First published 2001

British Library Cataloguing-in-Publication Data
A catalogue record for this book is available from the British Library.

ISBN 0-8264-4983-2

Typeset by Kenneth Burnley, Wirral, Cheshire.
Printed and bound in Great Britain by Creative Print and Design, Wales.

Contents

Foreword by *Canon Michael Saward*   vii

Introduction by *Ruth Gledhill*   xi

Acknowledgements   xiv

BIBLICAL PARABLES

STRANGE FIRES   *Albert Friedlander*   2

ASKING   *John Whittaker*   7

THE UNLIKELY HELPER   *David Tyrrell*   11

THE BRYLCREEM BOY   *Michael Topliss*   15

LAST OF ALL, AS TO ONE UNTIMELY BORN, HE APPEARED
ALSO TO ME   *Dominic Barrington*   23

153 FISH – OUR FIRST MEAL!   *Richard Dormandy*   28

REBEKAH   *Jo Bailey Wells*   34

SALVATION – WITH AN EXCLAMATION MARK!   *Ian Knox*   39

JOHN 12:24   *Norman Price*   43

SHARING TRUTH IN THE MARKET-PLACE   *Michael Botting*   48

JESUS WASHES THE DISCIPLES' FEET   *Barbara Glasson*   55

BELIEVING WITHOUT NEEDING TO SEE   *George Hore*   59

SOCIAL IMPROVEMENT

JOHN 2:13–25   *Graham Gillman*   64

THE GLORY OF GOD   *James Cocke*   68

BEING PART OF THE STORY   *Julian Cummins*   72

THE KEYS TO THE KINGDOM   *John Mills*   77

INCLUDE PEOPLE, DON'T EXCLUDE THEM!   *John Littleton*   82

YOU WERE STRANGERS   *Margaret Hay*   89

A LEPER CAME TO JESUS . . .   *Martin Boland*   95

HONOUR YOUR FATHER AND YOUR MOTHER   *Steven Katz*   100

CONTENTS

THE RELATIONSHIP WITH GOD

THOU DIDST FORM MY INMOST PARTS *Lesley Perry* 106

WHAT KIND OF RELIGION IS CHRISTIANITY? *Bill Wilson* 112

BIRTH AND DEATH AT CHRISTMAS *Gordon Giles* 116

A SERMON ON DEPRESSION *John Young* 121

HOW TO HOLD ON TO HOPE *Jayne Ozanne* 127

THE HOLOCAUST AND DIVINE SUFFERING *Dan Cohn-Sherbok* 137

JESUS' LAST WORDS: HOPE IN TIMES OF DESPAIR *Ken Paterson* 142

ENOUGH OF STUNNED SILENCE *Hugh-Nigel Sheehan* 148

TO LIGHT, OR NOT TO LIGHT? *Jonathan Wittenberg* 155

FEARFUL SYMMETRY *Neil Fairlamb* 160

THE DEATH OF GOD *Sir Alan Goodison* 166

EREV ROSH HASHANAH *Sheila Shulman* 172

SACRIFICE *Ronald Creighton-Jobe* 182

PENTECOST *David Hatton* 185

CONTENTMENT

LESSONS IN CONTENTMENT *Harry Young* 194

IF WE GET IT WRONG *Geoffrey Parkinson* 198

SERMON FOR TRINITY SUNDAY *Anthony Bird* 204

STRENGTH TO THE WEARY *Stephen Hance* 209

HARSH WORDS IN THE TEMPLE *Lawrie Adam* 213

FREE AT LAST *Rabbi Shmuley Boteach* 217

The Judges 224

Foreword

MICHAEL SAWARD

IS THERE ANYWHERE that I can go to church?' I asked the Army chaplain, three days after my arrival in Accra (in what was then called 'The Gold Coast'). Did I want to go to one or help in one, he enquired. I assumed that since I was a young subaltern, just turned nineteen, he meant run a Sunday School class. 'I don't mind helping,' I said. 'Right', he responded, 'you've got one'. And that is how I was handed a church of African soldiers, their wives and families, in a wooden hut, on the edge of the bush, and told to get on with preaching, Sunday by Sunday. It was July 1951 and I still have the sermons that I preached for the next fourteen months.

This morning, almost fifty years later, I fished out the very first one (of which I have no memory whatever) and found it was all about Daniel and the lions' den. I retold the story and asked my hearers whether they tried to be Christians without ever admitting to it or whether, like Daniel, they refused to hide their faith whatever the consequences.

Well, fifty years later I can see that it was lacking in many areas, a teenager's first attempt, but I am encouraged to rediscover that it was biblical, crisp, and had its focus on Christ and his demands. It required a response. I've heard many worse sermons from bishops and theological professors in the intervening half-century.

In October 1994 *The Times* launched its Preacher of the Year Award, whose aim was 'to encourage better preaching and to bring to wider notice those who possess the rare talent to rouse, touch and guide their flocks, not just through fire and brimstone but with compassion and topicality.' I was, at the time, amused. Where on earth in Britain were they expecting, at the end of the twentieth century, to find 'fire and brimstone' in the pulpit? Britain isn't exactly the American Bible belt.

This book, therefore, claims to offer some of the best sermons on offer in the year of the millennium. It is a slight irony, on this occasion, to have Jewish sermons in such a year since presumably the date does not provide many exciting resonances for the synagogue in what is now, for them, the year 5671. Be that as it may, 2000 has for most people in the United Kingdom, in spite of the unhappy experiences of Dome, Eye, and Wobbly Bridge, had some reference, however marginal or miscalculated some of the elements, to a carpenter from Nazareth in Galilee.

But why 'sermons?' Sermons are not exactly flavour of the year, are they? Back in 1994, Ruth Gledhill, *The Times* Religion Correspondent, quoted an about-to-be-published paper on the subject and began her piece by saying that 'preaching is dead and . . . is the most effective emptier of churches there is'. There were, it seems, 'a few wonderful exceptions' but in general they were 'dull, uninspiring, going nowhere, reflecting little stout belief, startling hardly anyone, converting few'.

Being a naturally 'diffident, modest, and shy' man ('ho, ho, ho' I hear my associates say) I was pleased to find part of one of my sermons quoted in the very same article. And, no, they didn't even shortlist me, so it's quite a flattering experience to have been asked to write this Preface six years later. Since I am at the point of retirement, I suppose it's the equivalent of an MBE or something of the kind. Presumably someone on *The Times* thinks: 'That should shut him up for a bit!'

So, I repeat, why sermons? In an age of two-minute soundbites (except for professional talkers like Jeremy Paxman) how can anyone hope to get a responsive audience for anything other than the verbal equivalent of a McDonald's cheeseburger? Junk sermons for a junkie generation? It's all too easy to blame the preacher. Why not blame the pew? Six hundred years ago a Dominican, John Bromyard, grumbled that the English were the worst sermons-goers in the world. 'There is', he complained, 'scarcely to be found a Christian nation that so rarely and unwillingly hears the Word of God'. So what's new?

Lord Habgood, the former Archbishop of York, chimed in more recently on the same note. 'How can people,' he asked, 'be expected to take Christianity seriously if all they know of it is a garbled mish-mash of irrelevant stories from the past?' He went on to maintain that 'widespread ignorance of the Christian faith among churchgoers as well as non-churchgoers is massive and alarming.' Most people get their understanding of Christianity and the churches not from preachers and worship but from the mass-media, which, as Harvey Cox put it, offer 'behaviour models directly contradicting the life-goals Christianity celebrates'.

All right. I'm a cleric and a preacher so you can call me biased. I'm certainly not complacent about a good deal of today's preaching but consider this: clergy are horrendously busy, have little study time, and, however sad it may be, are hardly going to be enthusiastic about detailed and careful sermon preparation if they know that even their own congregations despise preaching and would love to see it reduced to the minimum. Donald Coggan, a great preacher and a godly archbishop, put the consequence succinctly; 'Sermonettes make Christianettes'. Of course we clergy need to sweat to put the essentials of the faith into a concise and demanding format but as J. H. Jowett, the great Congregational preacher, once put it, 'you cannot drop the big themes and create great saints'. People remember John Wesley but forget that, as he once said, 'I offered Christ to the people for three hours'. Years later, Ruskin defined a sermon as 'thirty minutes in which to raise the dead'. It's a long time since I've heard a thirty-minute sermon. The old witticism that 'if you don't strike oil after ten minutes, stop boring' may have a powerful element of truth in it but nowadays (as in *The Times*' rules for Preacher of the Year) you've only got ten minutes. Last year's winner, incidentally, went on for fourteen minutes in the final, broke the explicitly-stated rule and romped home.

Which brings me to the question, 'what actually is a sermon supposed to be?' Phillips Brooks argued that 'a sermon is a piece of bread to be eaten, and not a work of art to be enjoyed'. Kierkegaard agreed with him; 'A congregation is not an audience for whose special benefit minister and choir give a performance.' There are not a few Christians, clergy and laity, who are uneasy about the Preacher of the Year competition precisely because they hold it improper for a sermon to be regarded as a 'performance' open to the same treatment as a play or a film for which theatre and cinema critics provide a judgement. That, I suspect, is too purist a view but the point is not unreasonable. If this is the Word of God being proclaimed then there is a real sense in which the hearer should be on his knees not his bottom, under judgement not dispensing it. Preaching as Lesslie Newbigin described it is 'the announcement of God's Kingdom, and conversion is conversion to his service. There can be nothing bigger or more relevant that that'. When the preacher forgets that, or ducks its challenge, he (or she) is failing in one of the most essential parts of their calling.

The old Franciscan, Bernardino of Siena, put the point most starkly. 'If you can only either hear Mass or the sermon, let the Mass go. There is less peril for your soul in not hearing the Mass than in not hearing the sermon.' In an age in which the major Christian churches are putting most of their eggs in the liturgical, eucharistic basket and diminishing the place of preaching, Bernardino needs to be remembered. One of the greatest preachers of the early twentieth century, P. T. Forsyth, held much the same view. 'With its preaching,' he declared, 'Christianity stands or falls.' The Scottish Presbyterian, Tom Allan, added that this statement was not, he thought, 'merely pulpit rhetoric' but a 'precise and careful statement of fact'.

But I've left one very important matter out. What are the judging criteria for a sermon? Is it merely a matter of who best grabs the audience and holds their attention? If that is the case, then all we're doing is judging technique. But what about content? Is this 'Preacher of the Year' or merely 'Persuasive Speaker of the Year'? Go for the latter and it's merely 'Who's the most exciting personality?' Would Adolf Hitler have won the award? Surely 'preaching' must relate to what is said as well as 'How does it grab me?'

When ten years ago I was appointed to be a Canon at St Paul's Cathedral I reminded the congregation on my first Sunday of one of the most famous of my canonical predecessors, the Victorian, Henry Liddon. It was said of him that his 'voice rang on, like a trumpet, telling of righteousness and temperance and judgement, preaching ever and always, with personal passion of belief, of Jesus Christ, and him crucified'. It's my goal, I told them, to be like that. That's what I understand preaching to be.

'The preacher's business,' said the great James Denney, 'is not to be original but to be true. If he has the gospel to preach, truth with saving virtue in it, he cannot repeat it too often.' What preacher could ask for more?

Introduction

RUTH GLEDHILL
Religion Correspondent of *The Times*

FEW PLATFORMS give one person the opportunity to speak for ten or fifteen minutes at a time without interruption, and usually without opportunity for questions or feedback from the listeners either. The Final of the Preacher of the Year Award must be one of even fewer platforms where six people in a row are permitted to do this. Wise preachers know how to use the privileges of the pulpit well. I attended one church service recently in a parish of a Tractarian tradition that had been beset by some divisive internal difficulties. The preacher spoke on the place of music in worship. But subtle references to harmonies, discord and political intrigue made it clear that there was more than one level to this talk. It was long, beautifully phrased and impossible not to listen to, the kind of sermon that makes the listener feel uplifted but at the same time slightly uncomfortable. I kept wishing he would finish. Every so often it seemed as though he would, but then would come another point, and then a counter-point. After nearly half an hour, he finally said: 'This is the end of the sermon.' You could hear a collective sigh whisper through the worthies of this parish, and the bishop, who happened to be present, even put his mitre on. But the preacher, who I predict will go far in the Church of England, might have finished preaching, but he had by no means finished talking. He proceeded with an extended finale, an anecdote about whether the best religious music should be heard in churches or, in the other venues where it is commonly heard, in concert halls. This sermon was one of the few that are truly unforgettable. It was pertinent but, in a delicate situation, not offensive. But even wise preachers can be caught short sometimes. I was told a story recently of a clergyman who was standing in for the vicar at a church. After the service, he was collared by an angry member of the congregation who demanded to know who had passed on such intimate information about him. In fact, the priest had not even written the sermon for that service, he had simply pulled an old one from his notebook written many moons before.

But to return to the theme of the first preacher, there is possibly an argument that what we do in the Preacher of the Year Award, in taking the sermon out of the context of a single act of worship and placing it in a competitive setting, albeit still in a place of worship, is equivalent to playing a Mass by Mozart in a concert hall: the work remains overpoweringly beautiful but, deprived of its religious setting, loses something of its spiritual significance. Some preachers who have been nominated for the Award have declined to enter a sermon on these or similar grounds. This is, to me, a pity because placing a sermon in an undeniably secular context helps bring religion to an audience that might not otherwise encounter it. Restricting Mozart Masses to church services would not, I think, get more people into church, but it would certainly mean that fewer people listened to Mozart. I would argue that a sermon is a thing worth listening to, whatever the context. In a service, however, the attention with which it is listened to, and the heed that is paid to it, can be to a great extent determined by its precise position in the service. Members of an Internet discussion list to which I belong, Christians on the Internet, recently debated this issue. Some preach after the second reading, some after the gospel reading, some before or after the Creed, some not at all. The introduction into the Church of England of the new liturgies in *Common Worship* has made possible the concept of a 'floating sermon', for example, preaching about confession and absolution immediately before confession. We asked all our 40 shortlisted preachers this year to tell us at what point in a service they prefer to deliver an address. Their answers are reproduced here, in the introductions before the sermons. Other traditions have sermons right at the end of a service.

But one enduring problem for any congregation is what to do during a sermon when listening is no longer possible. I consider myself fortunate in that I rarely hear the same person preach twice, because every week I must attend a different place of worship in pursuit of material for the 'At Your Service' column that appears in *The Times* every Saturday. Most church or synagogue goers are not so fortunate. Week after week they hear the same preacher preach. Of course the good preacher will keep the attention of most of them for most of the time, but even the best have the capacity to bore. And then the challenge for a congregation is of what to do now. The oft-cited advice, 'If you don't strike oil, stop boring', seems to be known to many worshippers but few preachers. Few are in a position to say, in the manner of Queen Elizabeth I: 'Of your sermon, we have heard quite enough.' The most famous occupation with which to while away a sermon is of course set out by P. G. Wodehouse in his 'Great Sermon Handicap'. But new sermon games are constantly developing and evolving, and some *Times* readers have been good enough to send in details.

Some choirs play 'hymn book pictionary', which involves sketching a picture to give clues to the line of a hymn, which then has to be guessed at by others in the stalls. For example, lines such as 'Sometimes a light surprises a Christian while he sings' lend themselves to this game. Points are awarded and the winner decided after a month.

One cleric advises youngsters to play the 'ABC game', a sport which, despite its name, has nothing to do with the Archbishop of Canterbury but involves listening for a word first beginning with an 'A', then a 'B' and so on. Counting the lights in leaded windows, the angels on a reredos or planks of wood in a ceiling are other diversions I have heard recommended. Those of a mathematical bent like to study the tables for calculating Easter. Others have been known to study the commands set out in the Table of Kindred and Affinity – 'a man may not marry his grandmother' and so forth. When I was young I used to attempt to memorize entire tracts of the *Book of Common Prayer*. (This did wonders for my command of the English language but gave me some rather unusual views about life which made coping with secular existence among my peers something of a challenge.) One strategy that does, in my view, go too far is that adopted by one acquaintance, who would make his views on a particular cleric known by ostentatiously flourishing and reading during his sermon a well-known book or novel, the contents of which could be guaranteed to be at sharp divergence with the views of the preacher. At the 1999 Preacher of the Year Award, held at Methodist Central Hall in Westminster, we coped with the concept of six sermons in a row by inviting the 1000-strong congregation to play 'sermon cricket'. This was based on a concept developed by Rabbi Jonathan Romain, a judge last year and this. He used to play this game when visiting different synagogues as a teenager. In this contest, the preacher is awarded one run every time he or she manages to mention God, four when he or she refers to the Ten Commandments and six if he or she raises both arms. At every mention of 'I', he or she loses a wicket. As with real cricket the object is to gain a high score with the minimum loss of wickets. Variations can be inserted, such as losing runs for the use of clichés. At the 1999 Award we had been going to award a prize to the winner of this contest as well as the main award itself, but in the end we lost our nerve, and just kept our 'sermon cricket' as something with which listeners could amuse themselves if listening to six sermons in a row became too much to handle. It is to be hoped that the growing practice of using sermons as a time to send text messages on silent but vibrating mobile phones – I know it happens because I've done it myself – does not bring such endeavours to an end. This seems unlikely, however, just as the continuing tendency for some in the choir stalls or pews to produce magazines, novels and maths homework during the sermon has not put an end to 'sermon cricket' or even the sermon – yet. And long may it never do so.

Acknowledgements

THANKS TO Peter Stothard, Editor of *The Times*, Ben Preston, Deputy Editor, Michael Grove, News Editor and John Wellman, Deputy News Editor. Richard Collins and Adam Fleming, students from Oxford University on work experience at *The Times*, whose help was invaluable.

BIBLICAL PARABLES

Strange Fires

ALBERT FRIEDLANDER

Rabbi Albert Friedlander, 73, is one of the country's best-known progressive rabbis. Married to the author Evelyn Friedlander, who is director of the Hidden Legacy Foundation, they have three daughters, Ariel, Michal and Noam, of whom one has also become a rabbi. Rabbi Friedlander was ordained in 1952 after studies at the Hebrew Union College in Cincinnati 1946–52. He served in congregations in Arkansas, Pennsylvania, and was founding rabbi of the Jewish Centre of the Hamptons in Long Island, New York. The family moved to Great Britain in 1966, where he became rabbi at the Harrow and Wembley Progressive Synagogue, and then went on to the Leo Baeck College where he became a lecturer, then Director, then Dean. He was appointed Minister of Westminster Synagogue in 1971, where he is now the Emeritus Rabbi. He was elected Associate President of the Council of Christians and Jews in 1999. He also serves as president of the London Society for the Study of Philosophy and Religion. He is a prolific writer and has authored more than ten books as well as libretti and articles in scholarly journals.

On the position of the sermon, he says: 'The sermon is still the centre of the worship service in the Jewish community, particularly when linked with the Torah reading. It therefore follows the two readings from the Torah and Prophets and should be an integral part of our worship. The minister and the congregation give each other authority in a religious dialogue which is part of their lives.'

Rabbi Friedlander's wealth of life experiences has given him a huge resource to draw on for sermons. For the past twelve years, for example, he has had an opening sermon at the Kirchentag in Germany, the biannual Conference of the Protestant Church, with an attendance of 200,000. 'At the Hamburg Kirchentag, I gave my opening sermon in the "Martin Luther King" church. I had marched with Martin Luther King junior from Selma to Montgomery. Years later, Martin Luther King senior took me to the grave. "Do you know who I am?" he asked me. "Of course," I replied, "You are Martin Luther King senior and we are at the grave . . ." He interrupted me: "You DON'T understand. I am Abraham, and this is my Isaac." When I recounted this, the church became very quiet, and I preached about shared grief and common goals.'

He tells another story about his preaching. 'In my first pulpit in Ft Smith, Arkansas, I was also a chaplain to the nearby Army camp, Camp Chaffee, and the soldiers came to town for the Friday night servce. At one point, a disturbed young soldier walked up to the pulpit and held his bayonet to my throat. "Don't frighten him", his friends called out to me. Frighten HIM? What about me? For the rest of the service, which I conducted at amazing speed, I spoke very softly. Afterwards, his friends came up to him, and he went with them like a lamb.' Rabbi Friedlander does have a quiet, gentle voice – but can roar like a lion when necessary. 'I once said to my chairman, "Max, why do you always sleep during my sermons?" "Rabbi," he said: "I TRUST you!"'

As an ordained rabbi, he uses the lectionary of texts read in synagogues. 'As a Jew who experienced the Holocaust, I found my faith deepened as I returned to my roots. In the end I have a questing faith which sees doubt as a necessary aspect of faith, and have a firm belief in the parallel pathways of religion which lead to God and to the encounter with other human beings. All of life is a learning process, and the sermon, as I see it, is a way of reaching out and of teaching. It is also an act of testifying, and must therefore be treated as an important task which demands much preparation, and the awareness of the others who are addressed and who interact with the preacher. A minister must never forget that he represents the people far more than him/herself. Incidentally, humour belongs to a sermon as a link between us; and listening to the worshippers, even to their body language, is vital at this moment.'

What interests him outside religion? 'Everything and nothing, since religion permeates my world. Nothing human is alien to me, whether in music, art, theatre, travel or books. As a devoted fan of Queen's Park Rangers, I am often found at the stadium (I have a season ticket). I read much poetry, and even write some. At present I am reading the latest Harry Potter book. It may well enter one of my next sermons.'

OUR ANCIENT SERMONS did not begin with the prescribed text, but turned to another part of the Bible. And so, let me begin with Psalm 30:

> ba-erev yolin vechi
> v'laboker rinah.

'Weeping may tarry for the night, but joy comes in the morning.'

In 1952, when Pastor Goes gave the *laudatio* for Martin Buber who was receiving the Peace Prize of the Frankfurt Book Fair, he expressed his delight for Buber's German translation. As with all poetry, it cannot be translated, but its meaning is:

'At even, weeping enters night, but in the morning, it's joy.'

Albrecht Goes particularly loved '*it's*': that sudden outburst which followed sorrow.

Is this a proper introduction for a Sabbath sermon? After all, the Sabbath is to be a totally joyous celebration of life. No funerals are held on the Sabbath, and its overriding message is of the Sabbath as God's gift of joy to sustain life. Yet sorrows endure: the Kaddish, the memorial prayer at the end and the Torah portion reflect *all* of life. Dark passages confront us with the abiding reality of pain. Again, as in the past, let me examine today's portion:

> Nadav and Avihus the sons of Aaron, each took his pan, and put fire therein, and put incense upon it, and offered an alien fire before the Lord, which he had not commanded them. And a fire went out from the Lord, and devoured them. (Leviticus 10:1–2)

Our Bible reading is integral to the Sabbath service. The ark, the breastplate of the Torah, the officiants and all of us at worship are drawn into the text. Perhaps we no longer think of the rabbis as priests in the world of today, even though we clearly fulfil priestly functions for the community. Of course, there *are* priests in all the sanctuaries of the world – but they often live apart from it. Does the world still listen to them – or has the world chosen new priests in our time?

A new type of priest is revered by the contemporary world: scientists, clad in their white garments, who work in strange places called Chernobyl, and Three Mile Harbour, and Sellafield. Suddenly, the Bible text has a new meaning: the slightest mistake on the part of these priests reaching out towards the mystery can bring death into the world. In biblical times, touching the Ark could kill even a pious priest. And the strange fires of Chernobyl were unleashed to spread destruction over the world.

Is that what happened in our text? I cannot accept this. True enough, there is a clue within it: *esh zarah,* a strange, an alien fire. Was *that* the sin which killed them? I do not like that sermon, because I have heard it too often from various pulpits. My own colleagues here happily attack traditional fanatics who lose themselves in the fire of intolerance against all those who differ from them in any fashion. The traditionalists, in turn, point out that 'strange, alien fires' are surely the rituals of non-orthodox communities who will be destroyed by God. The text has become a pretext to be used as a weapon against the neighbour. And I disassociate myself from both of these camps. The prophesied destruction does not come from God. but from flawed human beings. I recall a poem by Robert Frost:

Some say the world will end by fire,
Some say by ice.
I hold with those who favour fire –
But ice is also nice
and would suffice.

The destruction of the world is always imminent in a world filled with passion and hatreds, with fiery intolerance and cold, unfeeling apathy. When the sanctuaries are deserted, and when control passes to the market-place and to the laboratories, death doth draw nearer. And yet the holy places in this world are part of the world. It would be a dangerous illusion for us to feel that our houses of prayer are immune to the strange, destructive fires of the world: *we bring our own imperfections into our sanctuaries*. This insight is the heart of our biblical text today, and for thousands of years our tradition has struggled to discern the meaning of the death of the sons of Aaron and Elisheva.

The story is not a parable. It happened. Nadav and Avihu were the bright young stars of their time, born to the 'first family' in Israel, assigned to the noblest duties, struck down in the midst of their work. Why did this happen? The saddest and shortest verse in the Torah is the father's response:

va-yldom Aharon: and Aaron was silent.

The silence after catastrophe is part of human experience: think only of the survivors of the Holocaust who kept silent for decades after the event. But Aaron needed help. He had turned to his brother Moses, the leader of the people. And Moses said:

bikrovay ekadesh, v'al kol ha-am ekaved:
God says: I will be sanctified by those who are near to Me, and will be honoured before all the people.

Then, Aaron was silent. The answer had been taken out of the world, made a divine mystery. Just so, after the Holocaust, Martin Buber says that God turned away from the world for a moment. Aaron had to be satisfied with the answer.

WE are not satisfied, and still search for answers. The rabbis went back to the text, looking for the sins of Nadav and Avihu. Some saw the sins of the next generation, impatient to replace their elders. Other suggested they wanted to make changes, since they had made a sacrifice which God had not commanded. In the Talmud it states:

Four causes occasioned the death of Aaron's sons: They came too close to the sanctuary; they brought an untimely sacrifice; they introduced a strange fire, and they did not consult together on procedure.

That is a rational, almost scientific explanation which might even apply in an atomic laboratory. But – in God's House? Could God not accept good intentions? We might all stumble when we conduct prayers. And so the rabbis look for other reasons, and find them at the end of that Torah portion, where there is a prohibition against strong drinks:

Nadav and Avihu were roaring drunks, totally intoxicated when they tried to make their sacrifices.

In some ways, that answer makes sense. Why does the prohibition against drink become the concluding verse of that reading? The task which had been assigned to them demanded the closest concentration and dedication possible. Even when we shift our question back to Sella-field or Chernobyl, we realize that there are situations where the slightest mistake unleashes destruction upon the world. Even the best intention – trying to create genetically modified food in order to fight famine in a starving world – is filled with danger. Sober scientists warn of dangers here, and religious leaders say that we must not interfere with God's creation! Our tradition warns of another sin:

doche et ha-ketz – one must not hasten the coming of the Messiah.

That is God's decision. Did the young priests plan this? I do not think so. Were they drunk or evil? I doubt it. What remains? A mystery of faith, an encounter with God's inscrutable plan. Yet even when we accept this, our hearts cry out for the mourning parents. We meet them not only in the Bible, but in every generation. Once, children wept for parents, but in today's world, in Kosovo and Ethiopia, and in India it is parents who weep for their children. Their silence is not Aaron's acceptance of the word of Moses: it is the silence of despair.

We, too, must not be silent in these days. We have to cry out. We have to act, and by action bring hope into the world. Let us bind up one another's wounds, so that the words of the Psalm may resound through the world:

At even, weeping enters night
but in the morning, it's joy.

Let the true joy of the Sabbath leap out from the sanctuary and fill the world with joy.

Asking

JOHN WHITTAKER

Canon John Whittaker, 79, was appointed honorary canon of Manchester Cathedral in 1971. After a lifetime's service in the Church of England, he retired as Rector of Middleton in 1987. He and his wife Eileen, a retired teacher, had three children, Michael, Ruth and Philip (deceased). They have nine grandchildren and two great-grandchildren.

He says: 'I went up to Cambridge in 1939 to read English, having been accepted for ordination by the Manchester diocese, but volunteered for war service in 1940 during which I spent four years in the Indian Army, latterly with the rank of Major. I returned to Cambridge in January 1946 to read theology. I was ordained at Advent 1948, served as curate in two parishes and was incumbent in three, only changing parishes at the behest of my diocesan bishop. I was made an honorary canon of Manchester diocese and retired from the full-time ministry in 1987. However, once a priest always a priest, and I am very grateful to be wanted in that regard, having covered several interregnums, especially since I am not of a retiring disposition.'

There were several strands to this, but he converted chiefly through a school friend's desire for company during his confirmation course. 'I had no idea what it signified, but a year or so later the same friend said he thought I should be ordained. My initial response was to mimic a parson, but the idea stuck, and the rest followed. I always say that I was plucked out of the wilderness. Were I twenty years old I would wish to have the same vocation – if the Church would have me!'

When preaching, he follows the Church's Year. When asked once what he would like for an epitaph, he responded: 'He loved the Church's Year'. He believes a rogation sermon on Rogation Sunday speaks for itself.

He argues that no modern communication skills can ever replace the sermon, but there is more need now than ever for a priest to read as widely as possible, outside as well as inside theology. 'My own conviction is that there is more theology in English Literature than in the subject properly so-called. Therefore, while the parish priest needs a study he does not need an office. The parish does, but there should be others to exercise that responsibility. I liked this quotation from an obituary of Archbishop Runcie: "We've entered the era of the Management Church, you know – except a man be evaluated every other year he cannot see the Kingdom of God."

'The proper place for the sermon is after the Gospel at the Holy Communion,

as modern practice recommends, and probably after the formal Office at Matins or Evensong, and before the intercessory prayers. More informal services can have their own rules.

'It is important that the preacher should have some ability to stand outside himself, as it were, and seeing himself from that vantage point simply laugh. I like to recall a comment by a Boltonian deliberately made in my hearing: "It's all right yon job; it's nowt but talking".

'So I don't want to take myself too seriously. In the proper sense, nothing can be "outside of religion", but my wife and I enjoy walking, going to the theatre (though all too rarely), and spending time with our family and friends. Without Eileen my ministry would have been very incomplete. One pleasure of retirement is that we can share more time together. However, I would like to have the privilege of serving God as a priest so long as the brain will function and my legs will carry me.'

Text: John 16: 23–4.

> . . . if you ask the Father for anything in my name He will give it to you. Ask and you will receive that your joy may be full.

Excellent!   'Please can I have a new computer?'
Better still!   'Please can I win the lottery?'
The reply comes: 'No!'

Why not? The Bible surely says that if I ask God for anything He will give it to me, and the Bible is the Word of God is it not? Yes, but . . . there are three words left out – 'in my name'.

There is a similar example to this in Paul's letter to Timothy. It is often said that 'money is the root of all evil' – there was even a pop song in my youth which went, 'Money is the root of all evil. Take it away, take it away, take it away!' To which one Lancastrian said, 'Money might be the root of all evil, but give me a bit of "root".' However, this is another example of scripture being misquoted, for again there are three words left out. It should read, *'the love of* money is the root of all evil' and many of us would think that there is a lot of truth in that statement in this consumer-orientated society of ours.

However, let us get back to this 'asking' in the sense of asking God for what we want. Those three words 'in my name' mean 'according to my nature'. Anything we ask, in tune with God's will for us, He will grant. That was well understood by Our Lord's friends, and indeed by Jewish people in general in those days.

Like us, they gave people names to distinguish them from other people. We read also in the Jewish Bible – our Old Testament – of names being changed in adult life to fit in with a change in character. Thus one of the wandering tribe of Arameans, Jacob, had a name which meant 'crafty one'. If you read the first book of the Bible, Genesis, you will learn the reason. He kept deceiving his brother Esau. However, in adult life he was renamed *Israel*, which became the name of all his tribe and means 'perseverer with God' – a change indicating a change for the better in his character. Our Lord too was given other names. He is sometimes called *Emmanuel* which means 'God with us'. Again, in the nineteenth century there was a Jewish statesman who did not wish to disguise the fact that he was a Jew and consequently changed his name to *Disraeli* which means 'of Israel'.

We pray in Jesus' name. We often think of our praying, our talking with God, as asking, but of course it is much more than that. Another name for this fifth Sunday after Easter (or sixth Sunday of Easter as our new Lectionary so appropriately recommends) is Rogation Sunday. 'Rogation' means 'asking' and on this Sunday our ancestors asked for God's blessing on 'the fruits of the earth and the labours of men'. In other words, they asked God to bless the seeds which they had planted, praying that, come September, there would be a good harvest.

Most of us in our generation are not farmers but lots of us have gardens, and it is not too big a jump in imagination to empathize, to feel with, the farmers in a year which has particular difficulties for them. Yet 'asking' is more than that. It is a longing to be a better person in God's sight. One interpretation of the Sign of the Cross is that it is an 'I' crossed out; the desire to put God at the centre of our lives rather than ourselves. Put another way, it is a longing to make this world a better place. That surely would be pleasing to God. I don't mean big, grandiose schemes, but simply desiring to be sensitive enough to help in small ways where help is needed.

I live in one of the more pleasant districts of my town, but only a short walk away you can find an old mattress, a supermarket trolley and empty beer cans in abundance. A stream flows by this rubbish making it almost unreachable from the country lane just by it. 'Please God, stir some concern for our environment in those who despoil our town like this.' But again, prayer is not just asking. We need to say 'thank you' and 'sorry' as well as 'please'. And we need to listen as well as talk – at least preachers do!

In a cargo boat on one of the American Lakes an old Negro engine man was asked how he kept his engine room so bright and shining. He replied: 'Oh I gotta glory . . .' and

> Oh! You gotta get a glory
> In the work you do;
> A Hallelujah chorus
> In the heart of you.

> Paint, or tell a story,
>   Sing, or shovel coal.
> But you gotta get a glory
>   Or the job lacks soul.

Praying, asking, in the name of Jesus, is what gives a job its soul.

Note

The Runcie quotation came from Humphrey Carpenter's book *The Reluctant Archbishop*, p. 162. The negro spiritual he found in Jean Coggan's *Through the Day with Jesus*, p. 67, published by Mowbray in 1979.

The Unlikely Helper

DAVID TYRRELL

David Tyrrell, 45, a lay preacher in an independent Pentecostal church, the Open Door Fellowship in Glasgow, started out in adult life as a postman but now drives HGV lorries for the Royal Mail, which he has been with for 27 years. Married to Allyson, a part-time secretary, they have one son, Matthew.

'I became a Christian in the early 1970s through the ministry of Arthur Blessit – he carried a rather large cross everywhere he went. After the death of my uncle and aunt who brought me up, my faith deepened and grew,' he says. His vocation as a lay preacher developed over the years. He began in the Methodist Church as a local preacher and in the last 17 years has been involved with his family in the Independent Pentecostal Fellowship, where he is encouraged to preach by his pastor. 'Various other churches also ask me along to speak regularly. I have also been involved with various missions preaching in south-east India where many wonderful miraculous things happened.'

The sermon he submitted was one he preached recently before many hundreds of people in India. 'It spoke forcefully to those from the lowly caste system. It is all about loving those we despise. The Good Samaritan challenges us all that we are all equal in God's eyes.'

He believes the sermon is central to worship. 'The sermon should be given prominence, as it is God's Word that is being spoken to all who listen. To me it does not matter where the sermon comes as long as there is one. The preaching of God's Word will always bring a response from everyone who hears whether at home, in their seats at the Church or running to the altar. God's Word is powerful.'

Once, when he was speaking at Hartlepool, his Bible went flying through the air. 'It was a women's meeting in Hartlepool, and more than 100 women were there. Allyson was one of the national leaders with this organization and everyone knew her, so I was on my best behaviour. But I got so caught up in what I was saying that I lifted my hand too fast. My brand-new, rather large Bible took off and landed, bouncing, on a table where four or five ladies were peacefully sitting. It sent them rushing for cover as it bounded towards them like a bowling bowl towards skittles. The meeting took some ten minutes to get back to normality, as everyone was laughing and crying!' But that was nothing compared to what happened to him once in India. 'We had a herd of water buffalo driven between us in a stampede while we were preaching. We had to run for our lives. After it was all over we reassembled and continued our meeting.' Apart from preaching, he is a successful amateur painter, and is often given commissions to paint watercolours and oils. He keeps fit, goes regularly to the gym and plays sports with his family.

A TRICKY LAWYER asked Jesus a tricky question. This particular lawyer desired to inherit something by doing nothing to merit an inheritance. Jesus turned the question around – a very Jewish response to a question – and asked him;

'What is written in the law how do you see it?' The lawyer answered him by quoting the Old Testament Law – Deuteronomy 6:5, Jesus said 'Good answer, do this and you will live'.

But like all lawyers he was looking for a loophole in the Law, some hole of escape to slide through.

'Who is my neighbour?' He asks. In our multicultural world would we ask who our neighbour is? That group of people we do not like; the drug addicts or the pickpockets and thieves, muggers, or simply that person across the road we avoid at all costs.

Jesus then goes on to tell a story about a certain man, which tells us it is a true story – one which may have been doing the rounds so to speak.

This man went down to Jericho looking for a right royal time in the portal to Israel. A city renowned for its wickedness. But he got what he deserved we would say. Mugged and left for dead.

The first person to come upon this unfortunate man was the best one for the job of helping him. Yes, a Priest. Surely here is our answer to a sin-weary, beaten-up world. He knew all the answers. He knew compassion and love and he would certainly know God. Alas our poor man is looked at, given the once over and in summing up this situation the Priest says 'I can't help you, I don't want to get blood on my hands. The Law forbids I touch dead things.' Obviously he never took the poor man's pulse. Like so many today we haven't taken the pulse of the world. We have pronounced a benediction on a lost world.

Like Shakespeare's lines in The Rape of Lucrece:

> The patient dies while the physician sleeps
> The Orphan pines while the oppressor feeds
> Justice is feasting while the widow weeps
> Advice is sporting while infection breeds
> Our true hope passes us by but we cannot put our trust in men.

The second man to come into the story is a Levite – who also pronounced a post-mortem on the dying man. Unlike the Priest, the Levite could not enter the Holy of Holies or minister at an altar in

Jerusalem. From the tribe of Levi, they were purified. The Law of the Tithe enhanced the selection of the Levites. For in a sense this tribe was a tithe of all the tribes and it was to this tribe that the tithe was paid. A poor man on the road was robbed and had no money, not even any clothes and had nothing to give to the system, what we today consider a layabout with no potential, a carcass for the fires of prejudice. This Levite man had a place of responsibility and privilege in God's plan, his ancestor Phinehas stayed the plague in Num 25: 1–13. This particular Levite had no mind to stay the plague of violence on this road to Jericho. He knew his Laws; he was in a hurry to go to Jerusalem to act out a few more Laws to look good for the masses. Anyway nobody would see him or us pass by on the other side. The man was dying, leave him to die in peace and meet his Maker.

In the hymn 'Hear the voice of Jesus calling' one verse reads:

> Look the thorned crowned head is bending over thee,
> and the patient eyes are watching tenderly,
> watching for thy heart to yield, thy to lips to say
> Jesus Master take me save me here today.

Laws are a cruel schoolmaster; there is no compassion in the letter of the Law. People always quote laws and rules to us, you can't do this or that, keep off the grass, they never tell you of a perfect law.

The Law of Love

As Massinger says in the book the Old Law: 'The good needs fear no law it is his safety and the bad man's awe.' People today think our religion is a book of laws, burdens to be borne, pains to be endured. How wrong, how sad this thinking. Jesus said His burdens were light in Matthew 12. This Levite – a man of Law could not help the dying man.

The third person to enter the story was a hated man in Israel. They were considered squatters in the land of Samaria, a mongrel race of interlopers, no-good degenerates who had requested a Priest from the Jewish deportees in Assyria to teach them about Jewish laws and Jehovah Himself. The Talmud, a Jewish commentary, states Samaria as a 'Cuthite strip' or 'tongue'.

And here this despised man comes along. We have already decided that no good person is quite useless to help us, or anyone for that matter. Samaria was a place where malcontent Jews went to reside. Yet a rebel dissident shows compassion for the dying man. This Samaritan like a doctor, out on his calls, has all the relevant things for binding and dressing wounds. Notice Doctor Luke's account 'so he went to him and bandaged his wounds pouring on oil and wine'. Jesus left His eternal office to come and minister on our Jericho road. Seven things are recorded about this good man.

1. He bound up his wounds first. Jesus does the same for us and wipes the tears and blood away.
2. He administered medicines of oil and wine. The wine being symbolic of the Word of God, and the oil of the Holy Spirit. Such sweet relief from all pain and suffering.
3. He had his own transportation, his own ambulance – a humble donkey. God provides the way for the sick to come to His own hospital, namely through us to shoulder the load, quoting the words of a well-known pop song – 'He's not heavy – he's my brother'.
4. He reserved a room for this man. Jesus too has reserved a place in his Kingdom for us.
5. He paid all his expenses. This Good News is all of grace, we cannot pay; we are the beaten and the robbed lying at the side of the road.
6. He promised to come back. Jesus never leaves us in a fix or a sticky situation. 'I will never leave you or forsake you' Jesus says.
7. He guaranteed extra expenses for the sick man. There is always more of God, He can never be exhausted or used up. His love, compassion and grace go on for ever.

Of the three, who was the man's real neighbour? Jesus asks. Of course the lawyer had to say the Samaritan. What a lesson, what a profound truth. If we all put this into practice what a different world this would be.

There are no difficult rules or regulations to follow in this good news, just a step of love and compassion. When we cross life's road to help somebody in trouble, maybe a person who hates us or whom we even detest. This tricky lawyer was silenced and probably stunned by the simplicity and love contained in this story. May we be moved also.
Amen.

The Brylcreem Boy

Michael Topliss

Michael Topliss, a retired teacher and local preacher, has this year picked up his pension and his travel pass, a long-service certificate as a local preacher marking 40 years, and a fourth grandchild. He and Hilary have celebrated their ruby wedding at their home in Bloxwich, which they share with a couple of Border terriers, and from which they escape occasionally to a caravan on the Gower peninsula.

Michael is a son of a Methodist manse, and he was educated at Kingswood, a Methodist boarding school, and Westminster, a Methodist teacher training college. He is, however, or perhaps therefore, an active ecumenist, and long after early retirement from teaching he became a County Ecumenical Officer. He serves both Black Country Churches Engaged and CLASP (Churches Linked Across Staffordshire and the Potteries).

The subject of the published sermon chose itself, he says. 'When those verses form the gospel reading for the day, what else can you do?' But the decision to re-package the passage like this? 'Ah, well, it just came. And on occasions like that I like to spell "inspiration" with a capital "S".'

He has known both joy and embarrassment in his preaching.

'I cringe when I remember going back to preach in the church where I had been a Sunday school child. In the vestry a repectful young church steward asked me if I had been to the church before. "Yes," I said, "50 years ago." I didn't mean to put him down, but the moment I'd said it I felt a heel. A few weeks later, as chance would have it, the young man came to preach at our church, giving me an opportunity to be more polite. I complimented him afterwards on his brilliant, perhaps unique, pulpit use of a rare metaphor from engineering: "Recondition us, O Lord". "Every service should have a sparkling, memorable moment," I declared. But the smile of reconciliation did not appear. He was puzzled, perhaps annoyed. Apparently, recommissioning was what he had spoken of! (In case he should read this, let me add that a few weeks later I was prescribed a hearing aid.)

'I have a happier memory of finding in the pulpit a leather bookmark that had come from Edinburgh's Black Watch Museum. Remarkably, I had a line in that morning's sermon scorning our general lack of humility: "I preach in the old school tie; you may wallow in nostalgia for the regiment," I was to say. So there was an impromptu extension: ". . . like the previous occupant of this pulpit who's left the Black Watch bookmark behind". It transpired, how-

ever, that it was not left there accidentally. An appreciative member of the congregation had brought it as a present for me, and slipped it into the pulpit before the service. It seems he had – during his Scottish holiday! – remembered a sermon of mine from the previous year, a compliment in itself! I had preached on the first verses of St John's Gospel, and had begun by brandishing a collection of leather bookmarks – from holy places such as Canterbury, Iona, Epworth and Guiseley – before quoting Kenneth Grayston, who in his commentary on St John's Gospel had likened its prologue to a bookmark which might help the reader follow John's themes through the rest of the work. As this remembered idea had originated with Professor Grayston, I wrote to him to let him share my pleasure. And what did that gracious gentleman do? He sent me a leather bookmark from Bristol!'

Michael believes that preaching is vital. 'I have recently attended two services, one for a funeral, in which no attempt to mediate the Word was made. God forgive my resentment, but I continue to feel badly short-changed.'

SO IT'S A 'church weekend away' at some place that sounds quite impressive – yes, Willersley Castle by the River Derwent will do very well. Or maybe it's a Saturday Quiet Day, say just past Izaak Walton's cottage at Shallowford House. Somewhere where men keener on fishing than theology can slope off unnoticed and worship God via the beauties of nature: 'blue-domers' we used to call them. But a good number have stayed back this afternoon for it is very hot, and the minister has a workable gathering around him on the lawn.

'I've set you a question,' he says, 'that I want you to tackle in groups of about four.'

'Oh, no,' grumbles Pete, 'not discussion groups! I *should* have gone fishing.'

'So how many are we? About twelve? Right then, let's number off.'

'He always does this,' moans Jim. 'It's to make sure that we brothers are split up.'

'Now remember the number I give you as I go round: one, two, three, four.'

'Not again!' mutters Jude to his girlfriend. 'God, he's so heavenly-minded he's no earthly use: look, Josh, if you want groups of four from a dozen people, you must count just one, two, three.'

The minister looks dubious but accepts that arithmetic is not his strong point. And he numbers them one, two and three.

'Right, group one – will you go over there, in the shade by the old well. And group two – under that sycamore. And group three stay here. About twenty minutes, then? OK? Hang on – here's the question for you to tackle!' And he hands a piece of paper to the one in each group he considers a good leader. Except that Pete refuses the slip: ignores his group, and goes off to sulk at the gazebo.

Each leader reads the question through silently and, when they all settle, gens up the group.

'What he's asking us is: Who, of all the characters in the Bible, do we think a minister should seek to identify with, or, whom should he regard as his role-model?'

Meanwhile, this minister strolls away off the lawn, glances across at Pete, but decides he's just in a mood, and then he finds a deckchair in order to give the once-over to tomorrow's sermon.

But, it's a whole half-an-hour later when he calls them back: so that doesn't augur well for the morning service. This now is the 'plenary session' (if we're going to be formal) and we *are* going to be formal because the Reverend Josh has set up on the lawn an easel with a flip-chart. He explains to the company that the question has partly to do with his self-appraisal.

'Parsons and their congregations,' he says, 'do not always share the same expectations of ministry. So I'm interested to learn who people think a minister should take as his exemplar? Who do folk reckon I should be like? Group one – Andy.'

So Andy reports back from the first group. 'Well, you know I used to be a Baptist myself, but I don't think I have had undue influence on the group. John the Baptist is our ideal minister.'

Josh calls Matt up to scribe, so that the writing on the flip-chart will be legible, and asks Andy to explain their choice of John the Baptist.

'John was popular because he was very down to earth.'

('John was down to water!' calls Pete, who has returned to the bank of the lawn.)

'Those crowds followed him because he spoke their language, didn't beat about the bush, didn't spiel out the abstract nouns like some preachers do. He was a practical guy who told people quite plainly what they must do.'

Mary, from Group three, said she liked the idea of the parson having the common touch, but she wasn't at all sure about the authoritarian approach for this day and age.

'OK. Anything else. Andy?'

'Yes. We liked the simplicity of John's lifestyle. You'd never see John in a coat of many colours, just that camel-coloured sports-jacket.'

'What about his posh loincloth?' heckles Pete.

'Well it was good Walsall leather, I'll grant you. But it wasn't Calvin Klein, you know!'

Matt at the flip-chart chips in: 'Another thing. you wouldn't have to decorate the Manse and re-carpet the study before John moved in!'

(You could tell Matt was a Circuit Steward.)

And Joanna, a homely type, but nervous with it, says:

'And you wouldn't be expected to serve up *cordon bleu* if you had John to Sunday lunch.'

'And *he* was teetotal!' That's Pete calling out again. And that's a bit naughty because Josh is known to have visited a couple of French vineyards during his sabbatical and to have a nose (and a vocabulary) for wine like Jilly Goulden's.

'Time to listen to Group two!' says Josh.

'Well,' says Tom, 'we think Elijah is the fellow you should emulate.'

'Elijah?' query most of them, for their memories concerning the admirable qualities of Elijah are a bit rusty. Matt writes Elijah's name up on the flip-chart.

'We reckon,' says Tom, 'that Elijah's ministry was very powerful, and that his stance was evenly-balanced between the sacred and the secular.'

Josh asks him to 'unpack' their theory a bit.

'Right,' says Tom, 'the gist of it is: that the royal marriage of Prince Ahab to the green-eyed bitch of a princess from Tyre brought Elijah major problems when Ahab succeeded to his father's throne. It was head-to-head – Queen versus Prophet – on the fundamentals of religion and on social justice. It was hardline proselytizing and persecuting mission by the Baal-worshipper versus one man standing alone for the One God. Baal (and his female consort Asherah) supposedly specialized in fertility. *So* in the name of God, Elijah proclaimed a drought. It all climaxed in the challenge, the contest, on Mount Carmel with 850 dervishes prancing fanatically around the altar to no avail and Elijah taking the mickey telling them to shout a bit louder: perhaps Baal can't hear because it's his day off *or he might be stuck in the loo . . .*'

'Tom! This is a Christian gathering!'

'Oh, come on Joanna. You've read your Bible!'

'You don't expect church people to read their Bibles!' sneers Pete.

Tom ignores him.

'And then, Elijah drenches the sacrifice, and calls on God who responds with thunder and lightning, which destroys not just the sacrifice but the altar as well. The Israelites are convinced that 'The Lord, he is God', and the rains come and the ecstatic Elijah races the king's chariot home, running a marathon all along the valley of Jezreel.'

'Well, that's a tall order!' says Josh. 'But you said Elijah took a stand on social justice too. Remind me.'

'Naboth's vineyard.'

Josh cottons on, but Tom doesn't hear many pennies dropping. 'Don't you remember how one day Queen Jezebel found King Ahab lying on his bed in a thunderous sulk.'

(Tom now attempts an imitation of how Fenella Fielding might have played Jezebel).

'Diddums, what *is* the matter? And why haven't you eaten your supper?' But it takes a bit of wheedling even for her to get the reason out of him. It seems the king has set his heart on owning a particular vineyard but its Israelite owner refuses either to sell to the king his inherited family property, or to exchange it for another, for this has been passed down the generations.

'Sell, darling? Exchange? But you're the king!'

'I'm the King of Israel.' says Ahab.

'Yes, like Daddy is King of Tyre.'

'No. Israel is different. I'm not an absolute monarch like your Dad is. Israel is not like Tyre or Sidon, Ammon, Edom or Moab or anywhere else round here. And you're not the Queen of Sheba.'

'Oh, there, there, sweetie-pie. Cheer up duckie. Come and have your Horlicks. And don't worry about that vineyard. I'll sort out that little man.'

'And she does. And a dastardly business it is. Framed for blasphemy and treason, the innocent Naboth is summarily executed. And the triumphant Jezebel leads the pathetic Ahab down to the gate of the new crown property.'

(Tom's Jezebel has changed into Carol Smillie now).

'She blindfolded him and had the cameras zoom to catch the look . . .'

'You're making this up!'

He is a bit, but he's on his feet acting it out.

'. . . and they turn the key and she leaves him to wander through his vineyard, the property he has coveted so long. He's the happiest man on earth. What a wonderful wife: and the emerald-eyed, wealthy Tyrian beauty is such a fixer! Ahab, with his ambitions fulfilled, not a care in the world, strolls between the rows of vines and then hoping to admire and fondle another luscious-looking bunch of grapes he parts some leaves and there he discovers the unkempt head and the piercing eyes and the pointing finger and the scathing voice of the enemy he'd forgotten: Elijah.'

'Tom! Sit down for goodness' sake. Well now, Group three. Follow that!'

Now group three is the one from which Pete absented himself. So there are only three people in it, and two happen to be women, one with a different background, for she was actually born and brought up in Barbados.

Mary says: 'We too thought we should name one of the prophets and we thought Jeremiah would fit the bill'.

Matt's at the easel.

'. . . but in the end we thought better of it. And we have chosen a less well-known prophet: Miriam.'

Everybody looks blank. Phil runs his finger down and right through the list of books at the front of his Bible.

'How many r's in Miriam?' asks Matt.

'Why Miriam?' wonders Josh.

'We don't share the assumption that the model minister has to be a man, or high-profile, or perfect.'

'Amen to *that*!' says Pete.

'Part of the reason Jeremiah had appealed to us was that he was only a teenager when he responded to God's call: but Miriam was used when she was even younger than that. She had a vital part to play in Operation Survival by which Moses's life was preserved. You recall it was she who 'found' a Hebrew wet-nurse (their mother of course) so that the Egyptian princess could cope with the foundling from the bullrushes. And then Miriam evidently shared that imaginative flare for leading worship which seems to be a characteristic of many of the women ministers. We are told how when they'd crossed the Red Sea this prophetess took up her tambourine and led all the women in a dance of triumph and praise to God. But there's another thing Salome here has enlightened us about. Something she learned in her Barbadian Sunday School: but which was unaccountably omitted in the teaching the rest of us received. I mean, we all know how romance blossomed in Midian after Moses had rescued the parson's daughters from those yobbos at the well. But years later . . . he married again – a black woman! And Miriam and Aaron were rather outspoken – plain rude, in fact, about this relationship. And Miriam is stricken with a skin disease which turns *her* a totally contrasting white! She accepts that her prejudice and her criticism were wrong, for Aaron appeals on her behalf to Moses and Moses prays to God. She spends a week of penitence outside the camp. But such is the respect that the company has for her that they do not strike camp until she is back in communion with them and able to travel on companionably with her new sister-in-law. We believe all ministers are forgiven sinners.'

'I like that,' says Josh. 'And I'm sorry if sometimes we don't give that impression. But now, one last quick question before tea. In fact you can discuss it over tea. You can tell me your answer privately if your prefer. Who do you say that I am? I mean, to which of these characters you've chosen do you think I approximate?'

'Oh, come on!' says Pete scrambling up from the bank. He is holding an aerosol canister of hairspray gel, and he squirts it at the minister:

'You, Josh?' he cries. 'You're the Brylcreem Boy!'

'He's finally flipped!' says Barty.

But the minister smiles and puts an understanding arm round Pete's shoulder and leads him to the tea trolley.

Well, that's the end of the daydream.

Now listen to the Gospel:

(Matthew 16:13–20 is read.)

I'm sure you sussed out early that our Willersley Castle or Shallow-ford House was really Caesarea Philippi. And you knew that Joshua is an alternative form of the name Jesus. And you noticed that the men (indeed the women too) had the disciples' names? Then take away all the anachronisms which were included for amusement and who's to say that the original occasion wasn't *something* like that? Except, you're thinking, that last bit about 'the Brylcreem Boy'.

And yet, if you were a first-century non-Jewish inhabitant of the Roman Empire and the gospel story has come your way for the first time, that's the part of the story which then would have flummoxed you, in just that way.

'You are the Christ!' claims Peter.

The anointed one. The one with the greasy scalp. Oily-head! So 'Brylcreem Boy' is what our non-Jewish Greek-speaking Roman would have understood. He or she would not be familiar with the Jewish idea of anointing.

We are.

I remember as an irreverent teenager – that's another anachronism: 'teenagers' hadn't been invented in our day – looking forward to the Coronation ceremony not because it meant a day off school (though it did) nor even because watching the Coronation was going to be my first experience of television (though it was), but because I knew that the Queen was going to be anointed. And the very thought of the posh-est hairdo in the land being messed up by the Archbishop pouring a gravy-boat's worth of olive oil all over it excited me. When I learned she would be anointed not on the head but on the chest, I still thought it might be interesting.

What was the only bit of the Coronation ceremony that was screened off from the cameras? . . . The anointing!

But nevertheless in its symbolism for us, since Samuel's day, anointing has indicated God's approval of an earthly monarch's sovereignty.

So what is Simon Peter saying?

You are the Christ, the anointed one.

You are God's specially-commissioned:

> king, emperor, paramount chief, governor, tsar maharajah, royal highness, supremo, commander-in-chief.

He is acknowledging the totality of Jesus's Lordship.

And of course, yes, Simon Peter went on to demonstrate a sad mis-understanding of that Messiahship as Jesus was interpreting it, but we leave that for another day.

In relation to the eclipse, in some places for a very short time, they were speaking of the moment of totality. In relation to the Lordship of Christ, there's no eclipse, and the totality is eternal.

And at the end of the Methodist year or at the end of this

millennium *we* can come to Caesarea Philippi. And there let *us* face a self-appraisal.

There are only two important questions.

The second most important is the one that Jesus put to his disciples: he puts it to us. Not to us *all*. To *each* of us. French 'tu' not 'vous'. North Country 'thee'. 'Who do you say that I am?'

And the even more important question is the next one which we each put to ourselves: 'How does that creed (that belief about Jesus that I've just declared in my heart) affect the way I live from now?'

Last of All, as to One Untimely Born, He Appeared Also to Me

DOMINIC BARRINGTON

Dominic Barrington, 38, chaplain of St Chad's College, an independent con-
stituent college of Durham University of Anglican foundation, is married to
Alison, a music therapist, counsellor and flautist. Before moving to Durham
in 1998, he was curate of a three-church parish in the Diocese of Southwark
– Mortlake with East Sheen. He began training for ordination in 1992, after
a career in arts administration, including spending five years working for the
Arts Council, where he organized tours of contemporary music around Eng-
land.

'My faith emerged in my early teens, when I joined a church choir solely (so
I imagined) for the musical enjoyment that would bring. My parents were not
churchgoers and I had had no exposure at all to church prior to that point.
However, I was confirmed within six months, and knew that I felt a calling
to priesthood at that stage.*

'One of the joys of my current position is that it allows me the privilege of
ministering in a number of churches within this diocese and beyond, during
the Sundays of the university vacation periods, and in 2000 I was overjoyed
to lead the worship during Holy Week at Christ Church, Lumley, a parish
about seven miles outside Durham City, which had been without a vicar for
over two years. The sermon being published was preached at the Parish
Eucharist at Lumley on Easter Sunday morning, as the culmination of the
worship of the previous week, and the readings on which it was based are
those from the Common Worship lectionary of the Church of England.'*

As the sermon illustrates, he is a firm believer in the practice of using a text
from one of the readings which a congregation has just heard as the starting
point for a sermon, and then finding a way to relate the text, and the point of
the readings, to contemporary Christian life.

'My formal training in preaching, during my last year of theological study,
took place at the Graduate Theological Union in Berkeley, California, where
I was taught by a remarkable member of the Order of Preachers (the Domini-
cans), who stressed the importance of living one's whole life as a preacher, if
one is ever to preach effectively and with conviction. This has been a central
point of my ministry ever since. I am passionately committed to the need for
challenging preaching in today's churches, and it is in that spirit that this sermon was offered.'*

Text: Easter Sunday, Year B, Acts 10:34–43; 1 Cor 15:1–11; John 20: 1–18.

EASTER IS an odd time of year, isn't it? We arrive at Easter through the long haul of Lent, and the intensity of Holy Week, culminating in the anguish of Good Friday, when we commemorate one of the most certain and indisputable facts the Western world has ever witnessed. The clear historical fact that a Galilean peasant called Jesus was executed by the Roman authority in occupied Jerusalem on the eve of the Passover almost 2000 years ago.

Although many historians and theologians want to be cautious about placing too much literal, historical value on some of the events described in the gospels, only utter eccentrics would seriously try and maintain that Jesus of Nazareth was not crucified in Jerusalem on the day we now call Good Friday. And Good Friday is, of course, one of the key days of the Christian year, for it is the day when we are given the chance to understand more clearly than at any other time just how tremendous was God's love for the world that he could allow himself to take on our pain and suffering and die on the cross.

But, as all of us gathered here this morning know, the story doesn't stop with Good Friday. At some point in the darkness of the night between Saturday and Sunday morning, at some point in that utter darkness, something happened. Something that forged a link between the crucified Jesus, and you and me today, here on this Easter morning, all these years later. And something which is far harder to prove, or even, dare I say it, to explain. But something happened – of that we can be quite certain – that something happened is a fact as strong as the crucifixion itself. But what exactly was it that did happen?

Last night, some of you gathered here, in the dark, to commemorate that event of the darkness. And we heard what most people believe to be the earliest of all the Easter stories in the gospels – the ending of Mark's gospel, where the women find the empty tomb and flee in terror. And today, by contrast, we have had St John's rather longer, but no less curious offering – an offering which gives us both the story of the empty tomb as witnessed by Peter and the Beloved Disciple, and the story of Jesus meeting Mary Magdalene, who thinks he is the gardener. But what is it that is really going on?

Well – it's a good question. When we talk about Easter, we tend to talk about resurrection, and about Christ rising from the dead. And that is right, for that is what Easter, in one sense, is about. But when we turn to each other, as we should, and say 'Alleluia! The Lord is risen!' and when we reply 'He is risen indeed, Alleluia!' – when we come out with words like these, we often forget that the resurrection is not as straightforward as we say it is.

Take Mary Magdalene – a woman who clearly loved Jesus very much indeed. A woman who had performed the intimate service of wiping his feet with her hair, and covering him in tears. A woman who knew Jesus about as well as any woman could have done. And what do we find happening on Easter Sunday? She turned around and saw Jesus standing there, but she did not know that it was Jesus. What is going on? Even when he first speaks to her, she still thinks he's the gardener! The gardener, for God's sake!

And so it continues – the disciples go fishing and he's there on the beach, but they don't recognize him. He spends hours walking to Emmaus with two of his followers, and they don't recognize him. Truly, something odd is going on. This is supposed to be God's greatest moment – and nobody can follow the plot.

And think about it in the wider context. Do you know how many people came to Jerusalem for the Passover feast, even way back then, 2000 years ago? A fairly cautious scholar reckons that there would have been 300,000 and 400,000 people packed into Jerusalem, hanging around and inside the Temple area. If God had wanted to make a point in a big way, why did Jesus not appear solidly and soundly to all this great crowd of pious Jews who had come to Jerusalem precisely to have a religious experience?

It seems clear to me – if anything can seem clear about Easter – that whatever is going on here, it is, truly, very much more than a conjuring trick with old bones, to quote a famous retired bishop. If God had wanted Easter simply to be proof that he could effect a resuscitation then he could have had a much more dramatic way of demonstrating it than these curious, shadowy encounters with the risen Christ to such a few people as to hardly make it worth talking about in statistical terms. So what is going on?

Last of all, as to one untimely born, he appeared also to me.

There are two ways of viewing Easter, as far as I can see. You can see it as an ending, and a very glorious ending, to the story of Good Friday, and all that went before. You can say how wonderful it is that God did, in fact, raise Jesus from the dead, and that's clearly good news and shows that God can do wonderful things. And then you can say, apparently like the writers of the four Gospels (if you don't look hard at them), 'OK, story's over – that's all folks.' After all, it is the greatest, most bizarre, and most unexpected ending to a story imaginable. This kind, wonderful, magical man from Galilee, who works those fantastic miracles, heals people, preaches about justice, gets unfairly executed – and, blow it all, he survives. It's a great ending, do you not think?

Well, of course, the answer is 'no'. Because if Easter is the end of something, then whatever it was, it ended 2000 years ago, and we have no need to be here this morning. Easter is not an end – it is a beginning.

It's the moment when God said 'I've done my bit – I went and died to show how much I loved you. Now it's your turn.' Because, despite the miracle that we celebrate in the resurrection of Jesus from the dead, and despite our belief in an omnipotent God, actually he is a pretty powerless God in some ways. Think about the Gospel stories – and, indeed, about the whole of the Old Testament which preceded them. The Old Testament starts, probably, about 1200 years before the birth of Jesus, and we hear tales of generations of holy, God-fearing, right-eous men and women who try and do the will of God – and almost always they are anything but thanked for their pains by those around them to whom they preach.

And finally, in the fulness of time, God does it himself. He takes our flesh, and wanders around the Galilee healing, preaching and teach-ing. New versions of the Law made human in the Sermon on the Mount, wonderful, moving stories such as the Good Samaritan and the Prodigal Son, breathtaking examples of love and humility. And what does he get for his pains? The cross and nails.

And it would have been no different, I think, if Jesus had been raised on Easter Sunday, and plonked down right in the middle of the crowd-ed Temple area, with a divine thunderbolt, fireworks, smoke and all the rest of it. The penny still wouldn't have dropped for most of them.

And so, while it's true that Easter is, in one sense, about the resurrec-tion of Jesus, it is much, much more. Easter is the shock, the kick-start, to prove that the message of the Kingdom of God – the Kingdom of selfless love which Jesus proclaimed by both his life and, most supremely, by his death – Easter is the kick-start to get this Kingdom lived out in the world. And that requires us to do our bit.

Last of all, as to one untimely born, he appeared also to me.

Look back over the three readings we have heard. Mary meets Jesus in the garden, but he won't allow her to hang on to him – 'No, Mary, this isn't the end,' Jesus is saying, in effect, 'It's the beginning'. Look what he tells her to do, instead, "go to my brothers and tell them . . ."

And look at Peter in that passage from Acts. "You know the message God sent to the people of Israel, preaching peace by Jesus Christ – he is Lord of all . . . We are witnesses to all that he did both in Judea and in Jerusalem. They put him to death by hanging him on a tree; but God raised him on the third day and allowed him to appear, not to all the people but to us who were chosen by God as witnesses, and who ate and drank with him after he rose from the dead. He commanded us to preach to the people."

In other words, Peter is saying, 'God made it our job to spread the news.' Because, somehow, the news is more convincing when it is spread by people who have come to see and understand God's love for the world. The message of the Good News of God's love, at its most fundamental, isn't a message requiring drama and fireworks, it is a simple message of forgiveness, reconciliation, and love. And it's a message which can be delivered by all sorts of people – even ones you least expect.

And hence my choice of text this morning . . . *Last of all, as to one untimely born, he appeared also to me*. Because the early church never expected Saul the persecutor to be the one to work harder than any of them to spread this good news. I mean, really – what was going on? He was public enemy number one. He even admits it: 'I am the least of the apostles, unfit to be called an apostle, because I persecuted the church of God. But by the grace of God I am what I am, and his grace towards me has not been in vain'. And thus it was, Paul explains, that *Last of all, as to one untimely born, he appeared also to me*.

But even that was 2000 years ago, and since then a lot more people have come to know the message of the risen but wounded Christ. And it is my hope and prayer this morning, that many more yet will, like the beloved disciple, see and believe. But they will only do so if they are told about the good news, and, more than that, they will only do so if they see the good news – see the good news incarnated not by Bishop Jenkins' conjuring trick with old bones, but by you and me, as we minister in love and kindness to all those we encounter – the unlovable, even more than the lovable. And then we, in our own time, can tell our children and their children: *Last of all, as to one untimely born, he appeared also to me*.

Happy Easter to you, one and all. Amen.

153 Fish – Our First Meal!

Richard Dormandy

The Revd Richard Dormandy, 40, Vicar of Holy Trinity in Sydenham, south-east London, is married to Ruth, a counsellor and they have two children, Jamie and Woodie.

Ordained in 1989, his ministry in the Church of England began with a curacy in the same parish, which is designated an 'urban priority area' by the Church. After two years his vicar moved to be chaplain of an AIDS hospice. The parish had a long interregnum until Richard was finally instituted to the benefice.

He was brought up in what he describes as a 'warm, agnostic-christian-humanist family'. Going to church with school friends as a teenager, he saw other people with a dynamic, day-by-day, relationship with God. 'I was wary of being drawn into anything that was not authentic for me, but as I prayed to Jesus, worshipped him, and read the Gospels, I discovered him as a living reality, commanding and compassionate – in fact everything one might expect from the true God.'

He finds his vocation swings back and forth between being an evangelist and a teacher. 'I love preaching the Gospel and I love examining the meaning of the text in detail. I have always lived in London; I find it hard to imagine being anywhere else, though our three years in Cambridge, when I was at Ridley Hall, were wonderful. When the time comes to move, the way will open up, Jesus pointing down it.'

His sermon published here was inspired by the Easter story. 'The narratives in John are so emotive. I have a very strong, early personal memory of a family breakfast picnic in Kenwood. John's account of breakfast on the beach is full of lively recollection, the vibrancy of which is heightened by his use of language and imagery. I knew people would be able to relate to it! Interestingly, the first edition of this sermon was preached within my own inner urban context, and the second edition, the one I have submitted here, was preached to the tiny rural Cheshire parish of St Peter's, Delamere, where I was a guest. On both occasions there was positive feedback, even though the two sermons were substantially the same.'

He prefers the sermon to be at the heart of a service. 'Preaching based on God's word can be a life-changing experience for the listener, inviting them to believe or perhaps to deepen their existing faith. It is therefore an activity which requires substantial attention from ministers and the church. With the sermon at the end, it can be tempting for people, including the preacher, to think that he is "topping the bill." If we listen to conversations after the service, it is interesting to ask whether people are talking about God's presence in the service as a whole, or weighing up the merits of the preacher? I think I prefer to have the sermon presented centrally, on a bed of worship, giving a wider range of options for response, which can also be taken up in the prayers, and indeed, the creed – which no longer functions as a "badge of entry" but as an affirmation of trust in God. This is our usual practice in my church currently. Also, I think that normally the sermon should occupy a good chunk of the service, but one of my most memorable sermons consisted of five words: "Are you open to God?" – after which I sat down and let them sink in. It was even more memorable when I repeated them the following week!'

One of the most ticklish situations he has faced was not in the church itself, but on a carol singing outing to a drug rehabilitation centre, when he was still the curate. Four of them turned up with their song sheets. 'When we arrived the atmosphere was full of tension – they were in the midst of a "community pull-up" which meant they had been reading the riot act to one another for not pulling their weight or showing a responsible attitude. We were ushered quietly into a lounge to wait until things calmed down. We waited and waited. I had just about plucked up courage to emerge into the reception hall when the front door burst open and a whole troop of red-clad, harmony-laden, carol singers swarmed in, led by a jolly and exuberant "master singer". My first reaction was pure astonishment at the sight before me. My second reaction was to wonder how this intrusion of jollity would go down in the context of such anger. I was suddenly worried that our church would have to carry the can for these intruders' insensitivities, but with my little band of four we could hardly go out and say, "Oi – get off our turf!" There was no way we were going to join them, but we were stuck in the lounge. There was only one thing for it: the curate and his covert band of carol singers opened a narrow window and scrambled out on to the gravel below.

'The following day I phoned up the house, to try and gauge how things were. "Thank you so much for the carol-singing last night," they said, "it was just what we needed!"

"I'm so pleased," I replied, and we've never looked back. Nor have either of us known to this day, who the jolly intruders were. More recently, however, I did have the opportunity to relate the story to members of the community, who thought it was very funny.'

Besides preaching and evangelizing, he is a keen musician and songwriter. 'I am passionate about Latin American music, especially Cuban and Brazilian. I recently cycled 240 miles around Cuba and hope to return.'

Text: John 21:1–14.

I DON'T KNOW what paper you read, but I read *The Times* – partly because I can't understand *The Guardian* and *The Independent*, the *Telegraph*'s too tedious, the *Mail* and *Express* are too dull, the *Mirror*'s too short, *The Sun* is too obnoxious, *The Star* is too crude and the *Sport* is too far down the road to destruction. Apologies for my rudeness if you read any of those papers. In any case, as a typical cheapskate clergyman, the real reason why I take *The Times* is that it is by far the cheapest when you work it out words for pennies. And even if you only read 10 per cent of the words, you have a wide choice of which 10 per cent.

One bit of *The Times* I like to read about 10 per cent of is in the Saturday Magazine. It's a column called 'Our First Meal' – two people recalling the occasion of their first meal. Now I can't remember the first meal I had with my wife, but I can remember many other special meals, and this morning I want us to think briefly about – and apply – a highly memorable meal for Jesus and his disciples.

As is often the case with memorable meals, it wasn't simply what was eaten that was important, nor simply who took part in it, but also where and when it was – the location and the timing. This was a breakfast that took place a few days after Jesus' disastrous defeat by his religious and political opponents, his abandonment by God, and to cap it all, after a totally fruitless night's fishing.

The breakfast took place on the beach, as John recalled. He and the others had decided to go fishing because there was little else for them to do. Not long before, they had been key leaders in a new, vibrant, and charismatic religious movement. Now they had nothing. Jesus had been executed – they had no leader, no purpose, no point. Of course, it was true that by this time the risen Jesus had actually appeared to them, but they still didn't understand the implications of these appearances. Maybe they meant nothing more than the fact that a righteous man had been vindicated by God. Maybe they were hallucinations. I imagine the disciples' feelings at this point were rather up and down – and mainly down – because the full impact of the resurrection simply hadn't dawned on them.

Already there are some points of application for us – because everyone in this church today faces disappointment from time to time: and a crushing disappointment was what weighed the disciples down too. We face disappointments in our marriages, in our work, in our families, our communities and the moves we make, in our churches, our relationships or lack of them, and in ourselves. We go through phases where everything seems so positive – we feel great, keen, things are growing. Then we taste defeat. That oneness, that unity of purpose we shared, is damaged – perhaps dismembered – and the wounds are covered over, forgotten briefly with some new apparition of hope, but they're still there, they hurt, and they ache, and they come back when the weather's bad, or when we're tired, or at some other time, apparently out of the blue: we just can't get rid of them once and for all.

Peter, John, and the others went fishing. For three years they had been out of their depth, but safe behind the leadership of Jesus, trying to be apostles of a new teaching. Now, with Jesus gone and the bubble burst, they go back to what is familiar – what they're good at. We do the same, very often, when we come face to face with failure. We retreat into what we're good at. We long for the job before the one we have now. We play at being single again – close off in our relationships. In the church, we retreat into tradition – forms of service that feel safe because they are all about comfort rather than risk – and we'd rather die irresponsibly under the covers of our beds than fall foolishly, perhaps, on the battlefield.

'But that night they caught nothing.' The word 'night' in John's gospel, should never simply be taken at face value. It's one of his words that's dripping with meaning. Of course this expedition took place at night, but is was also a time of emotional darkness for these men – a time of groping, feeling for a mooring, searching for meaning and direction. They were in spiritual darkness too – in fact they had chosen it. Jesus, through his resurrection appearances, was already calling them to a renewed life of faith – but they chose to go back to their old life of fishing.

'But that night they caught nothing.' They couldn't see and they'd become de-skilled. They didn't know where the fish were. They didn't have the energy or vision for it. The fact was that Jesus had called them away from this way of being, and although they returned to it thinking it would be something they were good at – something to give them comfort – they were a flop.

Once again, the same is true of us. Faced with despair, we go back again to the place of comfort – but we forget that we are actually returning to the night, the darkness – in which our defeat will become even more crushing than ever before. As Christians we've been given the Word of God and the Spirit of Jesus to be our comforters – these lead us on into the light of day. But all too often we ignore the God-given sources, and turn instead to the hope of hiddenness, the icon of insularity – the night. And how bitter – when we catch nothing.

'As day was breaking, Jesus stood on the shore . . .' He'd been there for a while – making a fire, in fact, and getting some fish himself – but they hadn't seen him because they'd been so preoccupied with the fishing and the darkness of the night. 'He called out to them, "Friends, haven't you any fish?"' Of course, he knew the answer – just as they would later know that he was the Lord. "Not a thing!" they answered. "Throw your net on the right side of the boat and you will catch some."

When they did, they were unable to haul the net up because of the large number of fish.'

I want you to notice a few things about this. Firstly, Jesus calls them 'friends'. There was a lot he could have held against them – including the fact that they had moronically gone back to their boats. But he called them 'friends' – and he does the same for us. We change in our love for him, and our commitment to him, but he never changes in his love or commitment to us. No matter where we are, no matter how unfaithful we've been, no matter how deep we've sunk back into the night, no matter how much of a bog-up we've made of everything – he continues to address us as 'friends'. Jesus has established each person here this morning as 'friends of God' – it's up to you how you respond.

Secondly, Jesus reaches out to them right in the night of their despair. *He's* standing on the shore of a new day, but his word reaches *them* while they're still in the darkness. The word goes out, as it were, as Jesus' net – to bring his disciples in from their gloom. In our lives we need to listen for the word of God. It is there to bring us out of the darkness and into the marvellous light of his new day. His word goes out to us too, but we need to let it reach us. All over this country there are shrinking, defeated Christians and shrinking, defeated churches because they cover themselves with an old comfort – the way they live, they way they pray, the way they worship, the habits they renew. The word of Jesus, the word of God, which we hear through the Bible, will reach out and save us – but we must be prepared to hear it.

Thirdly, Jesus gives these failing disciples a new direction: 'Throw your net over the right side of the boat.' He spoke to them where they were, but he wanted them to move on. What is his direction for you? Did you listen out for it? What is his direction for your church? Do you meet together to pray about it? Do you prayerfully consider the needs of others living in the area and where he wants you to cast the spiritual net of mission? He *has* a new direction that will take us *out* of the darkness – but we have to listen for it with the *purpose of obeying it*. I don't know if any of what I've being saying this morning makes sense for you and for your life or your church, but I do know this: if those disciples had not listened to, received, and followed Jesus' new direction, they would never have caught the great draught of fish he intended for them. And *we* will never catch what he intends for us, unless we do the same.

Well, that brings me to a detail which comes a little later in our reading. When Peter and the others dragged the net ashore, they found it contained '153 big fish'. If you read the commentaries on John you'll find that all sorts of explanations have been offered to account for this very particular number. The best one by far is that those fishermen were so astounded by their catch that they sat down and counted them all out. The number of fish stuck in their memories just as, many years later, they could doubtless still feel the weight of those fish in their hands. '153 big fish'.

It actually *happened*. Jesus' resurrection – his alive-ness – actually made a difference to the real world. They knew it was Jesus just as truly as they could feel the weight of those fish sitting in their palms. And when *we* respond with faith to Jesus being alive today, we too discover that he actually makes a real difference to our real world.

'153 big fish.' It was a marvellous, unmerited, enormous gift of grace. Outstandingly generous and overflowing in abundance. How does *our* giving mirror the gift of God? Peter got the right idea. When John said 'It is the Lord' he jumped into the water and rushed to the shore. How generous are you in your worship? How abundant are you in your joy to meet the Lord? We come to church – presumably – for that purpose: Where's the joy? Or are our eyes still closed to the abundance of his grace? How does *our* giving mirror the gift of God? Do we offer him the fullness of our hearts? Do we offer him the fullness of our bank accounts? If your money is not fully and truly at Jesus' disposal then your heart never will be.

We're coming to an end – both of the sermon and the passage. Jesus already had a fire going with some fish on it, but he said to the others, 'bring some of the fish you have just caught'. Maybe it was because what he had was not enough for all to share. But more significantly, perhaps, notice how he wants them to join him – he wants them to bring their offerings, he wants to incorporate them into his plans. And notice how he gives them credit: 'the fish *you* have just caught'. He was the key player, but he's so pleased to affirm *their* role.

Jesus Christ is alive today – this morning – and he has plans that he wants us to join him in. He has plans for this church – for your life and mine – and he wants us to get together with him, bringing the fish that he's helped us catch – the little fragments of the dawn that helped us pull ourselves in out of the night. But we've got to pay *attention*, say *goodbye* to the false comforts we return so foolishly, listen to his *word* and follow him.

Maybe you feel you've been here before. I expect the disciples felt that too – it was as they were about their fishing business that he called them in the first place. Jesus' renewed call always echoes his calls of the past – but each time he calls us to a new future. How will you – how will this church – how do you as an individual – respond? Perhaps you too will end up with the first meal of a new day. 'Friends – haven't you any fish? Throw your net on the right side of the boat and you will find some.'

Rebekah

Jo Bailey Wells

Dr Jo Bailey Wells, 35, is the Dean of Clare College, Cambridge, the first ordained woman to be Dean of an Oxbridge college. Married to Samuel Wells, a parish priest, she began working life as Youth Director and Mission Pastor in an Episcopal Church in Minneapolis, USA, before moving back to Britain to become a research student at Durham University. She was priested in 1996. 'This job is liturgical, academic and pastoral – I strive to make the practices of the college human and its worship divine. I am often to be found with students in shared enquiry, personal turmoil, and emerging faith and vocation; and in quieter moments I make journeys of discovery in the pages of the Old Testament.' She has recently published God's Holy People: A Theme in Biblical Theology *(Sheffield, 2000).*

She was was brought up in the Church, but became more active in her faith as a teenager through confirmation classes and summer camps. The most significant experience for her was a 'gap' year spent working as a volunteer at a mission hospital in a remote region of Transkei, South Africa. 'In material terms I had everything and my local colleagues had nothing, but in spiritual terms the situation was the reverse. I learnt something there about what really matters, and I was in awe. A subsequent period as a volunteer teacher in Uganda, during the 1985 civil war, had a similar effect – so I have always looked to Africa as my spiritual home. Perhaps the church there may yet provide the needed inspiration for the Western church.'

She has always been attracted to the kind of work which is led by conviction. For her, this meant charitable work of some kind, either in relief and development or in the Church. 'My sense of call to ordination came about though the gradual elimination of other options – when logic overcame resistance. During my training and since during my ministry, this vocation has steadily deepened – mainly through sheer enjoyment and fulfilment of such work.'

The sermon published here was prepared for a series on Genesis, each one focusing on a different character. 'I chose a female character, and I was drawn to Rebekah given that she is such a complicated figure. She is so cunning and deceiving that it is not straightforward to claim her as God's instrument of blessing. Given the context in which the sermon was preached – in a college chapel, to graduates and undergraduates – I tried to dwell on the features of the story which might have relevance for students. Given that it is an academic context, I also tried to offer something interesting in terms of method for the way we read the Bible.'

In the service of Evensong, she prefers the sermon to follow after the readings (which should be read well!), in order that the rest of the service can respond to it, through prayer and music. 'The best justification for the relevance of the sermon today – as ever – is to interpret the readings, God's Word, so we may the better know and live our faith. Much of the Bible is so hard to understand that we need help and inspiration, and this is primarily what the sermon should provide. The challenge to preaching today comes from the fact that people seldom sit and simply "listen" – we are used to visual stimulation also – which underlines the need for the preacher to "paint" pictures and speak visually.' But talent and eloquence is not the whole story: the integrity and conviction with which it is prepared and delivered matters more in the end. The reason I felt good about this sermon is that it was a message I was preaching to myself during a difficult time.

Outside of religion her interests are artistic: painting, pottery, textiles – and generally transforming other people's junk into new treasure. 'This has such spiritual overtones for me – a second chance. A few years ago I renovated a tumbled-down old shepherd's refuge in a remote valley of the French Alps. It represents a touch of heaven, where my husband Sam and I love to go for mountain walking and lake swimming each summer. We have a golden retriever, to whom much devotion is accorded. She is chiefly responsible for organizing our days off, also spent walking.'

Text: Genesis 24:1–31; John 4:4–26.

I WOULD UNDERSTAND if after the end of this sermon you didn't want to stay for supper but made haste to the fountain in the middle of the college next door. You see, as far as I know, that's the nearest thing we have to a well round here. And as we shall see, it seems, according to the biblical tradition, that wells are the place to meet the person of your dreams. Rebekah is the first in a long line of women who meet their future partner through an enounter at a well. Moreover, each time it seems that God is not only fully present but making it absolutely clear who is the 'right' one. God's guidance concerning marriage seems to be made manifest at wells.

Don't take me too literally. But who am I to say that – especially with a surname like mine. Perhaps I must have such a thing about Wells that I married one. But it is interesting – isn't it? – that Rebekah and Isaac are 'betrothed' at a well, that their son Jacob meets Rachel at a well, that Moses finds his wife Zipporah at a well, and that Ruth and Boaz have their first conversation at a well. And there are many features in common running through these stories – all of which are most fully illustrated in the story of Rebekah.

The future bridegroom, or his servant as representative, travels to a foreign land. There, at a well, he encounters a 'maiden' – or several – always described as so-and-so's daughter. One of them, either the man or the maiden, then draws water from the well. After this she rushes home to bring the news of the stranger's arrival. And finally, a betrothal is concluded between the stranger and the young woman, usually just after a meal.

Now, one theory about all these similar stories is to suggest that they all stem from the same original story. Thus, for example, the story of Isaac finding Rebekah, and Jacob finding Rachel, is the same thing which has somehow become duplicated in the process of transmission. But this makes rather a nonsense not only of our sermon series – why waste time looking at both stories? – and it ignores all the subtle differences between them.

I want to suggest an alternative way of looking at them. Greek epic poets like Homer make use of 'typescenes' in their system of story-telling. These are certain fixed situations which the poet is expected to include in a work and manipulate for dramatic effect (just as we do in telling jokes about Englishmen and Irishmen). So here in Genesis we have encountered an ancient narrative convention. If this is so, then what is interesting about it is not the schema of the convention – that men meet maidens at wells when they travel abroad and return home with a wife – but what is done in each individual application of the schema to make it different. So we need to look carefully – for the sudden twist, that tilt of innovation, or even for a radical refashioning of the norm – for here will be the keys to its significance.

So, returning to this particular incidence of the betrothal typescene, what might we learn about Rebekah and about God's blessing to all people that began with Abraham? Now we are familiar with the patterns of the 'well' stories, we are better able to enjoy the allusions and the subtleties – just as with the genre of Englishman/Irishman jokes.

Genesis 24 begins with Abraham's fatherly concern that his young son should find a wife. Abraham appears to be more concerned about this than Isaac – throughout, Isaac is a completely passive character – and Abraham's concern is, of course, based on the fact that for God's promises to hold out – 'to your descendants I will give you this land', 'they shall be as numerous as the stars in the sky' – then there needs to be some children in the next generation. Fortunately Abraham has a faithful servant who sees this need more clearly than does Isaac, and does something about it – with the help of an angel who makes the travel arrangements. Meanwhile Isaac sits back, and lets others scurry around on his behalf.

Throughout we are assured of God's guidance in this matter. The servant pictures the circumstances in which he may find the right person for Isaac in his prayers beforehand, and, as the story goes, it happens exactly as he had hoped. So he can be sure he has found the right person. A friend of mine who feels he's missed the boat on marriage once said to me, 'I'm not fussy any more. There are only three qualifications for a person to be my wife: she must be single, female and a Christian.' Well, isn't Isaac lucky – Rebekah is also 'fair to look upon', she's from the 'right' family, she's carrying a water jar, and she gives him and his camels a drink . . . Oh that we all had such helpful angels, and guidance was so easy! Without lifting a finger, Isaac seems to have landed the jackpot.

Rebekah also shows immense initiative. A less polite description might be to say she's not backwards in coming forwards. In fact I expect she did everything her mother told her not to. Not only does she talk to a stranger, she has no hesitation in accepting gifts from him and puts on every nose-ring and bracelet she is offered. She invites the stranger to her home and runs back ahead of him to tell everyone the news. And when he invites her to return with him on the condition she will be loyal and true to Isaac, she is happy to leave immediately and doesn't even want to wait the ten days recommended by her family. From the very outset we see her as a powerful woman, self-possessed, sure to get her own way, not to be messed with. If Abraham is the patriarch of patriarchs, then Rebekah is the matriarch of matriarchs, more than a match for Isaac. Don't believe everything you hear about submissive women back in ancient times!

But this characterization soon develops in more disturbing ways. What might be described as Rebekah's initiative, on the basis of this story, turns into impatience and impetuosity before long, however. Likewise, Isaac's passivity brings him to the position of victim in the hands of the wily Rebekah. Of their twin sons, she favours Jacob, the one born last, and negotiates with him to deceive Isaac into giving his blessing to Jacob rather than to Esau, the first-born. The woman who was once an innocent maiden has become manipulative and deceptive.

Read this way, the text poses for us a big problem. What do we make of that oh-so-clear guidance that leads Abraham's trusty servant to identify Rebekah as the chosen one for Isaac? Was the servant wrong in thinking she was the one for Isaac, or worse still, did God mislead him in that decision? And if the patriarchs make mistakes, what hope is there for us?

The way the story of Rebekah is told provides a very clear answer to these questions. This re-telling of the betrothal typescene stresses God's sovereignty in the choice of Rebekah, as well as intimating that with this woman there may be problems. The problem is not naïvety.

The message is this. In choosing Abraham and his descendants as the means by which to channel his blessing to the world, God has chosen to work with humanity despite our unreliability, our inconsistency, our self-deception, our sin. He chooses imperfect vessels. It is not even that he chooses perfect vessels which develop imperfections. God chooses to work with broken pots.

There is not one single episode in the fulfilment of the promise of blessing to Abraham which suggests that human vessels work well. All the patriarchs and matriarchs are complex, compromised characters. Abraham pretends to Pharaoh that Sarah his wife is his sister. Sarah tries to take charge of God's promise by persuading Abraham to have a child with Hagar. And so it goes on, with Rebekah deceiving her husband, with Esau and Jacob fighting, with Laban palming off Leah rather than Rachel to Jacob . . . all the way to Joseph being molested by his brothers and sold off to Egypt as a slave.

But for some mysterious, even foolish reason, God does not give up with his promise to bless humanity. Blessing is his norm for us. That Rebekah fails to be loyal in no way brings the promise into jeopardy. Despite her deception and her manipulation the promise continues – and not only in *spite* of her but even *because* of her. Through Rebekah's deeds the blessing is directed through Jacob's line. Who knows how different it might be if it wasn't for Rebekah and her deception. What we do know is that – even in a person like Rebekah – the promise prevails. Whatever the circumstances, whatever our weaknesses, blessing is the prevailing norm for us under God.

Personally I find all of this very comforting. Nothing I have done can prevent God fulfilling his purposes – not just his purposes for those around me, but his purposes in me and through me. This is the heart of the encounter at the New Testament well, the encounter of all encounters. Notice again the features of a betrothal typescene: a stranger has wandered into a foreign land and meets a woman drawing water.

But this woman was no 'maiden'. Doubtless she was hanging around that well looking for the man of her dreams, the husband of God's choice. But she'd tried several men before, only to be hurt and disappointed. There was an aching void for sure guidance, for someone to trust, for God's blessing. Isn't that what we all long for? But feeling unworthy of any blessing and doubting her own value had brought her to give up all hope.

But at that well she met the bridegroom of all bridegrooms. She discovered the marriage made in heaven. And so she lifted her skirts and tore back into town, unstoppable with excitement. And through this broken vessel, the blessing of Abraham spread to the world.

Salvation – With an Exclamation Mark!

Ian Knox

Ian Knox, 56, was born and brought up in Yorkshire, but now lives in Coventry. He is married to Ruth, and they have four sons – Matthew, Jon, Andy and David. Their eldest, Matthew, works in the City of London, Jon and Andy are at university, and David is at a sixth-form college in Coventry. The other member of the family is Joker, a brood bitch for the Guide Dogs for the Blind, who has so far produced over thirty puppies.

Ian is a solicitor by profession, but left Coventry City Council where he worked as a senior solicitor in 1982 to take up employment as a full-time travelling evangelist. He works for the 40:3 Trust (a charitable trust, whose name is derived from Psalm 40 verse 3, 'The Lord put a new song in my mouth, a hymn of praise to our God. Many will see and fear and put their trust in the Lord.') In December 1998 Ian was made a Lay Canon by the Bishop of Bungoma in western Kenya. His work involves him in teaching and preaching evangelistically throughout the British Isles and abroad. He works with a team of other evangelists and many lay helpers in helping churches to share the Christian faith.

'I first trusted in Christ as a boy of seven, and my faith has been very severely tested through some difficult family bereavements, including the death of my mother when she was 45 and my brother who died from a terrible accident in Uganda when working as a missionary doctor in 1976, aged 28.' These experiences are described in his book, Bereaved, *published by Kingsway.*

How well the sermon works depends on how good the preacher is, he says. 'I believe that people should leave a service feeling inspired, enthused, challenged and uplifted, with something to carry them through the week. If a sermon can do these things then it should be towards the end of the service. If the preacher is not very good, then the earlier in the service the sermon comes the better, so that people can leave with the inspiration of prayers and hymns. This is why preachers need good training and the ability to convey the Christian message with enthusiasm.'

Earlier this year Ian was speaking in a pub at a men's meal. 'I was delighted with the great attention the men gave to my talk, and amazed afterwards to see all the men standing in a huge circle debating and discussing in a most animated way what had been said. They had no time to talk about anything else except the relevance of the Christian faith in their lives – most of them were people who rarely, if ever, set foot in a church.' On a recent visit to Uganda, in June 2000, he was further surprised when, having said something very deep about the cross of Jesus Christ, the congregation burst into spontaneous song. 'Not having expected this, I had to take a deep breath to wonder how on earth to follow their enthusiastic singing!'

In his spare time Ian loves gardening, particularly growing vegetables. He is a passionate follower of schoolboy rugby. His sons have all been in their schools' rugby teams and this season will be no exception. He and his wife enjoy walking in their local park with Joker.

I WAS WATCHING one of my sons playing rugby for his school. He's not wildly demonstrative, so he doesn't leap up and down like England's Ben Cohen. But he did score a try like Ben. As he got up, he quietly said, through clenched teeth, 'Yessss!' I could feel the exclamation mark of excitement – he was a winner!

There are bits of the Bible like that, where a writer seems to say 'Yesss!' with lots of 'esses' and an exclamation mark, as though he's got to say it or burst. Listen to these words of Isaiah as he launches into six thrilling verses which make up his chapter six:

I will praise you, O Lord.
Although you were angry with me, your anger has turned away
and you have comforted me. Surely God is my salvation;
I will trust and not be afraid.
The Lord, the Lord is my strength
and my song:
he has become my salvation.

He's pretty gee'd up, isn't he? He's almost breathless, unable to contain himself. Why doesn't he say, 'The Lord is my strength and song?' Of course, he does, but he actually says, 'The Lord, the Lord is my strength and song' – repeating 'The Lord' in his enthusiasm. It's as if he's realized for the first time how wonderful God is – like a first love affair, when you walk in the clouds with joy, or when a rugby player scores his first try.

He's almost become a Psalmist, singing his praises to the Lord. What's got Isaiah going like this? It's a combination of things. There is a rejoicing at God's forgiveness, when the opposite was deserved. He puts it in a delightful way: 'Although you were angry with me, your anger has turned away.' I like that! The concept of anger turning round and disappearing – I can almost visualize it. Forgiveness is one of our greatest needs. To know God's forgiveness is amazing. More than that, Isaiah has been welcomed back by the very God he has offended: 'You have comforted me'. It is the picture of an offended father embracing his wayward child back into his arms of love – beautiful.

He encapsulates the whole experience in the word 'Salvation,' with the meaning of healing and wholeness, bringing him 'strength' – from the negative to the positive. No wonder the Lord is his song! He's a happy man. When something excellent happens you want to share it with others so they can feel what you do, and experience it for themselves. My son's try, and his 'Yesss!' was not only for himself, but for his team to revel in five points gained. A first love affair is known by everyone because the lovers cannot keep the joy to themselves. Isaiah has you and me, and all his readers in mind, when he writes these dramatic six verses, as he enthuses us to discover what he now knows in his own life.

He wants us to *get it*. When he says 'I will trust and not be afraid' he wants the reader to say that with him. This 'salvation' is not meant to be a theory in Scripture, it is meant to be an experience in our hearts and lives. All the training in the world is useless unless it culminates in a try in a real match. Watching romantic films is a shadow for a real love relationship. 'Religion' is a poor replacement for a personal relationship with the living God. 'Come and know God as I do' Isaiah seems to be inviting us.

Secondly, he wants us to *grasp it*. 'With joy you will draw from the wells of salvation.' He's given himself away now – do you see how he's moved from 'I' to 'you'? He really does want us to be involved, and in a continuing, daily way. A rugby try in one game does not count in the next – another is needed. Falling in love one day means saying 'I love you' every day. Yesterday's water from the well will not quench today's thirst. We need, says Isaiah, to have a constant ongoing relationship with God and his salvation. The American evangelist Billy Graham was asked why he said he needed to be filled daily with the Holy Spirit. 'Because I leak' was his delightful reply!

If we are not careful, we block God's salvation out. We were on a family holiday in the Hebrides, walking across a beach, when we came across a little spring, bubbling up in the sand. One of our sons put his foot on it. The area all round became soggy, as the spring was squashed. How easily we can do that with God's love, not letting it flow through our hearts. The good news is that, as soon as my son lifted his foot, there was the spring, as clear and pure as ever. God's love waits to flow in the same way in our hearts, if only we let it. 'Do it!' says Isaiah.

Then, thirdly, he wants us to *give it*.

In that day you will say:
'Give thanks to the Lord call on his name;
make known among the nations
what he has done . . .
Shout aloud and sing for joy'.

Echoes abound through the Bible of Isaiah's desire that others should hear of God's good news. 'Tell out my soul the greatness of the Lord' is the hymn writer's paraphrase of Mary's song in Luke 1. 'We cannot help speaking about what we have seen and heard' is the reaction of Peter and John when told to be quiet in Acts 4. Good news is for sharing – be it a try, a new love, or God's salvation.

The next time you see a wild reaction to a try scored – at schoolboy or international level, or you meet a wide-eyed, over-the-top, 'I've fallen in love' person, remember Isaiah. You have his permission to get excited about God. And why not? His salvation, with its forgiveness and new life, is the best thing that can ever happen. Get it! Grasp it! Give it! With an exclamation mark.

Note
The 40:3 Trust website address:

http://www.xalt.co.uk/webspace/FORTYTHREETRUST

John 12:24

Norman Price

Norman Price, 73, of Cockington, Torquay, recently completed 50 years as a Methodist local preacher. Married to Joan, a retired school secretary, they have two children, Rosemary and Stephen.

After grammar school and Birmingham University, he became a teacher and lecturer in FE and was for 25 years until his retirement the head of Religious Studies at Torquay Girls' Grammar School. He has had four books published, three commentaries on the Synoptic Gospels and one on the Old Testament.

To a certain extent, he says, he 'inherited' his faith from parents and grandparents, but as a young man he was greatly influenced and encouraged by the preaching and ministry of The Revd William Hughes, a renowned Welsh preacher.

It came to a point where he had to decide between teaching and entering Methodist ministry. 'I decided to have the best of both worlds; to teach and to preach. So I had two types of "congregation"; Sundays and weekdays. But the classroom is not a pulpit, nor a pulpit a lecture lectern. I believe there should be a connection and correlation between teaching and preaching; that has been the challenge and the privilege. Both must have the sense of vocation. This sense has been strengthened and developed by people, young and older, coming to see how relevant religion is to life . . . the bread of life, not just occasional "confectionery". Also, to recognize that as far as biblical truths are concerned, there are many facets of truth and that moral and spiritual truths are as valid as those in an historical setting. Realization of this can provide paths to mountain-top views which can never be enjoyed from the foothills of extreme fundamentalism.'

The sermon published here arose from some thinking around the subject of the loneliness and futility of selfishness. 'The "dying to self" approach is an aspect of Christian teaching one feels is often under-emphasized in contemporary preaching. There is a need to contrast and compare spiritual poverty with economic prosperity.'

The sermon is a vital part of a religious service, he says. 'It should preferably be placed towards the end, and come as a culmination and climax of the service, which can be crafted to lead up to it. But such prominence must be deserved and justified by a relevance that reaches out to the congregation, both spiritually and intellectually. A sermon carelessly prepared and delivered will be heard with little interest or sense of involvement. I believe a sermon should have a base . . . which, to me, means a text; some background, to put it into context and to put the congregation "in the picture"; and a bringing up to date, with application to present-day issues. It is good to hear of sermons being "inspired", but true inspiration, whether of art, music, poetry or preaching, lies in spiritual reality.'

He recalls an incident in a service where he was a member of the congregation. 'A minister, new to that church, was taking his first service. When the time came for the sermon, he came from the pulpit and confronted the congregation. "Now" he said, "I'm your new minister . . . I want you to tell me what you expect of me." They were a bit taken aback, and there were one or two obvious replies. Then an elderly man, sitting by me at the back, got to his feet, trembling with the effort, and said, "I come to church, sir, to hear the Gospel preached, to know what the Lord wants of me in my life, and to hear of his saving grace and truth . . . and", pointing at the minister . . . "I shall rely on you, sir, to keep me informed."

'Every time I take a service, I remember his words and my responsibility . . . "I shall rely on you, sir, to keep me informed."'

His other interests include writing and music. He plays the piano and organ, which came in handy in one little country church, where he had to both play and preach. He also enjoys walking and is keen on conservation.

'Ignacy Paderewski was once asked about his reputation of being one of the world's finest pianists. He replied, "Compared to the composers – Mozart, Chopin, Beethoven – I am insignificant. My task is simply to try and interpret the work so that the listener is able to hear what the master intended."

'Applies to pianists . . . and to preachers.'

Text: John 12:24.

Unless a grain of corn falls into the ground and dies, it will remain a solitary grain; But if it dies, it will produce a rich harvest.

EVEN A CASUAL COMPARISON between the four gospels will show that the Fourth gospel is very different in character and composition to the other three. Matthew, Mark and Luke are known as 'synoptic' gospels because they share the same(syn) view(optic), or framework. Many scholars believe that Mark appeared first, with Matthew and Luke then using the same pattern of presentation as Mark, together with most of that gospel's contents, and adding their own material. But John's gospel has differences in style, language, presentation and purpose to the extent that prompts the question whether the Fourth gospel is more a theological interpretation of the life of Jesus than an historical record.

Such questions are complex and have been turned over in the field of biblical studies many times over the years, but another comparison, if not a contrast, is that whereas in the Synoptics much of Jesus's teaching is given to crowds, in John it is often delivered to individuals, or at least to small groups. One thinks, for example, of the meeting of Jesus with the Samaritan woman at Sychar and talking to her about 'living water', the conversation with Nicodemus about being 'born again', and the assurance given to Martha, after the death of her brother Lazarus, that he, Jesus, was 'the resurrection and the life'. And here, in the incident from which our text is taken, Jesus speaks to a few Greeks about the attainment of real life, a theme that runs right through John's gospel.

It may be maintained that the request by these men to see Jesus was motivated more by curiosity than genuine desire, but it would seem that there was more to it than that. They were probably proselytes, converts to the Jewish faith, on their way up to Jerusalem for Passover. They would have been familiar with the facets and philosophies of the Greek religions and one wonders whether a dissatisfaction with that background had led to an attraction to Judaism, but also whether they had, perhaps, become somewhat disappointed with certain aspects of Judaism. Was this the reason why they 'sought to see Jesus'?

Whatever the reason, they were resolute. They approached Philip, perhaps because he was on the periphery, but more likely because he had a Greek name and came from Bethsaida, a town which had a sizeable Greek population. Philip was a bit nonplussed, perhaps because he knew that Greeks were characteristically an inquisitive people, tending, as Paul found at Athens, (Acts 17:21) to seek after anything 'new and novel.'

Yet he sensed that there was something more serious in the request, so he enlisted the help of Andrew, who was also from the town of Bethsaida, and together they took the men to see Jesus. And Jesus, recognizing the need in this request to see him, said, 'Except a grain of corn falls into the ground and dies, it will remain a solitary grain, but if it dies it will produce a rich harvest.'

What did he mean? Many things. For example, he could have meant himself, because for much of his ministry Jesus was very much a solitary grain, in the sense that he didn't shake the world whilst he walked the shores of Galilee or the streets of Capernaum, and, on his own admission, sometimes he had nowhere to lay his head. It wasn't until that 'solitary grain' fell and died, and rose again, that the gospel and the Church were born and began to 'bring forth a rich harvest'.

The mighty growing from small beginnings is one of the great glories of Nature. The most magnificent rivers and most massive trees began from tiny tributaries and small seeds. And it is also true of great movements. The Christian religion has now reached every corner of the globe and its message translated into many hundreds of languages, but it began with one man and a few friends.

45

Take a grain of corn in your hand, or, for that matter, seeds of certain fruits and flowers, some of them looking little more than blackened grains of sand. Put them under a microscope . . . break them into pieces. What do you see? Can you see the power, the potential, the possibilities in those seeds? No . . . and you won't until you put them into the ground and let them die. Then, and only then, will you be able to know the harvest they can produce.

And what is true of Nature is true of human nature. Here were men who were seeking the secret of real living, the means of salvation of the soul, and Jesus told them, 'If you want to really live, then first of all you must die'. A paradox? Not in the least. The word 'martyr' comes from a Greek word meaning 'witness', which may well mean living for something, rather than dying for it. Jesus said that those who were serious about following him should take up the cross and 'deny themselves', which doesn't mean going about bowed down and looking as though we are bearing all the troubles of the world on our backs. It means the putting to death of our self-interest, self-seeking, self-gratification, self-importance, self-indulgence. It means putting ourselves second and God's interests first. When a person becomes immersed in merely their own personal ploys and pleasures, they become marooned on a very narrow neck of life, perhaps achieving fame and fortune, but in reality in being in great danger of becoming very lonely souls.

'What shall I render unto the Lord for all his benefits towards me'? asked the psalmist (Ps 116) and then gave the answer, 'I will offer the sacrifice of thanksgiving; O Lord, I truly am thy servant.' But such service and sacrifice isn't easy. Co-operation with God comes at a price, because it involves the willingness to put self way down the list of life's priorities. The farmer who in one of Jesus's parables, (Luke 12:16), thought that the celebration of success and reaction to a record harvest was simply to build bigger barns for himself, was described as a fool. The seed that falls into the ground and dies, or more strictly speaking, dies to itself, sets out the mystery of life through death because it quite literally empties itself of life in order to produce new life. In the world of Nature, it is the secret of fruitfulness and in spiritual terms it is the secret of salvation, since selfishness spells diminution of the soul.

So, what holds us back? If we call ourselves Christian, it is not an optional extra, it is an obligation. 'To give and give and give again what God has given thee', wrote Studdert-Kennedy, and St Ignatius prayed, 'Teach us, good Lord, to give and not to count the cost, to labour and to ask for no reward, save that of knowing that we do thy will'. And Isaac Watts sang, ' Love so amazing, so divine, demands my life, my soul, my all.'

Of course it's difficult. Self-sacrifice always is. Is there anywhere in the New Testament that indicates otherwise? No doubt, if the seed could choose, it might well prefer to remain a solitary grain, rather than being put into the earth to apparently die, but then there would be no harvest. Frances Havergal's words, 'Take my life and let it be consecrated, Lord, to thee', indicates unconditional surrender and no strings attached. It means letting go of ourselves and letting God take over. And if we wonder what he might want us to do, or where he might want us to go, the chances are that the demands will be more mundane than dramatic, but it is the level of commitment that counts.

We are told that we remember what we hear far less than we remember what we read or see, and if we doubt that, try asking members of a church congregation, after the service, what the sermon has been about! But remember this . . . God sees us not only as individuals, but also as seeds. And he looks at the possibilities and potential that lie in that seed. He sees the power for spiritual growth and goodness each one of us possesses.

We live in testing times, as far as the Christian faith is concerned. There is an obsession with materialism on a scale that not so long ago would have been thought unbelievable. The trivial and the transient are elevated and glamorized, whilst those things that would make for decency and good relationships are denigrated and often ridiculed. But rebellion against God and carelessness towards the trusteeship of his Creation doesn't mean we become religious refugees. It is very easy to retreat into a religious isolationalism and be satisfied with being a solitary grain. But if we do that, we mustn't be surprised if such isolation develops into insulation.

The prophet Amos wrote of ancient Israel, 'There is a famine in the land, not of eating of bread, but of hearing the word of the Lord', and his analysis applies to modern Britain even more than it did to ancient Israel. And it's a famine that will not be countered by the candyfloss of religious mediocrity, nor resolved by a pick-and-mix approach which seems so reluctant to portray Jesus as the Logos of God in human form. But such a famine can be alleviated by those who are willing, in Charles Wesley's words, 'to serve thee with single aim and eye, and to thy glory live and die'. One remembers the opening line of an old hymn which began, 'Have you had a kindness shown? Pass it on.' And the last verse ran, 'Live for self, you live in vain; live for Christ, you live again; live with him, with him you'll reign. Pass it on'.

Indeed . . . pass it on.

Sharing Truth in the Market Place

MICHAEL BOTTING

Canon Michael Botting, 75, describes himself as 'retired as far as clergy ever retire'. He and his wife, Mary, have two children and six grandchildren. His son is currently a churchwarden in Birmingham and possibly may train for the Church of England ministry. A grandson is considering full-time Christian youth work.

Canon Botting, a Canon Emeritus of Ripon Cathedral, studied science at London University and taught at a boys' preparatory school for two years before training for the priesthood at Ridley Hall, Cambridge, when he was 29.

Although brought up in a Christian home, it was not until he was a student at Imperial College, London, that through the ministry of the Christian Union his faith came truly alive for him. His call to the priesthood came some three years later when he was travelling on the London Underground during the run-up to Christmas and saw a whisky advertisement, surrounded by holly, with the words 'Unchanged in a changing world'. 'My mind immediately went to the text Hebrews 13.8 which refers to Jesus Christ as the same yesterday, today and for ever. Here we were at Christmas, about to celebrate the birth of Christ, and whisky was being promoted as the unchanging thing. It hit me for six – I just felt I was called to put the record straight. It just so happened that John Stott, Rector of All Souls, Langham Place, was leading a mission near where I lived. I went to see him, and he immediately accepted everything I had said as a call to the ministry.'

He became curate at St Paul's, Onslow Square, for five years and went from there to St Matthew's, Fulham. He was elected a member of the General Synod when it first started, and in 1972 went to St George's, Leeds, famous for the Christian social work in its crypt. In 1984 he was called by the former Bishop of Chester to help set up a diocesan lay training course, which had attracted some 2500 members by the time of his retirement at the age of 70. He is currently honorary assistant minister at his local church, St Michael's, Plas Newton, but frequently helps in other parishes, when there is an interregnum or the vicar is ill or on holiday.

One of the things that has dominated his ministry stems from his time at Fulham, when he noticed his church was getting lots of children in the Sunday School but he rarely saw their parents. So he started a 45-minute Morning Service based on Morning Prayer, without any psalms, and which he called a Family Service. It took off and drew in parents. Now very many churches in the country have a Family or All-Age Service. However, he believes that was the first. He has since written nine books on the subject of the Family Service.

'I believe that Christian preaching is the combined work of the Holy Spirit and serious study and hard slog by the preacher. However, in the case of the sermon I submitted, I go back to May 1982 when I was in the midst of leading an evangelistic conference at St George's, Leeds. This had involved a considerable amount of work and I had only two hours to prepare for an evangelistic sermon for the Sunday evening. Somehow the words just flowed on to my typewriter (this was before the word processor era!). I sensed I was being given that sermon. Some in the congregation came to faith that evening. With suitable revisions to suit different situations that sermon has been repeated well over a dozen times, more recently assisted with acetates. I believe it was the great Baptist preacher, Spurgeon, who said that if a sermon was not worth preaching twenty times it was not worth preaching once. In June last year (1999), during an interregnum at my own local church, Paul's sermon on Mars Hill (Acts 17) was the set reading, so I arranged to be the preacher. It was especially appropriate as there was also to be a public infant baptism, when some infrequent churchgoers were expected to be present. Once again the sermon was very obviously appreciated, so it seemed the natural sermon to submit to the Times Preacher of the Year Award. The subject obviously lends itself to evangelistic preaching, seeing it was really only a matter of updating that type of sermon from the Apostle Paul himself.'

He still believes the sermon should have a central place in a religious service. 'The Church of England believes in a balance of Word and Sacrament. In Holy Communion the sermon is rightly set in the Ministry of the Word section followed by responses in Creed, Intercessions and reception of the Sacrament. In Morning and Evening Prayer Services I am inclined to prefer the sermon to be near the end with a carefully chosen hymn for the congregation's reponse. I have plenty of personal evidence that God still uses preaching to bring people to faith. In the mid-sixties when there were two Billy Graham Crusades at London's Earls Court, with which I was offically involved, the large preaching stage was almost entirely taken up with seats for ministers of vaious denominations, who had all come to faith, and subsequently to ordained ministry, through the preaching of Billy Graham at Haringey in 1954.'

Canon Botting once preached a series of six sermons on a general introduction to the Bible. 'One of these was an outline of the Old Testament. To my horror I suddenly realized, as I came to the end, that I had preached for forty minutes! I hardly knew how I could face the congregation as I shook hands with them after the Service. But I had no need to worry. They had never had the Old Testament opened up like that and were fascinated. There was no complaint. Evidently people don't mind preaching provided it is interesting.'

An earlier sermon of his, included in the Fourth Times Book of Best Sermons, *was on the subject of 'Time'. 'At the very precise moment that I ended by saying "let us bow our heads for prayer", the church clock struck twelve. As some people said, "the clock seems to provide your prayer".'*

His other interests include writing, and he especially appreciated being asked by the chairmen of the Chester Diocese's Houses of Clergy and Laity to edit a Tribute Book for the Bishop, the Right Revd Michael Baughen, and his wife Myrtle, when they retired in 1996. 'Though it included sixty contributors, including eight bishops, two MPs and Billy Graham, the Baughens had no idea of its preparation until I handed them hardback copies at their Farewell Service in Chester Catherdral.'

He also enjoys opera, in good supply in Manchester and Liverpool. 'We further enjoy the theatre, especially in Chester, Mold, Clwyd and annual visits to the Festival Theatre in Pitlochry, Perthshire. This year we went to Ober- ammergau.'

Text: Acts 17:16–34.

THE STORY OF the Apostle Paul's visit to Athens, the seat of learn- ing of the ancient world, where he mixed with the so-called 'peo- ple in the street' of his day in the market-place, is remarkable in the fact that his world and ours are so alike.

The nature of the market place
What dominated the Athenian world that dominates ours?

1. Idolatry.

Athens . . .was full of idols.

Obviously modern British people do not build idols, but do have mod- ern equivalents, for example:

(i) *Luck.* People will bet not only on football pools and games of chance, but even, nine years ago, on who would be the next Arch- bishop Canterbury! *Reader's Digest* and other organizations also play on this in their promotional methods. An atheistic scientist once sent me a chain letter that I had to send to ten friends, warn- ing me of dire consequences if I did not do so, including imminent death. I ignored his demand and so far have managed to live anoth- er 50 years!

(ii) *The occult.* For example, astrology: believing the fanciful idea that in some way the movement of the stars, which can be determined scientifically in any case. can actually effect our day-to-day exis- tence. According to *The Sun* more than three billion people around the world, and in Britain 83 per cent of the population, study their forecasts everyday. But there is also the national fascination with tarot cards, Ouija boards, seances, celebration of Hallowe'en, etc., in which people are increasingly putting their faith. There is actually a book published with the title *Myths To Live By*! There is a very real truth in the statement that when people give up believing in God they don't believe in nothing but will believe in anything. The occult is, in fact, strongly condemned in the Bible.

2. Materialism.

A group of Epicurean . . . philosophers began to dispute with him (Paul).

Epicurus, an Athenian, taught that pleasure was the chief end of life. Though not an entirely ignoble cult it became the refuge for the hedonist, sensualist and sexual pervert, who welcomed any excuse for self-indulgence. In a nutshell: 'Let us eat, drink and be merry for tomorrow we die.' Would I be too far wrong in suggesting that our politicians play on the nation's basic materialism to win electoral support?

This attitude to life shouted at my wife and me when on holiday in the USA as every form of eating house competed for custom. Numerous TV channels informed us of all the drinks, gadgets, clothes, perfumes, cars we could not live a full life without. As my wife and I mingled with overweight, unhappy, people, in airport lounges, possibly living on large expense accounts , we longed for the simpler life, and neither of us are adverse to good food! But this American way of life is increasingly to be seen over here. Was not Lord Hailsham right when he wrote nearly 30 years ago: 'I am not at all sure that the introduction into the home of the most powerful advertising stimulant ever devised, giving rise to constantly increasing desires for new domestic expenditure, has not been an important contributory cause of wage demands and inflation which have so characterised the past 20 years of economic life.'

Jesus told a story of a man who had hoarded great wealth so that he could lead a life of total selfishess. At the end of the story God said to the man: 'You fool! This very night your life will be demanded from you. Then who will get what you have prepared for yourself?' Shrouds have no pockets!

We also need to remember George Bernard Shaw's observation that 'Death is the ultimate statistic, one out of every one dies'.

3. Agnosticism.

Paul said '. . . as I walked around and looked carefully at your objects of worship, I even found an altar with this inscription: TO AN UNKNOWN GOD.'

Agnostics are people who admit they are ignorant and know nothing definite about God. They often behave more like atheists, though I always say that an honest agnostic ought at least to pray to God every other day!

There seems much evidence of agnosticism in the meddling with the occult and with fascination with the New Age movement. We see it, too, in church where people still want just a little religion in their lives on certain occasions, or to play safe, so we see them in church for baptisms, weddings and funerals, and Mothering Sunday, Harvest and Christmas carols. People, like Paul preached to in the market-place in Athens all those years ago, are still with us. Perhaps some are here with us this morning.

The message to people in the market-place

1. There is a Creator of this world.

The God who made the world and everything in it is the Lord of heaven and earth and does not live in temples built by hands.

No one who ever lived can explain how something can be made out of nothing – we are all faced with this unsolved problem on this side of the grave. When people tell me dogmatically that they don't believe there is a God, I ask them to give me good reasons, for I believe the case for his existence outweighs the case against. For example:

(i) The wonder and purpose of creation – was all this just for me to live a selfish existence before going out into oblivion? The longer I live, and I'm nearly 74, the more I am amazed at my most incredible possession – my body. I find I am in the good company of the great seventeenth-century scientist, Sir Isaac Newton, who said 'In the absence of any other proof, the thumb alone would convince me of God's existence.' I would want to add my eyes. Bob Geldof, pop singer and inspirer of charitable relief in Africa said 'There's so much beauty out there. I wish I believed enough to pray.'

(ii) The 'god-shaped' gap in the human heart worldwide. As the Bible has put it '(God) has put eternity into man's heart'. Paul says much the same in the reading we heard. (Acts 17:26–28).

(iii) I have here a plastic and genuine flower. From your distance you are not likely to tell the difference, but why do some insist that one has a maker, but not the other?

2. This Creator is going to judge the world.

> God . . . has set a day when he will judge the world with justice . . .
> (v. 31)

I believe thinking people know there is meaning to the words 'right' and 'wrong'. I can't explain why I have a *conscience* unless I am ultimately answerable to Someone beyond this world. Quite often, when visiting the bereaved of people who rarely had any contact with the church, they will say 'He was a good man, Vicar. Never hurt a soul.' Why do people say such things unless deep down they believe we all have to give account for the way we have lived our lives on this earth? In many parts of the world, where Christianity has as yet made little impact, people are deeply aware of their sinfulness and go to aweful extremes to attempt to atone for it.

3. The evidence for this judgment is in Jesus.

> God . . . will judge the world with justice by the man he has appointed. He has given proof of this to all men by raising him from the dead.

I am sure that what we have here in Acts 17 is only Luke's summary of what Paul said in Athens that day. He would have had a great deal more to say about Jesus Christ. What do we make of the Man who has divided world history into BC & AD? Someone has spelt out three possibilities: Lunatic, Liar or Lord.

(i) *Lunatic.* Could it really be argued that the man who has inspired all the great advances in history in medicine, education, much art, music, literature, and vasts amounts of social work associated with the names of Wilberforce and Mother Theresa of Calcutta was a madman?

(ii) *Liar.* Jesus claimed to be God and lived on the assumption that he was. People sometimes say that they believe he was a very good man, but not God. But good men do not lie, certainly not on that scale, if Jesus is not God!

(iii) *Lord.* This possibility explains Jesus' perfect life, impeccable teaching, astonishing and meaningful miracles, his claim to die on the cross on the first Good Friday, to make available salvation from sin, and the resurrection from the dead to which Paul specifically refers. The most extraordinary fact is that many highly intelligent people have seriously set out to disprove the resurrection, with singular lack of success and been converted to Christianity in the process.

The responses from people in the market-place
The reading tells us there were three:

1. Some sneered.
2. Some wanted to hear more.
3. Some men and women believed.

I wonder what responses those who move in today's market-places, who are here this morning, are making.

Back in the late 1800s a rich Swedish tycoon woke up to discover the newspapers declared him to be dead. He had been confused with his brother who had died. The headlines called him the Dynamite King, for he had discovered blasting gelatin and invented detonators for explosives. As he read, the premature obituaries had a profound effect on him. Was he really to go down in history as the inventor of destructive devices? Was it too late to change? He decided not. From then on he put his wealth into a trust fund for the advancement of science, literature, medicine and world peace. To this day annual awards are given for service to humanity in these important fields. Few people today know of Alfred Nobel the Dynamite King, but all over the world the Nobel prizes are better known than most of the people who have won them.

What of your obituary? The response to make Jesus Lord could make a fundamental difference to your life and, in small or large measure, to this world.

Jesus Washes the Disciples' Feet

BARBARA GLASSON

*The Revd Barbara Glasson, 44, is a Methodist minister working in Liverpool
city centre. Married to The Revd David Glasson, also a Methodist minister,
they have three children, Emma, Robin and Alistair.*

*When she left school she went into farming, where she learnt how to
'watch flocks by night' and 'bring the harvest home'. She says: 'I also learned
to pick hops, as all good Methodists do.' She took a degree in Agricultural Sciences in Nottingham. 'Then I cloned potatoes and grew blue lettuces until the
call to the ministry could not be postponed further.' She worked first on place-
ment with an industrial mission on the Humber bank and then moved to
Merseyside. 'I am currently working in Liverpool city centre, where I am dis-
covering new ways of becoming "church". I am working with an ecumenical
team, in store chaplaincies and baking bread.'*

*She has a growing sense of being called to the margins, the place where
faith meets community. 'I believe that God is at work all over the place but
especially in unconventional people and settings. I have strong Nonconformist blood! I believe that faith is an open-handed gift for people like me
who struggle with churchy stuff yet wonder about the world. I have continually found that God can get us by the scruff of the neck and surprise us.'*

*Sermons, she says, need to be simple and deep. 'The sermon must respect
people's vulnerability, be more about God than personality, be spoken directly and from the heart. It should be given humbly and present more costly
questions than cheap answers.'*

*Her congregation is not all in one place. 'They are scattered all over the city
and I go and find them. I have learnt a lot about God in the wig department
of Lewis's.'*

*Her other interests are varied. 'We have a menagerie including chickens
(one with a Mohican hair cut), four Guinea pigs, three rabbits (one with killer
tendencies) and a rescued herring gull. I read Terry Pratchett books, write
depressing poetry and listen to Bob Marley.'*

Text: John 13:1–14.

WHILST I WAS TRAINING for ministry a special service of foot
washing was organized for Maundy Thursday. Each of us had to
choose a friend and suitably equipped with basins and towels we went

in pairs to wash the feet of volunteers in the congregation. My friend Cheryl and I, who had a habit of getting the giggles at inappropriate moments, (a habit I'm still trying to outgrow) were concentrating hard on the holy significance of what we were re-enacting. We did quite well, kneeling on the floor together, presented with the bare foot of our Tutor when she looked at me and said, 'I'll wash if you'll dry!'

I had thought, mistakenly, that as I was now mixing with Roman Catholics and Anglicans I was going to learn something remote and holy. Something that was erudite and beyond. But I realized with some surprise that as a mother of three children the task was strangely familiar. 'I've done this before'.

I've spent a good proportion of my life washing feet. I have washed baby's bendy feet and tickled their toes. I've washed the feet of an entire playgroup as they were caught after 'foot printing with paint' and before they walked all over the church hall floor. I've washed the feet of sick nine-year-olds who were boiling with a temperature. I've washed Grandad's feet when he was living with us and couldn't bend that far . . . and I've even grasped the ultimate challenge in cajoling 14-year-old boys to wash between their toes, which have become a health hazard, and to find clean socks!

So, what's so special about a foot? – it's just a frayed leg. I think we have to be careful about the point at which we enter this story. As a Christian Church we have used the story of the foot washing to assume that we are called to serve each other. The 'washing of feet' becomes the metaphor by which we understand that we are not called to be served but to serve. But it is only a small step to assume that we have to be willing doormats to be Christians.

We can get trapped in patterns of serving others that are not life giving. With such assumptions many people, maybe especially women, have got stuck in a cycle of servitude, guilt and low self-esteem. I sang as a child 'A servant with this clause makes drudgery divine, who sweeps a room as for thy laws makes that and the action fine' – not necessarily, it might just be drudgery and maybe you shouldn't be doing it.

So, let's revisit the story and ask what was really happening. A clue comes in the first line of the chapter, 'Having loved his own that were in the world he now showed them the full extent of his love'.

Here we have the reversal of roles which fills the Gospels. Jesus washes the disciples' feet. This is not a story about our willingness to serve the master. Nor is it primarily a story about our call to serve each other. It is a story about Jesus 'the Lord of heaven and earth' as he demonstrates to his friends the extent of his love. And we know that this action is simply a precursor to the demonstration of love that is around the corner. In the cross.

Hanging over the gospels, as over every human relationship is a question mark. The child asks the father 'How much do you love me?'

Jesus responds in words and actions, 'This much'. Enough to be born beside you. Enough to heal you, to eat with you, to be angry with you. Enough to pray for you without ceasing. Enough to tell you stories over and over. Enough to cry over your cities in despair and yet to forgive you everything. Enough to wash your dusty, smelly, weary feet.

And finally he will stretch his arms out as far as they will go, in a demonstration of suffering and embrace. 'This much'.

The story of the foot washing is not, fundamentally, a story about service but a story about love. Jesus washes the feet of all his disciples, even the ones who are to let him down. He washes their feet so that they understand that they belong with him. Jesus says to his disciples, in this simple, everyday, ordinary act, 'I love you, you belong with me'.

And that is how Christ comes to us. Not as a mighty and powerful overlord, nor as a tyrant who wants blood, nor as a demanding dictator who requires mindless obedience and squeezes all joy out of our bones. But as the God of heaven, kneeling at our feet, saying to us, 'I love you, you belong with me'.

In this way we are able to claim the fullness of life that the gospel offers. We are loved and we have a person to belong to. The destiny of all humanity is found in the God who serves us. Jesus says to us not, 'What can you do for me today', but rather, 'What can I be for you?'

Jesus says, to us 'What can I be for you today?'

Then he says, 'Now that I, your Lord and Teacher, have washed your feet, you also should wash one another's feet.'

Here is God's message for a tired, dusty, smelly world.

As we recognize God's amazing love for even us, only then can we claim the freedom to serve, not as drudgery but as transformation. The Lord who is prepared to engage in the everyday intimacy of foot washing, who is vulnerable to us and to our needs, who thinks that we are important enough to serve, gives us life. The world is offered life by the God of all creation kneeling at its feet.

And so we begin to be free. To recognize in the entire world the possibility that the mundane can be transfigured by the transcendent. Into the ordinary, everyday care for children, the elderly, and the disabled comes the recognition that Christ continues to meet us and to nourish us by his friendship. The incarnate, suffering God whispers in our ear, 'I'll wash if you'll dry'!

This reality is more eloquently put in the words of Brian Wren's hymn,

> Lord God, in Christ you call our name,
> And then receive us as your own,
> Not through some merit, right or claim,
> But by your gracious love alone
> We strain to glimpse your mercy-seat
> And find you kneeling at our feet.

Then take the towel and break the bread
And humble us and call us friends
Suffer and serve till all are fed
And show how grandly love intends
To work till all creation sings
To fill all worlds, to crown all things.

Lord God in Christ you set us free
Your life to love, your joy to share
Give us your Spirit's liberty
To turn from guilt and dull despair
And offer all that faith can do
While love is making all things new.

(Lord God your love has called us here . . .)

Author: Brian Wren
Source: *Hymns and Psalms, No. 500*
Methodist Publishing House: London (1983)

Believing Without Needing to See

GEORGE HORE

George Hore, 72, who is on the parochial church council of St Stephen's, West Ealing, tried twice throughout his life to get involved in church life but says he was never successful because he refused to argue when told of his 'uselessness'. Finally, the Bishop of Willesden, the Right Revd Graham Dow, took a stand on his behalf and he was commissioned as a lay assistant in 1999. An accountancy clerk, he worked in the City and then for the Midland Bank before becoming a volunteer with Age Concern in 1992. For 50 years until last year he was an occasional freelance contributor to Horse and Hound *and is a member of the British Equestrian Writers' Association.*

He has worshipped at churches in Devon and Worthing, but was for much of his adult life at St Martin-in-the-Fields, where he was a sidesman and on the PCC. Since 1990 he has been at St Stephen's in West Ealing, where he has served as treasurer and on the PCC.

'From my childhood in Devon I have been drawn towards the Church,' he says. In spite of two rejections when he tried to embark on an ecclesiastical career, he received much encouragement from people he encountered at places such as Cheltenham College, St Martin's and St Stephen's. He has dedicated his life to helping others. 'One of my regular visits is to a home for disabled ex-servicemen in the parish which, following on my work at Age Concern and St Martin's has given me empathy towards the less fortunate.' Although not ordained, he has a strong sense of vocation. 'At St Martin's we had a Monday evening service of prayer for sick people. One Monday a curate about to go into hospital asked me to lead the service in his absence. That led me to be invited to lead other lay services, such as "home going" prayers for local workers.' At St Stephen's he was also encouraged to develop his lay ministry, being invited to preach regularly. This inspired him to challenge his bishop on why the over-70s should not be licensed.

He has strong and well-developed views on preaching. 'For better, for worse, at St Stephen's main service, the Eucharist, the sermon follows the Gospel reading. On reflection, even at Matins or Evensong, the ideal position for the sermon would be after the second or third reading to illustrate clearly the relevance of the readings for today. This is vital because people imagine the Bible is archaic and that it and the Church have nothing in them to support people facing today's problems. Only through attractive explanations from the pulpit can people be convinced otherwise. It really is up to us. The

Apostles got the ball rolling by "gossiping the Gospel", surely we are told to "Go and do likewise".'

Like many preachers today, he has been confronted with the prospect of delivering his words of wisdom to an empty church. 'One Monday evening at St Martin's before the "prayers for the sick" the vergers wanted to lock up and reported, correctly, that the church was empty. I said I would carry on. The vergers were not amused. By the end there were twelve people in church and one came over and said it was the most moving service he had ever attended. This experience always makes me think of William Barclay's story of the curate who faced a congregation of two and was inspired by the phrase, "Therefore with angels and archangels and all the company of heaven".'

He is also something of a sabbatarian. 'With my equestrian journalism – now a thing of the past – I became increasingly uneasy about covering events on Sundays. I especially had a twinge of conscience after thinking about Psalm 20:7: "Some put their trust in chariots and some in horses: but we will remember the Name of the Lord our God". As at that time my "chariot" was a motor caravan, whenever it broke down I felt it was a judgement.'

Texts: John 20:19–31; Acts 4:32–5 (1 John 1:1–2:2).

Blessed are those who have not seen and yet have believed.

WHAT ARE the set readings for today trying to tell us? Remember that Acts 4, which is after Pentecost, says 'all the believers were one in heart and mind'. The other reading, also post Pentecost, is the first chapter of John's First Epistle and seems to clarify the situation a bit. One can almost imagine John across the years beginning to understand Thomas' dilemma. In verse 7 of the Epistle he writes, 'But if we walk in the light, as he is in the light, we have fellowship with one another'. Now that is precisely what Thomas lacked. Thomas was a pessimist. When Jesus decided to go to Bethany to see and, indeed, raise Lazarus, Thomas appreciated the danger Jesus was walking into.

Unlike Peter, when Jesus first foretold the crucifixion, Thomas did not argue but said 'Let us also go, that we may die with Him'. It is surely significant that he was not with the others in the Upper Room when Jesus made His first reappearance there. When many of us are overcome with grief we don't want to talk, we prefer to go into a quiet corner alone where we can share our heartbreak in silence. Some people feel ashamed when our feelings get the better of us. As a pessimist it is easy to imagine the even deeper sense of gloom that descended on Thomas. He wondered how he would rebuild his totally shattered world. Days before, Jesus would have snapped him out of it. But now Jesus was dead. It was unfashionable in those days to believe women, so when Mary brought the wonderful news back from the tomb would he have believed even if he heard it? After all he told his fellow apostles the conditions which would convince him of the resurrection. The following week a light, the light shone through his despair and immediately he was inspired to say 'My Lord and My God'.

This, surely, brings out the message for us today. It comes in that Epistle, 'we have fellowship with one another'. At Pentecost when the Holy Spirit came upon them they will have received that uncanny inner understanding which prompts compassion for the suffering of others. Thomas needed a shoulder to cry on, somebody to open his heart to, somebody he could trust. There are times you need just that; so do I. That can be achieved in 'that fellowship with one another'. That is what every Church, indeed every Christian, should be able to supply. Such fellowship binds 'all believers in heart and mind'. We must all pray that we can be guided into an embracing way so that no one in a parish feels ignored or left out. This is doubly difficult in an urban community.

One of the snags of the terrible expression 'do-gooder' is that there are some elderly, desperately lonely people who imagine that a genuine hand of friendship is just 'do-gooding' and prefer, like Thomas, to suffer alone. Tragically there are so many artificial barriers erected. Behind those barriers live people who would love to have someone to believe in, a real friend.

Through that fellowship and trust, once established, we really can believe even the seemingly impossible. Such Faith is truly blessed. Amen.

SOCIAL IMPROVEMENT

John 2:13–25

GRAHAM GILLMAN

Fr Graham Gillman, parish priest at the Roman Catholic Church of St Francis, Nailsea in Bristol, is a gifted preacher who has had many of his homilies published, including one in last year's equivalent of this book, The Fifth Times Book of Best Sermons. *He is also active in the healing ministry, and was a founder member of the Bishop of Clifton's Committee for Health and Healing.*

'On leaving school I trained in engineering, ending my apprenticeship as a planning engineer. I realized that this was not the career that I wanted, but that working with people was more important,' he says. 'I came from a family where my mother was Catholic and we attended church, but like many other teenagers I drifted, while at the same time I became more aware of the poverty and injustice in the world and wanted to do something about it. I thought that the path forward was through politics but, when on a youth exchange scheme in Russia, I became disillusioned by political philosophy and at the same time was impressed by the faith of the Christians that I met.

'On returning home my faith was renewed and my journey into ministry as a priest had begun. I still want to change the world and make it a more just and better place for people to live in, but it is not any particular political philosophy that will do this, rather the hearts of people being changed. That is why this particular sermon was given. I was impressed by the strength of Jesus' reaction to injustice and his concern for the poor. This made him do something about it and it challenged me to look at my own life and ask what am I doing to make our world a better place to live in. Perhaps when I was younger I thought that I would somehow change the world – now I am content to be a little bit more modest in my aims and hope that perhaps I can help a few people to see things in a different way and so play their own part in making our world a better place.'

Since being ordained as a priest most of his work has been in parishes but he has also worked as a chaplain to a sixth-form college, a polytechnic, and several hospitals. The healing ministry has been a central part of his life as a priest and in 2000 he celebrated the silver jubilee of his ordination.

'Life, for many people, has changed over the years, bringing more and greater pressures. So, too, for me – the demands of collaborative ministry require a more consultative approach. However, as a Catholic priest, I believe that I am ordained primarily to preach and teach. That is at the heart of any

priest's ministry. He must first read and believe the Word of God for himself and try to live it. Then he must share that Word and break it open for others, so that they too are nurtured and nourished by the Word of God. The sermon still has an essential place in our modern liturgy and should be based upon the Scriptures that have been appointed to be read on that particular day. Over a period of time the whole of Scripture should be read, proclaimed and broken open through the homily so that it becomes a living word for our own time and place.'

Text: John 2:13–25.

I'D LIKE TO BEGIN by asking you a question – when was the last time you got angry and lost your temper? One sort of anger that we can immediately think of is that of a child's temper tantrums: uncontrollable emotions, often born of frustration, cause the child to erupt into a fury of screaming, shouting and stamping of feet. The tantrum is usually guaranteed to cause the maximum embarrassment to mum or dad and, of course, takes place in a very public place like the supermarket, or even here in church. How many of us have seen parents squirming in mortification at their children's behaviour at such times and our hearts reach out to them?

Then of course there's another sort of anger – the violent, explosive anger so often seen on a Saturday night in our city centres. At throwing-out time, or earlier in the pubs and clubs themselves, fuelled by drink, a mere glance at another person can be the beginning of trouble. 'What are you doing looking at my girl like that?' and before you know what's happened, a fight has broken out – uncontrollable anger, flashes of temper, drink-sodden brains no longer in control. It's a pattern that's all too familiar to the police and anyone else in the city centres.

Today in the Gospel we hear of Jesus getting angry, but His is not a wild anger, lashing out uncontrollably, or indeed a temper tantrum. No, Christ's anger is a righteous anger, born of the wickedness he experienced going on in the temple. He was in God's house and he saw it being turned into a place of injustice. In His day, people went up to the temple to worship and offer sacrifice and they needed special temple money for this. What Jesus was angry about was the extortionate profits that the money-changers were making at the expense of the poor. No one objects to a reasonable profit being made, but the money-changers had a monopoly because there was no other source of supply and the temple authorities were countenancing injustice as the people were fleeced of their money. And when it came to offering animals for sacrifice – animals which had to be perfect, without blemish, and certified as such – these were being sold at inflated prices and huge profits made out of people's desire to worship and honour God. This behaviour so angered Jesus that He got a whip and drove the people out of

His Father's house – a house of prayer that had become a robbers' den. His was, indeed, a righteous anger.

Each one of us, come Judgement Day, will have to face God and answer for our lives: how will we answer? For most of us, it won't be what we have done that we are called to account for, but what we have failed to do. I don't suppose many of us here have robbed a bank or, indeed, coveted our neighbour's ox or ass (!). No, our sin will be what we didn't do; when we didn't get angry at injustice, when we turned away from situations that were wrong and said nothing. In history, situations and circumstances were changed dramatically because people got angry. Not far from here, a few generations ago, children were sent up chimneys to clean them, or down the mines to shift coal – children as young as eight or nine – and, far from being scandalized, people were expected to be grateful that the children had a job and could earn money for the family. It was only when people recognized this as a social injustice and got angry that they did something about it and changed society's values which then led to legislation about child labour.

In this century the greatest scandal has been the silence of so many, including the Church, in the face of atrocities such as the Holocaust, ethnic cleansing and the plight of the starving throughout the world. Even slavery has, in history, been condoned by the Church; indeed the institutional Church owned slaves at one time and it took the anger of righteous men, who saw the injustice of slavery, the injustice of one man owning another, to lead to a crusade which eventually resulted in the prohibition of slavery and freedom being proclaimed as the ideal for all mankind.

How do we behave in our daily lives? We are unlikely to be confronted by situations of enormous injustice, like slavery or child labour, but how do we react – in the office, at work, on the shop floor – when we hear of injustice, when we see wrong being done, when we see discrimination such as sexism, ageism, racism or even homophobia and anti-Semitism? Are we silent or does our anger, our righteous anger, speak out about the injustice and say that it is wrong? Racism is so deeply ingrained into our society today: only recently, in the Lawrence inquiry, we heard that institutional racism has become accepted, even in such good and law-upholding bodies as the Police Force. It is only when something shocking happens that our anger leads to action and brings about change. Racism is an evil that must be eradicated from our society, and this will not happen until people like you and I stand up and challenge racist statements and behaviour.

What about the office jokes; do we just listen to them or, worse still, join in? Have we the courage, as Christians, to refuse to be party to them, to proclaim them for what they are – smutty, dirty, degrading of others, or whatever? It is so much easier to remain silent, to pass by on the other side. In our own homes, when something on television goes against our values or principles, when we know that what we see is slowly corrupting society – do we actually switch it over, or off; do we complain about it? How many of us can say, with our hands on our hearts, that we have telephoned the BBC or ITV or have written to the Broadcasting Standards Authority? They do listen, and when enough people complain, they do act. As Christians, do we not have a responsibility to make our voices heard, to complain when something is broadcast that offends our values or our human dignity? Have we the courage to do something, or is it all just too much trouble?

Then there is the problem of published material – what newspapers and other publications do we have in the house; have we looked at our teenage children's magazines, so many of which are sex-obsessed, anything goes – dispensing advice on how to have better sex, without any regard to building relationships, commitment to marriage or any ideal that we hold important. Do we feel strongly enough to do something about it; do we have the courage to ban them from our homes and so face the complaints, and the caustic comments, of our own teenage children – or do we turn a blind eye and do nothing?

Each one of us will, one day, have to answer to God – not only for the things we've done, but for our silence and the things we've left undone too. As we reflect on today's Gospel, where Jesus acts with righteous anger against an evil that He sees, let it inspire us to look at our world, to take action against injustice and ungodliness and to work, instead, for love and a better world.

When was the last time you got angry?

The Glory of God

JAMES COCKE

The Revd James Cocke, 74, Vicar of All Saints' Headington, Oxford since 1957, has also been inspired in his preaching by his work as a hospital chaplain at the Nuffield Orthopaedic Centre in Oxford. Married to Margaret, a retired school teacher, they have four children: Hilary, Hugh, Fiona, Elisabeth. From 1944 to 1948 he served in the Royal Artillery and then the Royal Army Educational Corps before going up to Wadham College to read modern history. He was trained for the ministry at Wells Theological College and in 1952 was appointed Assistant Curate at Christchurch Priory in the Winchester Diocese.

'My faith became alive and relevant at the time of my confirmation in 1941,' he says. 'Compared with the stupidity of war, the Christian way seemed so much better.' His vocation as a preacher developed from his time at the College of Preachers in the days when the late Prebendary D. W. Cleverley Ford was Director. His sermon here, he felt, was relevant for the Sunday before Christian Aid Week, in its concentration on the 'social Gospel'. He believes the sermon should always come after the Gospel at the Eucharist, and either before or after the Intercesssions at Matins and Evensong. 'Preaching is always relevant because in preaching words become events. The preacher is involved in the science of hermeneutics; the hermeneutic interprets a reality.'

He tells the story of a dreadful road accident in Oxford, in which a young post-graduate student from overseas lost a leg. 'He came to the hospital where I am chaplain. He said "I believe I am going to grow a new leg. What do you think?" My reply was, "It will be a miracle if you grow a new leg, and it will also be a miracle, in my mind, if you learn to live with one leg – but it will be possible if you rely upon the grace of God, in Word and Sacrament."'

A STORY IS TOLD about a small boy who unwisely threw a pebble at one of the stained glass windows in the local church. Fortunately for all concerned, only a tiny part of the window was broken by that pebble.

The subject of the window was the Christmas story; and at the bottom of the window were the well-known words from St Luke's account of the birth of Christ: 'Glory to God in the highest'. The pebble which had been thrown by the boy had gone straight through the letter 'e' in the word 'highest'. Even with the removal of that letter 'e', the text still made sense. It now read: 'Glory to God in the high st'. The high street in any city or town stands for, and represents the day-to-day life of the local community. There is a famous high street in the centre of the city of Oxford – known as The High. This street with its lovely sweeping curve is one of the most famous and most beautiful streets in the whole of Europe; as you cross Magdalen bridge, you find the tower of Magdalen College on your right; travelling up The High, you pass The Queen's College on your right and University College on your left. You see the unique All Souls' and some of the buildings of Brasenose and Oriel. There are shops and there are banks and there are hotels. Some members of the local business community lived at one time over the high street shops, before houses were built in the suburbs. The High stands for the local community.

Here in the suburb of Headington we find Old High Street and we find New High Street. In these two roads, which are very near the centre of Headington, there are homes and shops. We talk about the high street banks. We recognize the truth of the high street image or picture; it stands for all that is involved in a living community. As a result of the throwing of the pebble, the familiar words 'Glory to God in the highest' had become 'Glory to God in the high st' – it had proved to be an inspired throw.

The story of Jesus of Nazareth is all about God revealing His Glory in the least likely of places – in the common ways of life – in the high street. After his birth in a stable at the back of a pub, it is recorded that the angels sang 'Glory to God in the highest'. His birth was the beginning of many scenes of glory. Before we proceed any further, it is essential to recognize that the Glory of God means the presence of God. There were some moments when a few people were aware of God's glory before the birth of Jesus. The Old Testament prophet Ezekiel, was able to report 'this was the appearance of the likeness of the Glory of God'; but this was an exceptional case. When Moses had asked of God: 'Show me thy glory', the answer had been: 'while my glory passes by I will put you in a cleft of the rock, and I will cover you with my hand until I have passed by; then I will take away my hand, and you shall see my back; but my face shall not be seen'. With the coming of Jesus, all this is changed. The glory becomes personal; and it is unique. The glory seen in Jesus is a once only event. There are all the years leading up to this manifestation of glory; and there are all the years which have followed this manifestation of glory. We can lift Shakespeare's famous words from Hamlet and apply them to Jesus; 'we shall not look upon his like again'. His glory was truly unique – the glory of God. There is the glory of his humility in his home life at Nazareth – the humility of obedience to Mary and Joseph. There is the glory of his humility in his willingness to learn an artisan's trade of carpentry. With the beginning of the three years of public ministry, there are further signs of glory.

The first eleven chapters of St John's Gospel have been called 'The Book of Signs'. When the author of the Fourth Gospel writes up his account of the wedding at Cana in Galilee, when the water tasted like wine, he says 'This beginning of his signs did Jesus in Cana of Galilee, and manifested his glory'. The miracles of Jesus are signs of glory. The raising of Lazarus is for the glory of God: Lazarus dies – his sisters are bereaved – Lazarus is called back to life. And it is all 'for the glory of God'. The glory reaches its climax in those events, which are always at the centre of Christian worship – the death and the resurrection of Christ.

St John sees the Cross of Calvary as the throne of glory. In one of the great hymns of Christendom, the writer says that God: 'Fore-ordained the Prince of Princes. For the throne of Calvary'. The evangelists see the cross from different perspectives. For St Mark and St Matthew, the cross is a gallows – a place of darkness and dereliction. For St Luke, the cross is a pulpit from where the Lord speaks about forgiveness, eternal life, and serenity. For St John the cross is the throne on which the Lord reigns. He reigns on the tree; and from the tree he proclaims the victory which he has won over the evil powers of sin and death. He is in control on the cross; it is a picture of self-giving love to the uttermost – and thus a picture of supreme glory. He makes arrangements for the future of his Mother and for the beloved Apostle from the cross. He utters his plea for the allegiance of men and women of all ages from the cross. And He proclaims his victory from the cross – 'It is finished' – 'It is accomplished'. He is indeed the King of Glory; and that glory is seen above all else on the cross.

In this life of glory in Jesus, we see a mixture of being in the Church and with a community of faith, and being out in the world. St John's Gospel, which contains scene after scene of glory, is written round three Passover festivals. At the first of these Passovers, 'Jesus went up to Jerusalem – to the Temple'. This is a Church scene. The Lord is seen in the Temple. He recognizes the importance of the Temple. He is aware of the need for worship in the Temple. Because the Temple is important, the Lord cleanses the Temple for its proper use – the worship of Almighty God. His glory came to the Temple. His glory is seen in the Temple. And at the same time, much of his public ministry was carried out in the open – in the eyes of the world – in the high street. He ministered to a woman at a well in the open air; he feeds the five thousand in the countryside; he cures a blind man by the roadside. Here we have three open air miracles – three signs of glory. The Crucifixion takes place in the open. This is not a Temple – not a Church setting. It is a public execution, which becomes an open air scene of glory. Some of the resurrection appearances are Church scenes – behind closed doors. Some of the resurrection appearances take place in the open air – like the breakfast event by the Sea of Tiberias at the end of a night's fishing. St John begins his Gospel on the note of glory; the climax of his account of the incarnation comes with the words: 'we beheld his glory'. This theme of glory never departs from this Gospel. It is there in the Church scenes, and in the high street scenes.

The Church, of which you and I are members by virtue of our baptism, is called in every age to reflect something of the glory of the self-giving love of God revealed in Christ Our Lord. There is nothing particularly glorious or sacrificial about doing that which pleases or appeals to you. It is no hardship for me to sit down and listen to a recording of Mahler's 5th Symphony by Sir John Barbarolli – 'glorious John' as Ralph Vaughan-Williams called that great conductor of the Hallé Orchestra. Glory is seen in the lives of the members of God's Church when you and I take on some task from which we naturally shrink – the task for which we look for excuses. Before ascending the throne of His cross, the Lord went into a garden for a time of prayer. 'Glorify thy Son that the Son may glorify thee' he prayed. These words are at the heart of his prayer of consecration. He did not pray for a way of escape. He prayed that He might glorify the Father. This Sunday brings us once again to the beginning of another Christian Aid Week. Few, if any, wish to deliver and to collect the Christian Aid week envelopes. And yet we all know that we live in affluence in suburban Oxford compared with most parts of the world. I can think of some families who were on, or very near, the breadline in the Parish where I served as an Assistant Curate from 1952–7. I know of no family on the breadline in this Oxford parish in 2000. The truth of the matter is that there are undeveloped countries among the family of nations in the world. There is an imbalance in the use of the world's resources. There are the rich and there are the poor. There are the sick and there are those who are without proper medical facilities. There are the homeless and there are those who are dying in dreadful conditions. We can ignore them. We cannot deny their existence. The glory of Christian Aid Week is seen when Christians, not wishing to go out into the high street with envelopes and Christian Aid leaflets, actually do so. Christian Aid Week calls for glorious action. This week is given to us – to the whole Church – not just for the sake of those in need of help. This week is given to us for our sake in order that we may identify ourselves more closely with the self-giving love seen in the Lord of glory. It has been said of Cardinal Manning, Roman Catholic Archbishop of Westminster in the second half of the 19th century, that 'his true glory was his sympathy with the poor'. May that be true of each one of us. The path of duty is the way to glory.

Being Part of the Story

Julian Cummins

The Revd Dr Julian Cummins, 45, is a non-stipendiary curate at Lower Wharfedale, a parish in North Yorkshire between Leeds and Harrogate. His wife, The Revd Daphne Green, is stipendiary curate of St Michael's, Headingley in Leeds and they have two children, Olivia and Caroline. From 1981 to 2000 he was managing director of Avista, a public relations agency in Leeds, and continues to play an active role in the business. He is also non-executive director of a manufacturing business.

After graduating in history and theology from King's, Cambridge, he went into marketing management for Procter & Gamble and Terry's of York before setting up Avista. He has also served as a Leeds city councillor and has twice stood as a parliamentary candidate for the Liberal Alliance. He has also found the time to serve as a board member, with the Regional Development Agency, Yorkshire Forward, to be a CBI regional council member, and to study for an MBA at Bradford University and a PhD at Leeds University in 1999. Not surprisingly, after his ordination to the diaconate in 1997, he was invited to chair the Church of England Investors in People Task Group from 1999 and to chair the Churches' Regional Network from 2000.

'I've always tried to search out God's presence in the world, particularly in the interface of faith, government and business,' he says. 'Working with the challenge of doing so has brought me closer to the truth of God's presence in Christ in all the suffering and glory of creation.'

For years, he resisted ordination and lived a busy and fulfilling life in politics and business. 'But it wouldn't go away. The birth of our children forced to me to reflect on what really matters in our lives. Priesthood for me has not been an alternative to active engagement in the world, but the place from which I engage.'

This sermon came out of a desire to connect the events of Holy Week with those of everyday life today. He examines Seeing Salvation, *one of the most successful exhibitions ever staged in the Sainsbury Wing of the National Gallery in 2000. 'Holy Week accelerates in a blur of violently opposed emotions from Maundy Thursday to Easter Sunday – drama, tragedy and joy in quick succession,' he says. 'How do you connect these events with everyday reality at home and at work? How do you deepen understanding and engagement with a story that is at once familiar and unfathomable? Reflecting on this, I chose to preach from lived experience on TV and at work, making connections between the everyday and the great truths of Easter.'*

His marketing background gives him a helpful perspective on the place of the sermon in worship today. 'Sermons are just a form of communication, and the listeners are in charge.

'We expect communication to be fast, focused and interactive. We expect it to be of the highest quality, but to respect our own contributions. Sermons should reflect these expectations. I favour three minutes at the beginning of the service setting the scene, preferably interactively, and a more reflective five minutes after the Gospel. Sermons should encourage connections, and should not close off the answers.

'They should offer insights, and encourage listeners to develop them. I would like to use sound, light, pictures and video, though you can go a long way with words and actions. As such, sermons play a vital role in worship.'

His busy life has also led to the occasional mistake of the kind everyone makes, while the new technologies which create the business mean also that errors are more easily rectifiable. 'Immediately after priesting, I was due to lead services in three of our four churches on a Sunday morning. I arrived just in time for the 9.30 at one of them to find it locked. I'd come to the wrong church, and with five minutes to go I had no idea in which of the other three villages there was a congregation ready and waiting. Thank God for mobile phones, tolerant parishioners and Sunday morning roads!'

He considers himself fortunate to be able to combine interests in church, business and the social and economic regeneration of Yorkshire so that one flows into another. 'But for complete relaxation, I favour a small boat, a long sea journey, and no sight of land for days.'

TWO WEEKS AGO we had the great privilege of visiting the exhibition *Seeing Salvation* at the National Gallery. Many of you will have seen Neil MacGregor's remarkable series on BBC2 that accompanies the show. The last is tonight, and focuses on depictions of the resurrection in Western art. If you are like me, you will face an anguished choice between that and another unmissable resurrection, of Jenny Agutter in the re-make of *The Railway Children*, and will be thanking God for the video recorder.

I doubt very much if BBC and ITV schedulers discuss the theological significance of their programme timings, which tonight seem particularly inept. The story of *The Railway Children* is, of course, a story of crucifixion and resurrection. The loving father is falsely accused and imprisoned, the family leave to live in isolation and poverty, they befriend strangers and neighbours. Then through another stranger truth is established, goodness vindicated and the family reunited.

Such a bare account says nothing of the landslip, the theft of the coal, the waving of the banners, the birthday party for Mr Perks and the incomparable scenery of the Yorkshire Pennines which made the 1970 version such a firm favourite. Watching tonight, we will be fighting to keep them out of our minds to appreciate the new edition, and to understand the timelessness of Nesbet's story which lies behind them both.

Seeing Salvation addresses the same challenge on a larger scale. For at least 1700 years artists have sought to capture the truth of crucifixion and resurrection in paint and stone, marble and glass. They have faced the essential duality of Christ – his human nature, depicted in the style and form of each generation and culture, and his divine nature transcending every one of them. Jesus has appeared as Italian peasant and Flemish burgher, as Indian prince and as nineteenth-century Englishman. He has appeared in painful torture and in exalted glory. Each one is different, yet each one reflects the central truth that we celebrate this Easter day.

The great strength of *Seeing Salvation* is that it asks us to make a personal response to these paintings and sculptures. The arrangement is not chronological, and makes only incidental reference to the history of artistic technique. Rather, it gathers them under great themes of passion and compassion, of praying the passion, of the saving body and of the abiding presence. It asks us to respond as whole human beings, in our emotions as well as our minds. It asks us to peel off the layers of intellectual defence and to become part of the story that is depicted.

It asks us to respond as we do to *The Railway Children,* not as a curio of Edwardian life, but as a living drama of a family like yours and mine. It asks us how we would behave if disaster befell us, whether we would show courage and love, whether we would retain our confidence and faith. Visitors to the National Gallery have been asked to say what most struck them in *Seeing Salvation*. It is startling to find that the most frequently mentioned issue is the role and nature of suffering.

Startling, because suffering is something we don't talk about much today. Much of our lives are lived within a culture of managerial optimism. We believe that if we get our vision straight, organize ourselves properly, and deploy our resources correctly, we can sort out the problems that face us. I certainly live within that culture as a Board Member of our Regional Development Agency, Yorkshire Forward. We set targets for new jobs, for inward investment, for halving the number of deprived wards and for reducing carbon emissions. We seek to cut through bureaucracy, implement action plans and maximize effectiveness. And I make no apology for that way of working. It is certainly preferable to any alternative I can think of.

Yet we look around us and see ample evidence of failure and muddle, suffering and disaster. Last year, 110,000 people were killed in armed conflicts around the globe. Global warming is not a theory to people inundated through rising sea levels in Bangladesh. We can also find evidence closer to home. We find it in the persistence of high levels of teenage pregnancy, in ever-rising marital breakdowns, in people devastated by the decline of traditional industries.

In tackling these challenges, we face intractable trade-offs. We seek greater labour market flexibility to respond to international competition. Yet we know that labour mobility makes it more difficult for families to support each other. We seek policies supportive of the family to help with care for the old and young. Yet we know that they can threaten the viability of firms facing a gale of international competition.

Managerial optimism needs to be set in context. It can take us so far but no further. And the place it brings us to is the foot of the cross. It brings us to the point that our best endeavours, our deepest strivings, our hardest work somehow do not deliver everything we hope for. We find it in our jobs, in bringing up our children, in caring for our wider families. When things go wrong, we can blame each other, use the benefit of hindsight to imagine different strategies, or just walk away from it all. But we know it is to no avail, that the perfect outcome is always outside our reach.

Peter sought every possible means of securing a perfect outcome. He must have felt on top of the world at the triumphal entry to Jerusalem on Palm Sunday. When it all went wrong and Jesus faced arrest, he sought a military solution, cutting off the ear of the High Priest's servant. Then in the darkest hour he reinterpreted his career, denying he had anything to do with Jesus. How often we do the same, reacting to disaster with force, then quietly tiptoeing away and denying responsibility.

To the foot of the cross we bring the things that don't work in our lives. Love that is going cold, intractable problems with family or neighbours, dead-end jobs or insufferable loneliness. We also bring the things that are going swimmingly at the moment. New-found love, promotion at work, schemes that are reaching fruition, all the things that we know could be quite different if we only pause to think.

The great truth of Easter is that the bedraggled failures at the foot of the cross became the confident church of Pentecost. They became apostles because they had experienced the risen Lord, the Christ who would be with them to the end of time. Every failure, every disaster, had been transformed through the gate of the cross to the glory of resurrection. For two billion people across the world today, it remains the guiding principle of life. In the single movement of crucifixion and resurrection, all our suffering is caught up in the vindication and glory of the risen Christ.

It is this which enables us to persist with love when we know it may end in tears, to persist with practical action when we know it may end in failure, to pick ourselves up and try again. Tonight, a new generation of railway children will get into scrapes with the coal and weep over their absent father, will wave flags and befriend Mr Perks and through the kindly stranger find their family vindicated. This is crucifixion and

75

resurrection played out in fictional lives that speak to all our hearts.

So it will be for many of us in the last episode of *Seeing Salvation*. And as Easter Christians it is in our grasp to be more than spectators. We can be characters in the story. We can be bearers of the light that stands in this church. In the words of the *Exsultet*, we can be people who rejoice in shining splendour, radiant in the brightness of our king. This is the great hope that Easter holds out to us. That we will be people transformed by the great reality of Easter day, that all our hopes and longings are vindicated in the ultimate truth of resurrection. It is a truth and a hope for us all to make our own. Christ is risen. He is risen indeed. Alleluia! Alleluia!

The Keys to the Kingdom

JOHN MILLS

John Mills, 79, a retired solicitor, is married to Eirene, formerly Chief Pharmacist with CMC Vellore, India. They live in Bournemouth and have one daughter, Dr Christine Boardman.

This Remembrance Sunday sermon reflects his background as a Lieutenant in the Royal Naval Volunteer Reserve during the war. He served in one of the Malta convoys, in naval ships escorting Atlantic convoys, and then in the invasion force to France on 'D-Day'. He took part in the invasion of Malaysia shortly before the Japanese surrendered.

After the war he qualified as a solicitor and started his own legal practice. At that time he also trained to become a Methodist local preacher and is still preaching about six times a quarter.

'I remember as a young man my faith was suddenly enriched when I stopped thinking about myself and lost myself in prayer for others. Having my own legal practice has made it possible through the years for my wife and myself to get away to more than twenty Lay Witness weekends in the southern part of the country. These greatly deepened our faith.'

Like so many preachers today, he is possessed of a natural modesty. 'I have few of the natural abilities which congregations expect of their preachers. I only started training to preach so as to be better able to lead a young men's Bible class; since then almost every sermon I have preached has started as a little introductory talk to the weekly intercessory prayer meeting at our church which my wife and I have attended most weeks since it started over 50 years ago.

'To me, the final preparation of a sermon during the following months is as interesting and challenging as playing a game of chess; then on the rare occasions when I believe I have the right message, like Jeremiah, I find 'God's word is in my heart like a fire, a fire shut up in my bones' (20:9). In this case I had been meditating on this particular subject for a sermon for some time.

'My experience is that I am able to preach with more freedom after the sermon has been given several times; this luxury is possible because I am sent to many little chapels in the villages in Dorset and Hampshire.'

The sermon published here uses the biological information given by Dr Marshall in his sermon 'The Pearl of Great Price', published in the very first Times Book of Best Sermons. *'While I find much encouragement from reading the sermons published in this series of books, their greatest value to*

*me is when I find one which throws some light upon an aspect of divine truth,
which I do not hesitate to use in the villages where I preach. Perhaps some
hard-pressed preacher will find in it something of use.'*

*He always addresses the congregation at the end of a service because he
believes the reading of the Word and the Intercessions prepare the hearts for
the message which then comes through the 'foolishness' of preaching. 'As
Paul says, "How can they hear without a preacher?" (Rom 10:14).'*

*He and his wife keep one day a week for walking in the country and he
plays tennis three times a week.*

The Keys To Heaven

Jesus said that the Kingdom of Heaven is like a merchant looking for
fine pearls. When he found one of great value, he went away and
sold everything he had and bought it. The Kingdom of Heaven is
truly the most priceless possession for any human being, so valuable
that we have to be willing to forgo and sacrifice everything else to
receive it.

Jesus deliberately chose pearls rather than diamonds or other
gems to illustrate the Kingdom of Heaven because they are created
by living creatures; other precious jewels are mined from the earth.
Pearls are found in the shells of oysters where the sea temperature is
warmer than around these islands and biologists tell us that they are
created as a result of damage suffered by the oyster when its shell is
penetrated by some tiny boring parasite or by some grains of sand.
The natural reaction of the oyster is to exude a powerful liquid
which surrounds and covers the intruder to stop the pain. Nature
completes the miracle when the liquid solution rapidly solidifies to
become a beautiful smooth round pearl. For us it may seem a far cry
from the glittering sparkle of a necklace of pearls to an injury felt by
a small shellfish at the bottom of the sea, but there is a direct connection. The oyster forms one of the world's most precious gems in
order to stop the pain caused by the grit or sand thereby illustrating
the amazing link between what is of special value in life and suffering.

John The Divine (the writer of the book of Revelation) tells us in picture language that there are twelve gates into the New Jerusalem and
that these gates are made of pearls. No one can enter the City of God
except through a gate of pearl; the entrance for everyone into Eternal
Life is through one of these gates. How are these gates of pearl created?
Just as God in his wisdom gives to each oyster a precious solution to
surround a injury, so God gives to each person a way to live with each
problem which he or she experiences by surrounding it with divine
love. Divine pearls are created though the experiences of an individual
and so they cannot be mass-produced.

If serious difficulties just happen in our lives, the question we have to try to answer is whether God is calling upon us through these problems to make some pearl for him. We must try to look upon these difficulties as a sharing in the travail of Christ, who ever lives to make intercession for us.

Where a son or daughter falls in with the wrong company, the pain and distress caused to the parents can be likened to the grit which enters an oyster. It is part of God's pattern for our lives that every young person shall have the freedom to choose their own way. So where a son or daughter goes wrong, the distress and anguish of the parents will create a divine pearl within their hearts.

St John tells us that there are different gates into the Kingdom of God. Jesus used the parable of the sheep and goats to explain that those who spend their lives helping others will be welcomed into his kingdom; that is, people who give practical help to those who are in difficulty.

We think today especially of four young people who have lost their lives this week whilst working abroad for Tear Fund, and those who have risked their lives serving in the armed forces in Northern Ireland to bring about a political settlement or are now serving in Kosovo and East Timor.

There are also other challenges which call for different forms of courage. There may be circumstances when, because of our Christian commitment, we have to be willing to accept heavy burdens and responsibilities which can and do result in disappointment, frustration and even anger.

I wonder how many of us here have undertaken some work in the church with the best of motives but somehow things have gone wrong. A horrid irritation has come into our hearts like the grit in an oyster, yet, if we persist, a beautiful pearl can be created in our lives. Just as God gives to an oyster a powerful solution which enables it to turn the irritation into a smooth round pearl, so God blesses the problems in our lives by touching them and turning them into something of eternal value. It is God's love which is the powerful solution which works a miracle in our lives it; creates within us something both of beauty and of intrinsic value.

Think of the lovely words of Jesus – come unto me all you who are weary and burdened and I will give you rest, take my yoke upon you and learn from me; you will find rest for your souls for my yoke is easy and my burden is light.

Last summer I bought a backpack as a present for my wife and she tells me that they are now becoming the in-thing in the towns. These backpacks are like a ladies handbag but they fit on the back like a rucksack used by walkers. In effect Christ is saying take my backpack (my rucksack) on your back and put in it compassion, kindness, humility, gentleness, patience, courage and above all put in it love. Christ's backpack fits easily and its burden is light because it brings rest to our souls; as we share in Christ's heartache we discover that it opens up for us the very gates to heaven.

Dr Paul Brand was brought up in very primitive conditions in the hills in India by his missionary parents. Later when he qualified as a surgeon he returned to India accepting a small fraction of the amount he was earning in this country.

In his book *Pain; the Gift Nobody Wants* he tells us how a young missionary couple in India travelled a long distance with Anne, their only child, to get help from him. He performed a routine operation removing a section of the bowel, but within a week the parents returned to Paul as the wound had not healed; he re-stitched the wound with most meticulous care and then, when it still did not heal, he tried protein and transfusions. Anne would lie with a sweet and trusting smile; she did not feel much pain but grew thinner and Paul's eyes filled with tears when he had to tell the parents that she had died. Paul felt like a miserable failure even though he suspected that no doctor could have saved her and for 30 years he remembered Anne with a sense of failure; he couldn't forget her.

When visiting America years later, out of the blue came an invitation to take part in a church centenary, and he remembered the name of the pastor; it was Anne's father. When the pastor introduced him, it was as the doctor who cried at Anne's funeral; I've told you about him, he said, and the congregation nodded knowingly. He tried to say a few words about Anne but broke down. Round the table at lunch, Paul met all the children of the pastor who had been born after Anne; Paul had gone to the church in a state of guilt and embarrassment but was treated as a beloved dignitary.

To share in God's Kingdom of love and peace we may have to dive deep into the ocean of life, accepting its risks, its disappointments and its sorrows. As we carry our yoke, that is, our backpack filled by Christ to overflowing with love and kindness, it will not be too heavy for us to carry. When a young girl was seen carrying her little brother; a kind passer-by asked her, 'Isn't he too heavy for you to carry?' She explained that he wasn't heavy, he was her brother. Travelling with God's backpack will bring rest to our souls as divine love fills our hearts and inspires our prayers. Jesus shares our sorrows and gives us his peace. Divine love surrounds our sorrow, creating a divine pearl.

There is a lovely song by Graham Kendrick explaining that Jesus has put a song into our hearts, turning our sorrow into dancing and changing our tears of sadness into rivers of joy.

We can sing with William How

> From earth's wide bounds,
> from ocean's farthest coast,
> Through gates of pearl
> streams in the countless host,
> Singing to Father, Son, and Holy Ghost,
> Alleluia!

(A note from John Mills: Dr Paul Brand is a former colleague of his wife and is now living in America. He called to see them on 22 November 1999 on his way to India and agreed the personal illustration could be used in the sermon.)

Include People, Don't Exclude Them!

John Littleton

Fr John Littleton, 40, is a Roman Catholic priest in the Archdiocese of Cashel and Emly in Ireland. He was ordained priest in June 1986 after which he did postgraduate studies in theology. He went on to teach theology, liturgical studies and religious studies in various colleges and institutes in both Ireland and England, spending six years on the teaching staff of St Patrick's College in Thurles, the Catholic seminary in his Archdiocese. Originally from County Tipperary, he currently works as a curate and assistant pastor in the parish of Doon in County Limerick where, in addition to parish ministry, he is involved in school chaplaincy work. He still works as an occasional and visiting lecturer in theology and religious studies, and preaches at least twice every weekend and often during the week as well.

'I have been involved in adult religious education throughout Ireland for many years and I am well known as a retreat director and preacher', he says. 'I am a member of the College of Preachers in the UK and have been awarded a Visiting Fellowship at the College of Preachers in Washington, USA during the autumn term of the academic year 2000–2001. Many of my homilies and sermons have been published in theological and pastoral journals in Ireland, Britain and America and I am a frequent guest contributor to radio programmes dealing with religious topics.' He is also currently the Director of Ecumenism for the Archdiocese of Cashel and Emly.

'My work enables me to enjoy and develop my interest in communication. I enjoy the challenge of conveying complex concepts in relatively simple and meaningful language', he says. 'I have always had an innate sense of the presence and activity of God in the world and in my life. While I cannot explain it logically, I believe that the universe could not possibly exist as it is without some greater power sustaining it and guiding it. It can be difficult to accept this sometimes, especially when witnessing the effects of violence and evil; however, it is precisely on such occasions that I have an even greater need to believe that God exists.'

His family was significant in his faith development. 'Family prayer was important in the fairly traditional Irish Catholic home in which I was reared in the 1960s and early 1970s. Sunday attendance at Mass was the norm and religious topics were often discussed in the home. My parents had a great respect for priests and fostered in their four children a reverence for the Church and its representatives. There was daily reference to God both at home and in school. In hindsight, these events and experiences shaped my world and deepened my faith.'

The most difficult question he is asked today is, 'Why are you a priest?' He says, 'Generally eager to discuss all issues, I find this to be a question that I can never answer with ease. It is difficult to find suitable words that totally satisfy the questioner. However, I know in my heart that, while there are several other careers I could have pursued successfully, I would not be as fulfilled and content as I am working as a priest. Being a priest is more important than doing the duties of a priest although, of course, one follows from the other.'

He chose as the subject of this sermon, 'Include people, don't exclude them!', because, for him, it was the central theme of the prescribed Old Testament and Gospel readings for the particular Sunday he was preaching. However, he believes it is in any case a theme that merits frequent reflection in the lives of Christians. 'People are so quick to exclude others, to judge them unfavourably, simply because they are different or because they do not conform. Jesus never excluded people. In fact, he deliberately invited those whom other people had excluded to assume a pivotal role in his ministry and teaching. The attitudes and behaviour of Jesus must become normative for all Christians if they are to be credible witnesses for the Kingdom.'

He says preaching is still relevant and central to today's worship environment because, for many people, gathering at formal worship provides the only opportunity for catechesis. 'The preacher needs to be aware of this in preparing and delivering the sermon. Also, the preacher needs to realize that, unlike most other gatherings of people, church congregations consist of many different age groups and people of varying levels of interest.

'Preaching is about proclaiming the word of God. As such, preaching is a sacred task and the preacher shares in a wonderful privilege. Proclaiming the word of God is about announcing it publicly, heralding it so that people may heed it, notifying people of its message so that they can respond, pronouncing its teaching, declaring publicly its challenge and going on record about its immediacy and relevance. The preacher's task, therefore, it seems to me, is to awaken a living faith in the listeners so that they may turn their minds and hearts towards God and be renewed in their commitment to Christ's call to discipleship. Thus the preacher has a serious obligation to devote time and attention to careful and proper preparation of his/her preaching; otherwise Christ may be hindered from being truly present and active in the preacher's words.'

He finds it sad that many priests and ministers seem to settle for so little in their preaching. 'Regrettably, an activity in their ministry which has the potential of being so powerful and influential is often rendered ineffective and redundant. They are frequently complacent and indifferent about the centrality and significance of preaching. They seem to be without the conviction of the great biblical role-models; there is no awareness or sense that they are meant to be crying out, or shouting out, the word of God. Imagine the difference if, for example, all preachers combined the fearlessness and urgency of the Old Testament prophet Amos with the zeal and faith in Christ of the New Testament preachers like Peter and Paul!

'All too often preachers fail miserably in communicating the message of God's word and its truth. In my opinion there are three obvious explanations for this. Firstly, failure to adequately prepare for preaching, with an accompanying lack of competence and confidence, results in unconvincing, mediocre homilies and sermons. Preachers need to engage with and struggle with the word of God through personal prayer and contemplation. Without prayer and contemplation they will never begin to appreciate its inexhaustible richness and splendour and they will never accurately present its message to their listeners. There can never be a satisfactory substitute for prayerful dialogue with God's word when preparing to preach.'

It also concerns him when a preacher appears to have a particular agenda, such as when preaching about parish finances or peace and justice. 'They often gain the reputation of being single-issue preachers, having become extremely insensitive to the need of their congregations to hear the truth of God's word proclaimed in its entirety.' An apparent desire not to offend and upset congregations can in addition lead to a dilution of the teaching of Christ and his Church. 'By being vague and general in their preaching preachers fail to make the practical connections that are necessary if people are to understand the lessons and challenges of the message of God's word. The content of such preaching is destined to be bland and impoverished. Pure exegesis of the Scriptures is not sufficient; the preacher needs to relate the message contained in the Scriptures to Church doctrine and to the importance of witnessing to Christ's teaching amidst the problems and circumstances of contemporary life. Basically, then, many preachers appear to lack the courage of their convictions and are unsuccessful in communicating and proclaiming the complete truth of God's word.'

One of the main factors contributing to this growing malaise and dilution of the content of the faith and the effectiveness of preaching is, in his opinion, a 'false notion' of compassion that is characteristic of much preaching. 'All preachers, like Christ, must be compassionate. To be truly compassionate means to be sympathetic; it means to be understanding, kind, helpful and merciful. However, it can also involve firmness and other qualities less readily identifiable as compassionate qualities. Equally, genuine compassion requires that the truth be proclaimed without compromise. Whenever the truth is compromised, compassion is false and, ultimately, unhelpful. True compassion desires what is best for the person in accordance with God's will revealed to us through the authoritative teaching of Christ and his Church. Preaching, of course, has to be pastoral. But being pastoral does not mean pandering to what people want to hear. It means having the courage to preach the salvific message of Christ which they need to hear. The preacher is called to be a prophetic figure in today's world. In this way the preacher effectively contributes to the building of the Kingdom of God. This can only be achieved, however, in the spirit of John the Baptist who, in his preaching, always acknowledged that "He must increase, but I must decrease" (John 3:30).'

Texts: Leviticus 13:1–2, 44–46; Mark 1:40–45. Bible: New Revised Standard Version.

SEVERAL YEARS AGO a friend was diagnosed with a life-threatening disease. He was devastated. However, his devastation on being told by the doctor about his serious illness faded into insignificance when compared with the devastation experienced after he informed his family and some of his close friends. Unfortunately, his disease was also infectious. So most of them changed their attitudes and behaviour towards him. Admittedly, this was because of their fear; and fear leads to exclusion. So they avoided him. They were no longer available to meet him. They offered excuses, which he realized were rather silly, for not being able to invite him to their homes. He was not contacted on important occasions such as birthdays, Christmas and Easter. He felt abandoned because, ironically, those who were dearest to him were anything but nearest. Not surprisingly, he became depressed and this depression resulted in a further deterioration in his physical condition.

Feeling rejected and dejected, he returned home to live with his mother. Then everything began to change. She loved him as much as when he had lived at home during his childhood and adolescence. Although her worry was apparent, she was not afraid to touch him and nurse him. She was available for him at all times. She did not resent him for being ill and incapacitated. In fact, she was very pleased that he was living at home again. Through her unconditional love and care, his sense of dignity and self-esteem began to return. Eventually his depression eased and he was able to cope with his illness much more courageously and effectively. There was such a contrast between the response of his mother to his illness and the response of other family members and his close friends.

What a contrast, too, between the Old Testament Reading and the Gospel Reading today. Both readings deal with the treatment of lepers, people who have a life-threatening and infectious disease, although the approaches are radically different.

In the Old Testament Reading, from the book of Leviticus, an exclusive approach is the norm. We are told:

> The person who has the leprous disease shall wear torn clothes and let the hair of his head be dishevelled; and he shall cover his upper lip and cry out, 'Unclean, unclean'. He shall remain unclean as long as he has the disease; he is unclean. He shall live alone; his dwelling shall be outside the camp (Leviticus 13:45–46).

Lepers are to be segregated from other people and excluded from society. Lepers must be clearly identifiable so that they can be avoided. They are banished to the margins of society, stripped of their dignity and shunned. Lepers are rejected and dejected people. However, in the Gospel Reading, from Mark, Jesus adopts an inclusive approach. We are told:

> A leper came to him begging him, and kneeling he said to him, 'If you choose, you can make me clean'. Moved with pity, Jesus stretched out his hand and touched him, and said to him, 'I do choose. Be made clean!' Immediately the leprosy left him, and he was made clean (Mark 1:40–42).

Jesus refuses to exclude from his group the leper who speaks to him. He is happy to touch the leper. He wants to cure the leper and he does so. He respects the leper's dignity. Jesus responds to the leper's proclamation of faith and trust. He brings healing into the leper's life. Jesus certainly treats him differently. In fact, Jesus always looked towards the edges of the crowds gathered around him and he invited those who had been banished, for whatever reason, to assume a centre-stage role – often much to the annoyance of the other people who were present.

Thankfully, leprosy is no longer a commonly occurring disease. However, we need to acknowledge that there are many forms of leprosy, in addition to the physical disease. Many people judge others to be modern-day lepers and embarrassing sores in society; by condemning and excluding them they make them into social outcasts.

A relevant current example here in Ireland is evident by our treatment of refugees and immigrants. Condemning attitudes and excluding behaviour towards refugees have been exhibited by some Irish citizens. Other examples of modern-day lepers who are banished to the margins of society are homeless beggars and 'down-and-outs', people suffering from AIDS and those who are HIV positive. People who speak about the need for acceptance and tolerance in our society often display their true prejudices when dealing with members of the travelling community.

Excluding such people from the very heart and love of the community is sinful. To exclude them is to exclude God. As Jesus said, 'Truly I tell you, just as you did not do it to one of the least of these, you did not do it to me' (Matthew 25:45). When we sin, we reject the presence of God in our lives. We banish God's life from our hearts and we exclude God's guidance from our decision-making. Little wonder, then, that our relationships (with ourselves, with other people and with God) begin to disintegrate when such sin is a reality in our lives. The only cure is to be reconciled with God and with other members of the wider Christian community.

Jesus is the only person who can reconcile us with God after we have sinned. As he did when he met the leper asking to be cured, Jesus stretches out and touches the sinner seeking forgiveness, with the assurance of his unconditional love and mercy. Jesus always wishes to bring healing and acceptance into the life of every sinner – if only they could believe that he is the Son of God. Yet the sad experience of many people is that they never truly accept that their sins are forgiven. Sometimes I encounter people who are afraid to meet God in death because, not really believing in his forgiveness, they are fearful of God's judgement and eternal punishment.

As we read the gospel stories we discover that many people, particularly the scribes, doubted the ability of Jesus to forgive sins because only God could forgive sins. They did not believe how easy it was for Jesus to forgive sins because they did not believe that he was the Son of God. But Jesus surprised them by proving that he could forgive sins just as easily as he could restore health and wholeness to the leper.

The ministry of Jesus focused on his invitation to undergo conversion and on his forgiveness of sin. This ministry is still alive and active today in the life of the Church. There is a fundamental question for all of us who claim to be Jesus' disciples. Do we really believe how easy it is for Jesus to forgive our sins? Do we really believe that Jesus is the Son of God with the power to forgive us? Regrettably, many people do not believe, as evidenced by their attitudes and beliefs. There is no reason, except lack of faith, why we should not believe that sin can be cast out from our lives.

A question people frequently ask me is: What is the most serious sin? Strange as it may seem, the most serious sin is refusing to believe the word of God. The word of God teaches us constantly – and with certainty – that sin is forgiven. At times, though, we apply the same standards to Jesus as we apply to ourselves and, because we find it difficult to forgive, we imagine that Jesus is like us. Fortunately, Jesus is very different from us in this regard. Jesus desires to forgive our sins and he readily does so. The forgiveness of sin, like the curing of leprosy, is not a big deal for Jesus! In contrast, we are usually quite successful at introducing unnecessary complications to situations requiring forgiveness and healing. It seems easier to exclude.

When we refuse to believe that Jesus can forgive sins, and when we refuse to accept the forgiveness that God offers us in Jesus Christ, then we are denying the truth of God's word. To deny the truth of God's word is the most serious of all sins because any approach to categorizing the gravity of other sins must begin with accepting the truth of God's word. The truth of God's word has to be our reference point. We should not be fooled into thinking that the message of today's Gospel Reading is not relevant to our lives just because we do not suffer from any form of physical or emotional leprosy. If sin – especially serious sin – permeates our lives, then the implications may be very serious. There may be the possibility of eternal consequences unless that spiritual leprosy is removed from our lives through the process of reconciliation.

Jesus challenges us today, as we listen to his words, to stop treating people as lepers. He also challenges us not to remain lepers, according to our own estimation, because of shame or guilt or self-pity. He invites us to be compassionate and kind so that we may facilitate the process of healing and the restoration of wholeness in the lives of broken and shattered people. Such compassion can be as simple as a welcoming smile, an encouraging word, a loving gesture – anything that gives an otherwise dejected person a renewed sense of dignity and self-worth. But such compassion may also be as risky as giving someone a second chance when no one else will do the same or forgiving someone who has hurt us deeply.

Returning to the story about my friend, thankfully he has made a complete recovery much to the surprise of his so-called friends. He continues to live with his mother and now he cares for her because, with the passing of the years, she has become infirm and housebound. I remember him telling me that he learned two important lessons during his illness, lessons that are applicable to all of us. Firstly, when we are judged to be lepers, of whatever kind, we quickly discover who our true friends are. Secondly, everything – even what seems to be unimaginable – is possible when we experience unconditional love and tender care. Today we are reminded again that Jesus is a true friend to all lepers, all sinners, and that he loves us unconditionally. If only we could do likewise. Include people, don't exclude them!

You Were Strangers

MARGARET HAY

Margaret Hay, 58, is a Colonel in the Salvation Army and a member of the Penge Corps in south London. She works on the chaplaincy team at Rochester Prison and Detainee Centre, where she is also the Foreign Nationals Co-ordinator in the race relations management team.

She and her husband Laurence have four children, Mary, Jeremy, Michael and Susanna, who are all grown-up. She began her career as a secondary school teacher in Wellington, New Zealand, but then trained as a Salvation Army officer and from 1968 has worked for the Army in educational and pastoral work, first in Zambia then New Zealand, Hong Kong and now in Britain.

'I grew up as a child of Salvation Army officers, hearing my father, not a scholar but a gifted orator, preaching to congregations with a mix of saints and red-blooded sinners. The subterranean sounds of childhood are of father preaching the Word at the Army hall, and, through the thin walls of "the quarters" in which we lived, men weeping as they bared to him their scarred souls. So two things were early on the pulse; the power of preaching, and that its proper focus was beyond the church building.

'The early '60s was the era of vibrant ecumenical youth conferences in NZ, and I was invited to attend one where daily Bible studies from 1 Peter 2 were led by Philip Potter, then General Secretary of the World Council of Churches. My little gold light of childhood trust burst into a blue-green flame of conversion and of vocation to teach in Africa as I heard: "But you are a chosen race, a royal priesthood, a holy nation, God's own people, in order that you may proclaim the mighty acts of him who called you out of darkness into his marvellous light."'

So following study, marriage, teaching, Salvation Army training and the birth of her first child, she set off to take the Gospel to Zambia. 'Not for nothing, after all, had I been named Evangel after a feisty SA officer of an earlier generation.'

She continues, 'I found to my surprise that God was already there, deeprooted in the people and in the fabric of the gold, green and purple landscape. And so, also, I found in Hong Kong, where I saw young colleague Salvationists passionately studying theology with other believers from the range of Christian traditions, elevating the Word in worship, and expounding it in Army halls, on basketball courts with at-risk youngsters, and in assorted eateries to sinners and saints alike.'

She says the task of the preacher is to let the Word speak. 'The unbound Word which leapt in my 18-year-old spirit as Philip Potter preached from Peter leaps again 40 years later as now, at Rochester Prison and Detainee Centre, I hear the Bible read Sunday by Sunday. An inmate serving time for a grievous crime recently read to us sinners gathered in the chapel those same words from 1 Peter that had seized my heart years before. My scalp prickled.

'My preaching these days is mainly one-to-one in the cells of the prison and with asylum seekers in the detainees' wings. The task is more listening than speaking, with the Word interlaced into the stories of the lives I am honoured to share, reminding me of St Francis's injunction: "Preach the gospel at all times; if necessary, use words."

THE LITTLE METHODIST CHAPEL in the village of Norton, Northamptonshire, has seen better days – it's in danger of demolition in fact, and is being used meantime by its owner, the local repair expert, to store his spare gear. I clambered over old beams and machinery up into the impressive carved pulpit where, from on high for two centuries, preachers must have proclaimed 'thus and thus saith the Lord' to perhaps 20 – or when it was a packout, 30 – members, eyes upward, my grandfather George a child among them.

In 1874, George, now a five-year-old, left the chapel with a Bible under his arm, presented by the good believers as he set out with his family for a new life at the bottom of the world in New Zealand. The current owner of the chapel hasn't been to London since 1953, and it's certain that my forebears hadn't ventured to the big smoke either until the start of their odyssey, undertaken because of poverty and a dream.

George's parents were not writing people, so we know nothing of the voyage, and have to imagine it in the words of others, like the Australian poet Les Murray, wondering how such voyagers fared 'on the Sea of Sweat, the Red Sea' where the boatload headed for the strange south 'paid salt tax day and night, being absolved of Europe'.

The ship left the deathly chill of Gravesend on 25 February 1874 and arrived in New Zealand on 1 June, the first day of the southern winter, so no harvest could be hoped for within a year of leaving the old country they called 'home' even to the next generation. Did my great-grandfather, I wonder, when the first fruits of their slog, the wheat harvest of February 1875, was finally reaped, open George's Bible from the Norton chapel and read to the family from Deuteronomy 26, the primeval liturgy of strangers in a new land giving thanks to their God.

When you have come into the land that the Lord your God is giving you as an inheritance to possess, and you possess it and settle in it, you shall take some of the first of all the fruit of the ground, which you harvest from the land that the Lord your God is giving you, and you shall put it in a basket and go to the place that the Lord your God will choose as a dwelling for his name.

'When you come into the land . . . and you possess it' – well, not exactly – they were labourers under New Zealand's stark mountain spine as they had been in Norton's mellower meadows, but God had given these strangers a harvest and a hope, and God was to be honoured.

The jewel of liturgy now in Deuteronomy 26 is in letter and spirit at the heart of the Pentateuch. Over time, individual and communal affirmation was formulated to give appropriate weight to the archetypal underpinnings. The worshipper was to bring the basket of first fruits, recalling his ancestor Jacob and the past experience of his people.

A wandering Aramean was my ancestor, he went down into Egypt and lived there as an alien, few in number, and there he became a great nation, mighty and populous. When the Egyptians treated us harshly and afflicted us . . . we cried to the Lord the God of our ancestors; the Lord heard our voice and saw our affliction, our toil, and our oppression. The Lord brought us out of Egypt with a mighty hand and an outstretched arm . . . and he brought us into this place and gave us this land, a land flowing with milk and honey. So now I bring the first of the fruit of the ground that you, O Lord, have given me.

And once the offering had been made, the injunction was: 'then you together with the Levites and the aliens who reside among you, shall celebrate with all the bounty that the Lord your God has given to you and to your house'. 'Celebrate,' not tolerate, 'with all the bounty', not the bits and bobs. The landless and aliens, sojourners, strangers, were to be given equal status with native Israelites – like them, at home, well in, favoured but accountable. 'You shall not wrong or oppress a resident alien, for you were aliens in the land of Egypt.'

These days I work at HM Prison and Detainee Centre Rochester in the chaplaincy team and as Foreign Nationals Co-ordinator, my right to work in England based on my relationship to the five-year-old George, dead now for half a century. Much of my daily work is with the nearly 200 asylum seekers held at Rochester, who can claim no such grandfatherly favour or show acceptance under any immigration scheme such as my fortunate forebears had gained in the 1870s. Poverty, which drove my great-grandparents, is present for most, mixed with a web of other conditions they had not known in nineteenth-century Northamptonshire: cities plagued by poverty, the dismal tyranny of dictators, civil war, banditry and spiralling injustice. Yet asylum seekers are so readily and scornfully branded as mere economic migrants and labelled 'bogus', a word which, as Donald Macintyre of *The Independent* wrote, 'miserably stereotypes a hundred different stories of pain, aspiration for a better life, hunger, the entrepreneurial spirit, and all those other reasons for emigration through the ages, and then wraps them up with sheer unadulterated criminality'.

Realism is essential, and no one would suggest that, given the 55 per cent rise in those seeking asylum in the past year and in view of the domestic problems we face, that the UK can receive all or most of those who wish to come. Quotas and entry criteria are necessary in a world still 'groaning in labour' to be free from 'its bondage to decay'.

But realism mixed with racism is a dangerous cocktail. As *The Independent* pointed out in its editorial of 5 April, asylum seekers have one thing in common with Britons born and bred – not all of them are angels, but there is still a widespread popular presumption that all asylum seekers are criminal.

A couple of weeks ago, for example, I stopped on my bike to chat to an elderly neighbour painfully making her way on a Zimmer frame up to the local shops. Health enquiries led to a tirade about how she had been paying taxes for 50 years but couldn't get a hip replacement with the NHS, while she had seen in the tabloids that some asylum seeker with several wives and homes and numerous children enjoying the fat of the land. Sad as I was to see her painful condition, I had to tell her what I had left that morning out at Rochester; the usual mix in the two detainee wings of depression, anger and anxiety, with good cheer, cynicism and courage, as the men went to education courses, played endless games of pool, took their scheduled visits escorted by prison officers to the library and gym and, funds permitting, to the canteen for precious phone cards and cigarette papers, the whole routine surrounded by endless hours in the cells.

When asking inmates where they are from, the soft but fervently spoken names of homelands imprint the ear – Kosovo, Somalia, Sri Lanka, Afghanistan and the rest, some of the world's most dangerous destinations. You cannot spend your days talking to men who have left oppression and civil wars, and made their way across the world, and who if deported face incarceration and terror, or those from former Yugoslavia whose family members have been killed, or those with wives and children in England whom they risk losing if deported with no means or money to be reunited, or those who have borrowed unimaginable amounts from loan sharks to make the trip, or a man thrown into the sea off the ship on which he had stowed away with nothing but a life-jacket – you can't spend your time like this and not be changed.

And you can't be with the most desperate, those using the only weapon they have in the end – food and water refusal – and see the lips blistering while the spirit struggles with astounding resilience – you can't be with such people day after day and still sleep soundly under the duvet in a double-glazed, two-up-two-down in Bromley. You can't because such protests are costly – costing not less than everything – how can we go on with our tidy lives pretending that other lives aren't being sacrificed in our community, while asking, 'Lord, when did we see you?' or without enquiring why people should be going through such searing suffering.

And what's Deuteronomy 26 got to do with it? If I read it right, it's a foundational document of the faith: 'Then you together with the Levites and the aliens who reside among you shall celebrate with all the bounty that the Lord your God has given to you and to your house.' Celebrate with the stranger in the face of life. Resist the pull to the centre. Find Christ in the alien.

We should have learnt by now what happens when we start batching people, fanning fear and ignorance, and firing loose cannons like the words 'bogus' and 'flood' to describe asylum seekers.

Let's not start there. Let us start with the triune God: the Father, revealed in the too-familiar but still not known 'God so loved the world'; the Son, our Lord Jesus, who would tolerate no exclusion, and whose word was always 'come', not 'come if . . .'; and the Holy Ghost who, Hopkins wrote, 'over the bent world broods with warm breast and with, ah, bright wings'.

Start, I say, not with a fortress and drawbridge mentality and narrow notions of what the country can be expected to manage, but with the very nature of the All-in-all as we embrace the spirit of Deuteronomy 26 – the sharing of God's bounty with strangers.

The world is in deep trouble, with mercy in short supply, and the tide of pain and sorrow enough to freeze the blood. It is awash with movements of people, millions unanchored and uprooted with no place to land or stand. We have the makings of a world neighbourhood, but have lost the sense of neighbour, of one world where the rights of all are respected, and all are gathered into a single human family. The French economist Jacques Attali portrays a bifurcated world: rich nomads, nowhere, nothing beyond their reach, and poor nomads denied almost everything, nowhere to call home.

In such a world we must articulate a theology of the stranger. But the intrusion of strangers on our turf – of the 'other' in culture or faith, in socio-economic status, can befuddle, intimidate and infuriate us. How is it that we forget so casually the injunction: 'you shall love the stranger for you were strangers'? How is it that the best we can manage is truce, when the only resolution is embrace? How can we learn to extend hospitality, to see the stranger who retains her strangeness as a gift to us, one who completes us?

'A wandering Aramean was my father . . .' The sense of being a stranger seems to be the starting point if we are to be responsible agents of our faith, equipped to exemplify and testify to it in a pluralist society. In prayer we may, through a painful exodus, move outside the circle of egocentricity, conformism and inertia, and find ourselves in the sphere of God's influence in company with a certain stranger whom the world did not recognize. Like him, we may live as if the poor matter, and look for the day when the downtrodden may finally come into their own. Further, we may make it known to others that, since in his own body Christ has 'broken down the dividing walls', they 'are no longer strangers and aliens but citizens with the saints and members of the household of God', and also that we are invited to go with God, the inveterate crosser of borders, restless, always leaping and luring across boundaries toward the horizon, with us to the end of the age.

A Leper Came to Jesus . . .

Martin Boland

Fr Martin Boland, 34, a Roman Catholic priest, has since October 2000 been assistant priest of Our Lady of Lourdes, Wanstead, Essex. A cradle Catholic, he was brought up in a relaxed Christian atmosphere. 'I suppose I was unconsciously a child of the Second Vatican Council,' he says. Although the Catholic faith was important in his family and schooling, he never found it oppressive or sombre. 'I don't recall any of the guilt or angst that seemed so much part of the literature and films that dealt with Catholic life. My faith seemed a natural way of worshipping God and a way of not being too po-faced about the whole religious enterprise . . . if there was any guilt in my life then it was probably the guilt of not having any of the feelings of a Grahame Greene Catholic!'

However, as he got older, he became aware of a tendency to take much of what he believed for granted. He addressed this when he went up to St Andrews University in Scotland to study English and theology. 'At St Andrews I had the privilege of having four years to reflect more seriously on what I believed; to have those beliefs challenged in an adult environment and to consider the consequences of presuming to call myself a Christian in a largely secular and spiritually indifferent society. It was during this time that my sense of vocation became more focused.'

Up until that point he had never seriously contemplated becoming a priest, although his younger sister has reminded him that as children they did play at priests and congregation. 'I would bully her into being the sole member of my congregation and I would be the priest with ice-cream wafers and Coca-Cola as makeshift bread and wine!'

The social life at St Andrews centred around two focal points – pubs and churches. 'I visited these focal points regularly and misspent time putting the world to rights with youthful zeal and wrestling with the question of how best to live my adult life. This was a privileged time of trying to discern what my fundamental option in life would be and if that option was to be Jesus Christ how that would manifest itself.'

After university he spent a brief year teaching in a girls' school and then decided it was about time that he laid to rest the nagging intuition he had developed that indicated he might have a vocation to the priesthood. Accepted by the Church, he was sent to the prestigious English College in Rome by the Bishop of Brentwood, and the next six years were spent in study and prayer. 'At times I clumsily tried to discern God's will for me. When I finally discerned that it was time to stop discerning there was only one realistic option for me . . . on 14 September 1996 I was ordained to the priesthood at St Edmund the Confessor in Loughton, Essex.'

His time at St Andrews and in Rome was not only personally formative but helped shape his understanding and appreciation of the art of preaching. The theological faculty at St Andrews served also as a college for future Presbyterian ministers and so many of the preachers he listened to came from this Christian tradition. 'I would often sit transfixed by their eloquence, learning and the length of their sermons. These were sermons for real men and women – thirty or forty minutes of effortlessly keeping a variety of ideas in the air. But what impressed me most was how these preachers spoke with conviction and loving tenderness of the ways of God as revealed in the Sacred Scriptures. While they rarely ducked hard theological questions, they never fudged the truths contained in the scriptures. They exhibited an honesty and courageousness that I would later attempt to emulate.'

But the art of homiletics is also taught with serious dedication at the English College, where the seminarians must count as one of the most critical and alert congregations in the entire English-speaking world. 'The priests and deacons who dared to preach to them often looked like men who would rather take their chances with a Colisseum full of starved lions. Yet this gladiatorial atmosphere produced many fine homilies – homilies that were witty, well-crafted but above all, conceived in prayer. During my time in Rome I began to appreciate that the authentic homily is not just a verbal scrap of entertainment or erudition but that it had to be inspired by prayer. If prayer has not been part of a homily then, to my mind, no matter how exciting it is as a piece of rhetoric or oratory it remains spiritually stillborn.'

Since returning from Rome, he has been the assistant priest in two parishes in Essex – St Peter and St Paul's, Ilford and Our Lady of Lourdes, Leigh-on-Sea. Catholic homilies are traditionally far shorter than Protestant sermons – they can be as brief as one or two minutes. The sermon published here is, in this tradition, brief, but it packs an incredibly powerful punch. It shows the priest's constant awareness of the need to keep his homilies alive. 'There is a danger that one's preaching can become stale and colourless, especially if one is expected to preach every week and sometimes two or three times in a week. Preaching fatigue can begin to set in and in order to combat this tendency, I find I need to feed my preaching with study, with prayer and with a constant eye to "the joy and hope, the grief and anguish of the men and women of our time", as the Vatican Council called it in the encyclical Gaudium et Spes. *It is important that my imagination is attentive not only to the detail of my parishoners' lives but also to the issues that confront the men and women of our crooked age. So, for me, an evening at the Royal Court or the latest Spike Lee film isn't only an excuse to escape the parish. These excursions outside my "religious world" nourish my thoughts and are fed back into my preaching in some shape or form.'*

He says it is not just the content of homilies that can become stale but also the presentation and delivery. 'There was a time when I wandered around with the routines of the comedians Jack Dee and Al Murray playing in my Walkman in an attempt to learn something about timing, patter and the power of the punch-line. I'm not sure this experiment improved my preaching but it did keep me amused. However, I am convinced that preachers need to be open to the advice and example of all those who are gifted in the art of presentation and we shouldn't be ashamed to beg, borrow or steal from them if it might help us communicate the good news of God's grace.

'Finally, Jesus Christ must be at the heart of all Christian preaching. Gimmicks, stylistic slickness and theological smartness may amuse a congregation but the homily is an empty, hollow exercise unless it helps people deepen their understanding and love of the person of Christ. For me, this is the bottom line.'

Does preaching have a future? 'The answer must be an emphatic "yes" because we have been commissioned by Christ himself to "Go into all the world and preach the Gospel to every creature." (Mk 16:15). Such a commission cannot be ignored, especially in our society where there is an urgent need to proclaim the mystery of Christ to men and women who find themselves spiritually incomplete and aching for meaning in their lives. In our dot com world, where individuals find themselves locked in front of computer screens and increasingly have less sense of community and healthy relationships, there will always be something potentially inspiring and morally invigorating about people coming together to listen to passionate heralds of God's word. I believe that while people may wish to flirt with virtual realities they will always crave the reality of this world, of other people and God.

'Preaching in our particular moral and spiritual climate is no easy task. It seems to me that preachers have to be willing to subvert the cultural signs and theories of our secular age in order to expose the eternal truths revealed to us by Christ. Today preaching is a subversive activity and for this to be done well preachers need to be ambitious, prayerful and not take themselves too seriously.'

Texts: Leviticus 13:1–2, 44–46; Corinthians 10:31–11:1 and Mark 1:40–45.

A leper came to Jesus and pleaded on his knees: 'If you want' he said, 'you can cure me.' Feeling sorry for him, Jesus stretched out his hands and touched him . . .

Ricki Lake. Kilroy. Trisha. Jerry Springer. Oprah. Montel Williams (well, that's enough about my daily television intake). Of course, they're all chat shows – programmes where people, whose lives are often coming apart at the seams or who are damaging others, appear in a sort of public confessional. The audience jeers, bays for emotional blood and offers snap judgements: 'You're better off without him . . . kick him to the kerb . . . he's a dog and you're a whore . . . get a life.'

These programmes are both ethically repulsive and voyeuristically compulsive. But in an extreme way they remind us of the human tendency to make crude judgements about people based on what they look like . . . how they speak . . . what they've done, achieved or acquired in their lives. The smallest detail, episode or moral foible can colour or discolour our view of the whole person.

We judge the guy on the pavement with the anorexic dog and the cardboard plea for money.

If I tell you I've got lung cancer – your response and attitudes would generally be positive and sympathetic . . . you'll probably even overlook the fact that I smoke forty cigarettes a day. But if I tell you I have contracted AIDS – then your attitudes, your questions and judgements may be less clear cut.

If Posh Spice and David Beckham go on a trolley dash around Harvey Nichols – virtually nobody raises an eyebrow.

But if Mike Tyson spends his money on Rolex watches and sports cars, then, for some people, this is vulgar, shallow and becomes an ethical issue or even the cause of moral indignation.

It is easy to make judgements about people.

It is not so easy to show people compassion.

Jesus reaches out to those excluded from society and he reaches out not with a politically correct word or a token gesture . . . he reaches out with compassion.

He touches the leper.

He takes this disfigured, afflicted, rejected creature in his arms and holds him.

He risks contaminating himself.

Christ's touch is a touch that melts barriers.

His is a touch that breaks the human rules of quarantine.

His touch holds the whole person – not just their actions – not just their weaknesses – but he sees and embraces the whole person in all their complexity, fragility, dignity and beauty.

One summer, while I was a student, I had a job cleaning pots and pans in a university hall of residence in Victoria. The hours were long, the pay seemed fantastic and my grumbling bank manager was silent. Late one night, while waiting at a bus stop, a down-and-out staggered up beside me. He was elderly. His clothes were stained with vomit and the scum from sleeping rough. His eyes were glazed with alcohol; his breath was thick with a night's heavy drinking.

I asked him where he was heading.

– Back to the hostel . . . I stay up Pimlico way, you know it?

I said I didn't and he recommended it to me, describing it as if it were a four-star hotel.

– Why do you come down to Victoria? I asked.

– I come down to be with me mates . . . they're all down here and I go into the Cathedral . . . I say my prayers . . . I speak to Jesus.

– What do you say to him?

– To who?

– To Jesus . . . you said you spoke to –

– I ask 'im . . . I ask Jesus . . . I say Jesus tell me if I should live or die.

– And what does Jesus say to you?

– Say? He says nothing. He never speaks to me . . . never . . . he just touches me.

And with that his bus pulled up and he staggered on to it, showering the night with obscenities.

(preacher holds out his hands)

Now we must be Christ's hands.

We must be the touch of Christ . . .

. . . a touch for those who feel the breath of sadness

. . . a touch for those worried by madness . . .

. . . a touch for those who find themselves ridiculous

. . . an arm for those limping through life . . .

. . . an embrace for those trapped by the glamour and addiction of sin . . .

. . . a caress for the wounded and lost in life's no-man's-land.

The hands of Christ.

The touch of Christ.

The compassion of Christ for our crooked age.

Honour Your Father
and Your Mother

STEVEN KATZ

Steven Katz, 51, Rabbi at Hendon Reform Synagogue in north London, is married to Sandra, a dental practice manager. They have two children, Danielle and Laura.

Rabbi Katz, a finalist in the 1999 Preacher of the Year Award, studied history at Queen Mary College, London, before moving to Leo Baeck College in north London to train for the ministry. He was ordained in 1975 and went straight to Hendon.

His inspiration throughout his ministry has been his father, Arthur, a rabbi who 'lived as full a Jewish life in retirement as when working.' Although he finds his faith is challenged when members of his congregation experience pain and hurt, his faith is deepened through seeing 'the incredible goodness, the profound selflessness, which men, women, children sometimes express in their daily lives.' His 'nourishing faith in God' has been installed in him by 'the survival and vitality of the Jewish people and Judaism in the face of two millennia of harsh persecution coupled with the sheer miracle of life and the wonder of nature.' He believes that Judaism possesses insights, often reaching back four millennia, on a whole range of issues including God, family, war and peace, charity, work and medical ethics.

After 25 years as a rabbi, when he has experienced illness and suffered bereavement himself, he has learned how to empathize with members of his synagogue. He says he has 'counselled congregants in ways that have emphasized the enormous potential for good and bad possessed by us all and the imperative need to embrace religion so that we recognize and express the good within us.' He believes that preaching is an essential teaching tool. He is working hard to offer formal and informal Jewish education to children and adults to equip them with a full knowledge, understanding and appreciation of Judaism.

The sermon here grew out of his concern for the family. 'The family, its stability and strength underpins society. Its fragility in recent years requires the attention of all religious leaders and I am sure that family remains an essential subject of sermons preached in all houses of worship.' He is concerned that the family unit is fragmenting as GPs and the social services play a less active role. He believes that society is suffering because those who are vulnerable at times of bereavement, divorce and the like often have no one to turn to for spiritual, physical or emotional support.

He believes the content of a sermon is more important than where it occurs in the service but appreciates that a sermon is not always welcome: 'The smiles and suppressed applause when I announce "NO SERMON" are truly humbling.'

His other interests are reading, theatre, cinema, sport and going to football matches at Highbury. 'Arsenal is my second house of worship!' He plays competitive tennis on a weekly basis and follows football, cricket, tennis and golf.

Text: Exodus 20:12.

AMERICAN JEWISH COMEDIENNE Rita Rudner once said, 'I won't say that my parents were over-protective, but even the tricycle they brought me for my fourteenth birthday had seven wheels and a driver'!

Jewish lore and legend are replete with many examples of pure parental selflessness and sacrifice. But we need not search lore and legend for such examples. One of the most moving and memorable pictures of recent years is of Jewish parents on German railway station platforms in 1938 and early 1939, bidding tearful goodbyes to their children who were heading for a haven of refuge on these shores, in what came to be called the Kindertransport. For a parent to draw a child close, to clutch a child to one's chest in a warm, loving embrace is natural, instinctive, but to send a child to an unknown destination, to an uncertain fate, in the fragile hope of securing his/her physical safety, is an expression of supreme parental love.

Added to this example of parental emotional courage, come heroic examples of parental love from the concentration camps of frail and famished Jewish parents linked to life by the flimsiest of threads yet intent on sacrificing their meagre portions of watery potato soup in order to give their child a lifeline. We know that it does not require a commandment, God does not need to speak amid fire and thunder. He does not need to bellow over nature's most spiritually defining pyrotechnic display at Sinai to instruct a parent to love his/her child. A parent's love for his/her child comes nearly always naturally, instinctively therefore no need to enshrine in the Torah a commandment to love one's child.

But a child's love for a parent, especially the love of a financially independent adult child for a lonely, ageing sickly parent is not so intuitive, not so instinctive. And so the fifth of the Ten Commandments instructs us 'Honour your father and your mother that your days may be long on the land which your Lord God has given you.'

Out of the counselling situations which a rabbi encounters the great majority are family rifts. Cruelties that streak the human personality tend to come out most vividly at home. And of these family rifts the one that causes the deepest, most lingering hurt is that inflicted by an adult child on a lonely, ageing, vulnerable parent. At first glance the commandment of 'Honour for one's parents', *Kibbud Av Va'Em*, is anodyne, obvious, not meriting additional commentary or further elaboration. But the second part – the promise of lengthy life as a reward for those who embrace this commandment indicates that the commandment is neither anodyne nor obvious for it has in mind not the young child living at home who depends physically and emotionally on his/her parents, but rather the older, independent adult child. The promise of long life to a young child, who thinks that life goes on forever, is meaningless. However, to an older adult child whose face and body and receding hairline bear the tell-tale signs of the relentless advance of years, the reward is more real, more tangible.

Too often the unfeeling, uncaring adult child will have an encyclopaedia of excuses for his neglect of the Fifth Commandment. In a world of greater mobility, more and more adult children live in other parts of the country or even abroad, but geographic distance need not mean, should not mean, must not mean, emotional distance.

Sometimes the adult child pleads the competing needs of other family members, but our hearts and our diaries are big enough to embrace all family needs. Sometimes the adult child requires a cavernous reservoir of emotional courage because time and age may have ravaged both the mind and the body of the ageing parent and it hurts the adult child too much to bear witness to the distressing signs and symptoms of the remorseless march of ageing. But pain is as much a part of life as joy. If we hide from pain we hide from life. When visiting parents we must be as ready to listen as to lecture, to hug as to be hugged. Listen to this beautiful reflection of a non-Jewish daughter, her words so warm and wise on her duties to her mother:

> You bathe the body that once carried you,
> You spoonfeed the lips that kissed your cuts and bruises,
> You comb the hair that used to playfully cascade and make you laugh,
> You arrange the covers over the legs that once carried you,
> The naps are more frequent then once they used to be,
> You accompany her to the bathroom and wait for her to return to her bed.
> You never thought it would be like this – that's the price of love.

It is this depth of sensitivity that underpins the *mitzva*, the commandment of *kibbud Av Va'Em* and the rabbis of the Talmud and invested the *mitzva* with added significance. The *Tanya d'vei Eliyahu*, a midrashic work, says 'The whole world belongs to God and all God wants is for us to honour our mother and father.'

The Talmudic rabbis tell the story of Dama ben Netina, a royal governor who lived in Ashkelon, who had a chance to make a lucrative sale. Unfortunately the key to the jewels was under his father's pillow and his father was asleep. The buyer kept raising the offer, but Dama ben Natrina refused to wake his father. Soon the buyer left. Only after his father woke did Dama find the buyer and sell the jewels at the original price, not a penny more. 'I won't a make profit out of honouring my father!'

You might say, 'Lovely story, but it demands too much of me, I can't give that much, I can't be that much, I can't love my parents that much'. However, the joy of Judaism is that not only is it so challenging in its expectations of us, it is also so fair and realistic in those expectations, in those ethical standards that it sets before us. Judaism's standards and expectations are exalted but attainable. Observe that the Fifth Commandment does not say love your father and mother, or even like them. It does not say obey your father and mother, or even agree with them. But it does say 'honour them'. The rabbis define honour more precisely. 'Do not sit in their chair or publicly contradict them, don't raise your voice to them, provide for their needs including food, shelter and medical care.'

Sixteen million of the United Kingdom's population of fifty-nine million are over 65 years of age. Moreover in the first quarter of this century the over 85s group will double in number, so more and more of us will be blessed with the privilege and responsibility of caring for, or arranging care for, elderly parents

Again you might say, 'All right, I get the message. I accept I have a responsibility, a *mitzva*, to carry out towards my parents, but what of other family relationships?'

Why is that of child and parent singled out for inclusion in the Ten Commandments?

What of the relationship between husband and wife? Is not the Almighty Himself portrayed by the rabbis as the supreme marriage maker? Does not the relationship between husband and wife at its most harmonious create stability in the home, a stability that percolates through society? In 1998 there were 300,000 new marriages in this country, but 160,000 divorces. Moreover, the number of Jewish women battered verbally and beaten physically by their husbands increases consistently and contemptibly year on year. Surely there should be a place for the husband–wife relationship in the Ten Commandments you may argue. And what about the relationship between siblings? From the time of Cain and Abel, Ishmael and Isaac, Esau and Jacob and Jacob's sons, they have constituted a powder-keg of complex character contrasts, juvenile jealousies, and lingering adult animosities.

And ironically of all the family relationships we are given, or form, in the normal course of life, none lasts longer than that of siblings. So surely you may argue for one of the Ten Commandments to demand respect between brothers and sisters. Why is respect for parents highlighted?

Two answers – one is obvious. Parents give us life, and they give us love. But second, not only do they give us life; but they teach us how to live, they not only give us love, but they teach us how to love. They are the transmitters of Judaism, from parents, from their faith and their practice, from their lips and their hands, we learn or should learn about the other nine Commandments, not to kill, not to steal, not to cheat on a relationship, we learn about *Shabbat*, and to put life into a perspective that is not blurred by false idols such as self-centredness and so we come to hear the mention, and see a glimpse of God. 'I am the Lord your God.'

As early as the Middle Ages, theologian Rabbi Levi ben Gershon argued that Jewish parents represent Jewish history even as they are duty bound to transmit Jewish history.

Listen to the words of the American rabbi Morris Alder who was so tragically gunned down in his pulpit in 1966. 'Judaism begins in homes where Judaism lives in the atmosphere and is integrated in the normal pattern of life. It begins in homes where the Jewish words re-echo. Where the Jewish book is honoured, and the Jewish song is heard.

'It begins in homes where the child sees and participates in symbols and rites that link him to a people and a culture. It begins in the home where into the deepest layers of a child's developing personality are woven strands of love for and devotion to the life of the Jewish community.' Is Adler describing an unattainable idyll, a Garden of Eden scenario? It can be our own back garden scenario.

To this day a parent's posture to Judaism is crucial in determining whether Judaism lives and thrives for another generation and therefore the reverence due to parents from their children should be accorded an honoured place in the Ten Commandments. And finally what of the promise of long life to those children who comply with 'Honour your father and your mother'. Does that mean that where lives are cut short prematurely they are punished for neglect of this commandment? Of course not. Saadiah Gaon the tenth-century philosopher recognized that the child, the adult child who honours his ageing vulnerable parents will not only be carrying out the responsibility of 'Honour your father and your mother', but will be setting an inspiring example for his/her own children which they will go on to emulate – so perhaps not only adding years to their parents lives, but certainly life to their years. Psychologists tell us that in old age loneliness poses a greater threat to good health than obesity, smoking or high blood pressure.

May you in the congregation blessed with parents, remember that each loving visit, each loving phone call, each loving errand, will certainly add life to your parents' years, and in so doing you may also add years to their life – is there more fitting a reward to give our parents who gave us life and filled our early years with their love and guidance and is there anything more precious we wish from or for our children?

'Honour your father and mother.'

That is God's instruction to us. 'So that your days on the land God has given you may be long'. May that be our reward – yours and mine.

THE RELATIONSHIP
WITH GOD

Thou Didst Form
My Inmost Parts

LESLEY PERRY

Lesley Perry, 48, moved in August 2000 from being Press and Communications Secretary to the Archbishop of Canterbury to become Director of External Relations for Universities UK (previously the Committee of Vice-Chancellors and Principals of the UK). An ordained priest, she was the first woman ever to celebrate communion in the chapel at Lambeth Palace. She started her career at The British Council, where she was an officer for thirteen years, finishing up as Parliamentary officer for three years. This was followed by four years as Head of Public Affairs at the Royal Institute of International Affairs at Chatham House.

Her faith dates from her childhood. 'As a small child, I was taken to the local village Sunday school in Yorkshire, and thoroughly enjoyed being an angel in the nativity plays each Christmas, delivering harvest festival goods to the old folks home, and keeping the animals together at Rogation services. I enjoyed the Bible stories which formed the backbone of our Sunday mornings. I always believed in God, having some hazy idea of an old man with a beard who lived in the sky. Although that picture metamorphosed into an even hazier one of a formless "entity" over my teenage years, it was not until I went to university (King's College, London) to read history that I began to question what God was really like. There I met people who were not only regular churchgoers but who had a vibrant faith that was both fascinating and interesting and I started to delve deeper into my own feelings about God, and who I really thought he was.'

She joined the Christian Union, and started to go to Church regularly, and found it easy to stay interested surrounded by like-minded others, but much harder when she started work. She had a difficult ten years or so after university when she left the Church and came back several times. Her mother's death when she was 30 sent her back to Church for comfort, and this time she stayed, finding a spiritual home at St Barnabas, West Kensington, which was the first church plant from Holy Trinity, Brompton.

'It wasn't long before I started to want to give something back to the Church, and worked in a variety of areas – teaching the 3–5s at Sunday school, cooking for the old folks' Saturday lunches and finally, training as a home group leader. I led home groups for St Barnabas for several years, and in the meantime, started working for the Archbishop at Lambeth Palace. When the vote went through which enabled women to be priests in Novem-

ber 1991, I had to do some hard research, thinking and praying as I had quite a conservative view of the subject and I had never really thought through my own feelings about whether women could be priests. I was surprised by my findings – not only did it seem eminently right that women could and should be priests, but people had also begun suggesting I should think seriously about the priesthood myself. For some time I asked myself "Why?" but gradually found I was asking "Why not?" so I began the long, slow process of discernment and training which eventually led to a wonderfully joyful priesting ceremony on 2 July 2000. I trained part-time for three years, combining a busy job with evening teaching and weekends away, which was in turns tough and exhilarating. I like to think the training informed the Lambeth Palace job, so there were benefits to both, but perhaps others are better judges of that than I am!'

Her present pattern of ministry combines full-time work with parish-based ministry at All Saints in Fulham. 'Not surprisingly, perhaps, I think that this model is one which is increasingly useful and appropriate for the Church, and I am content to stay with it as long as God calls me to it.'

She chose Psalm 139 to preach on because it is one her favourites. 'Not only is it a wonderful Psalm of comfort, it is obvious from the context that the author was going through awful trials, and feeling quite bloodthirsty about the evil he saw going on around him. But there is a faith and hope that clings to God's intimate love in this psalm that has given me strength over the years. When it came up as the psalm on an evening I was preaching last October, there had also been a series of newspaper articles about the potential problems of Y2K. It seemed like an ideal opportunity to explore some of the psalm's themes with the congregation.'

For her the sermon is still a central part of a service, particularly for teaching and encouraging people. 'It should relate to the readings, and come soon after them, so a theme or thread can be clearly discerned. With all the pressure on time today, it isn't easy for people to spend time reading the Bible, and being fed by the word of God, so to my mind, the sermon should be designed to help that process. Ideally, too, the hymns and prayers should tie in, so that the overall message is "portable" and can be remembered and thought about during busy weeks.'

She has not been ordained for long, but has already faced one of the most difficult challenges imaginable, taking the funeral service for a friend of her own age. 'Although he was of Jewish origin, his wife and daughter wanted an Anglican funeral and marrying the two faiths to ensure both sides were included at such a sad time was quite a challenge.'

Another recent experience left her feeling enormously privileged. 'When I was ordained, the Archbishop asked me if I would like to celebrate the Eucharist in Lambeth Palace chapel, which I did on 12 July 2000. I was the first woman priest ever to celebrate in this particular chapel, and it was an awesome (in the sense of being filled with awe) experience – I was deeply aware of the weight of history in the thirteenth-century chapel. Cranmer's room, *traditionally the place where the Archbishop is said to have written the Prayer Book, overlooks the chapel, and the ghosts of previous Archbishops seem to hover close by. I celebrated again before I left, on 19 July, feeling much more at home the second time . . .'*

Text: Psalms 139:1–18.

Lord thou hast searched me out and known me.
Thou knowest my downsitting and mine uprising;
   thou understandest my thoughts long before.
Thou art about my path, and about my bed:
   and spiest out all my ways.
For lo, there is not a word in my tongue:
   but thou, O Lord, knowest it altogether.
Thou hast fashioned me behind and before:
   and laid thine hand upon me.
Such knowledge is too wonderful and excellent for me:
   I cannot attain unto it.
Whither shall I go then from thy Spirit:
   or whither shall I go then from thy presence?
If I climb up into heaven, thou art there:
   if I go down to hell, thou art there also.
If I take the wings of the morning:
   and remain in the uttermost parts of the sea;
Even there also shall thy hand lead me:
   and thy right hand shall hold me.
If I say, Peradventure the darkness shall cover me
   then shall my night be turned into day.
Yea, the darkness is no darkness with thee, but the night is as clear
     as the day:
   the darkness and light to thee are both alike.
For my reins are thine:
   thou hast covered me in my mother's womb.
I will give thanks unto thee, for I am fearfully and wonderfully made:
   marvellous are thy works, and that my soul knoweth right well.
My bones are not hid from thee:
   thought I be made secretly, and fashioned beneath in the earth.
Thine eyes did see my substance, yet being imperfect:
   and in thy book were all my members written.
Which day by day were fashioned:
   when as yet there was none of them.
How dear are thy counsels unto me, O God:
   O how great is the sum of them!
If I tell them, they are more in number than the sand:
   when I wake up I am present with thee.
                       (BCP)

MAY I SPEAK and may you hear in the name of the Father, Son and Holy Spirit. Someone said to me the other day that he thought we'd all be heartily sick of the millennium by 1 January. He wasn't referring to the reason why we are celebrating the millennium, the anniversary of Jesus Christ's coming to earth, but to the hype around it.

I know what he meant. The prophets of doom have been at work for some time. 'Look at this century,' they say, 'we have made more advances in 100 years in sciences, in technology and medicine than ever before, but equally, we have had the worst world wars ever, and our technological advances can kill as well as cure.'

There have been some horrible natural disasters this year too . . . like the earthquakes in Turkey, Greece and Taiwan and some man-made ones as well, like the Paddington Rail crash. Despite reassurances, no one really knows whether the millennium bug is going to disrupt all our lives by seizing up the computer systems we have come to rely on to make life run smoothly. An Italian newspaper, *La Stampa*, was wringing its hands recently over all these things and proclaiming them to be the beginning of the Apocalypse at the end of this millennium. It was the same a thousand years ago – Wulfstan, Archbishop of York preached a 'fire and brimstone' sermon on what Satan would do once he was released from his 1000 years of captivity.

By and large we're far too pragmatic in this country to be quite so hysterical, but there is a sense of insecurity at the moment, a wondering about the future. All of us know people who are struggling with enormous burdens – sickness, unemployment, bereavement, or loss of direction. Apocalypse or not, sometimes it all gets a bit too much and we all need someone to turn to for comfort and understanding. Well, whether we're single, married, old, young, sick or well, today's psalm gives us just that. God, it says, is not only watching from far off. He is intimately concerned with us, with who we are, and what we will do. This care started even before birth, when our cells began multiplying for life. More than that, God actually set that process in train. 'Thou didst form my inmost parts, thou didst knit me together in my mother's womb' . . . One lady actually walked out of Church when she first heard this psalm . . . the idea of being so intimately known to God shocked her so much, she had to run . . . I hope none of you are going to walk out, but the idea of being intimately known to someone we don't necessarily know so well is rather shocking!

If we ask people today what they want most, many will say 'a loving relationship where I am accepted for who I really am . . .' It's a wonderful ideal. But if we're honest, for many of us also, that is probably a mixture of 'who I am, and who I want you to think that I am'. We all like to present our best side, but, says this psalm, God knows it all. God knows when we will sit down and when we will stand up. He knows what we will do and say even before we know it ourselves. Wherever we go, whether we walk out of Church in a panic about being known, we cannot escape this God. He is the Creator of all, and is present everywhere . . . in heaven, in hell, and even if we run away, 'on the wings of the morning and in the uttermost parts of the sea' . . . God is there, and we will not escape him. This is not said to make us afraid. This God who is omnipresent is not a malevolent force. This psalm is about being known and loved so thoroughly that there is nowhere we can find ourselves that is out of the reach of God's reckless love.

Thompson's poem 'The Hound of Heaven' captures this sense of relentless but loving pursuit – it begins 'I fled Him, down the nights and days; I fled Him, down the arches of the years; I fled Him, down the labyrinthine ways of my own mind; and in the mist of tears' . . . It ends, 'by me that footfall: Is my gloom, after all, Shade of His hand, outstretched caressingly, "Ah, fondest, blindest, weakest, I am He whom thou seekest! Thou dravest love from thee, who dravest Me"'.

It may be a temptation to say, 'well, if God is so all-powerful and omnipotent, I don't need to do anything – it'll all just happen'. But I don't think that is what is intended here. The psalm is not *carte-blanche* to abdicate responsibility for our lives, rather, it is to take full responsibility for them. The Collect for today reminds us that if we live without reference to God, we will not please him . . . More than that, as the New Testament reading from St John's first Epistle told us, God wants us to pass on the love that he has for us to others – if we have and we give to those in need, God's love can live in us.

Rather than sit back and do nothing, I think this psalm is saying 'nothing you can do will ever put you outside my love, so go ahead and take some risks for me!' The message, once we've got over the shock of being known so intimately, is to accept the security of that love and to let it make a difference to our lives in what we do for others and in what we let it do for us.

We may say, 'But I have so many problems, how can just being known and loved by God solve them?' I don't think the psalm is saying that it will. I have a friend who has cancer. This psalm tells her that God has formed her, and knew this would be part of her life. She finds God very difficult to take in her situation. Undeserved and unexplained suffering, whether it be of Jews in a concentration camp or of terrible sickness, is an age-old problem that people have wrestled with since time began. Jesus knew the pain of undeserved suffering and died an undeserved death on the Cross. In one sense, there is no answer to suffering this side of Heaven, but what we do know from the psalm, and the Cross, is that acknowledged or unacknowledged, God is still with us and is still present in suffering. Suffering and crises can make it difficult for us to see God's love personally . . . surely the message of our psalm and the challenge for us, the Christian community here and worldwide, is to be the embodied love of God for those who are being tested.

There's a story about a small boy who was wide-awake and frightened one dark night. 'Daddy', he called, 'come and see me ... I'm lonely.' Back came the sleepy reply from a father tired of getting out of bed ... 'Don't be lonely, God is with you.' There was silence for a moment then the little boy said – 'I know God is here, but I'd rather have someone with skin on!' And that's where we come in – we can be 'God with skin on' for each other. As we allow God to love us, and know us intimately, we can share that love with one another, when times are good and bad. The great drama of creation and redemption is not yet finished. The faith that clings to God's intimate love described in our psalm, and seen in Jesus, will, one day I'm sure, find every anguished moment will be understood and all the tears will be dried. This is a psalm to draw comfort and strength from, and to go forward trusting in God's love whatever the new millennium might bring.

What Kind of Religion is Christianity?

BILL WILSON

The Revd Bill Wilson, 57, is Vicar of St James', Sussex Gardens in Padding-ton, central London. He is married to Anne, a teacher, and they have three children.

He was conscious of a vocation from the age of twelve, and was determined by the time he left school to offer himself for the ministry in the Church of England. He was ordained deacon in Manchester in 1967 and priested in 1968, beginning his ministry at St Margaret's, Hollinwood in Oldham. After nearly four years there he became Vicar of St James', Oldham where he stayed for eight years, moving then to Holy Innocents at Fallowfield, Manchester, where he remained for fourteen years. He then left Manchester and moved to Paddington.

'When preparing sermons I am guided by the content of the given readings for the particular occasion, the most important of which is the Gospel read-ing. I see the sermon as the continuation of the proclamation of the Gospel and so in the Eucharist it quite properly follows the reading without a pause. I have no reason to question the sermon in itself as an effective medium of communication, though style and content often leave much to be desired. I have always found that people listen attentively to intelligent, well-delivered, challenging and gimmick-free sermons.'

Outside the Church he enjoys architecture, motorcycling and fitness train-ing.

IS CHRISTIANITY A RELIGION formulated by philosophers, who have come to the conclusion that belief in a god is a logical necessity?

Is it a set of regulations put together to control people with the promise of eternal happiness if they stick to the rules?

Or is it a construct to soften the misery of human existence with the prospect of better things in the next world?

Although these things have all been part of our tradition they are in a sense aberrations.For Christianity is a *revealed* religion.

It rests on the conviction that God has disclosed himself.

The rumour of God's existence seems to have originated in a nomadic people in the Middle East, the nucleus of the community known as the Hebrews.

The first stirrings of a response to this ever-present, all-creating and sustaining, loving God, our tradition locates in the man we call Abraham.

Abraham left the security of his native city at the behest of this God and went on pilgrimage to another, *promised*, land.

This small community gradually took on a more defined shape.

There was a cultus, with a priesthood and carefully regulated rituals.

Eventually a temple was built, to be the home on earth of this invisible, ever-present God.

As time went on there developed among these people the conviction that one day God would act decisively to *save* his people.

For the Jewish people of the first century this became the expectation that one day there would be a new king to make them an independent nation again, God's *chosen* people. No wonder King Herod was disturbed when astrologers from the East came looking for the new king. Herod made every effort to ensure the extermination of every child recently born in Bethlehem.

Things turned out very differently, of course, and the king who came, so our tradition asserts, was to bring in a kingdom of peace and reconciliation to God for all the peoples of the earth.

So immense was the love God had for his creation that he sent his own Son, his word made flesh to dwell on the earth, to show, to embody that love.

This is the heart of the Christian tradition – the conviction that God acted decisively and in this way to fulfil his desire for us, his children, made in God's image.

Jesus of Nazareth is not merely a *messenger*, as John the Baptist was.

Jesus is the light itself, shining among us and telling us in human terms of the heart of God.

If you want to know what God is like, look at Jesus.

If you want to know what God is like, see that birth in a stable among the poor and dispossessed.

If you want to know what God is like, see the man nailed to the cross, his life-blood pouring away out of love.

This is the central message of the Church.

And it is the mission of the Church to lead people to perceive that love and begin to return it.

Can we do this?

Can we, all of us, get to grips with this mission?

Can we explain to others what it is that makes Christianity distinctive, what makes us belong to the Church, put it at the centre of our lives?

This enterprise is urgent.

It's urgent because the love of God for us is urgent.

It demands a response, when so much has been given.

113

It is urgent because we are surrounded by the deepest ignorance of Christianity.

People have not turned away from the Gospel, the Good News.

No.

They haven't turned away from it because they haven't heard it!

There are many reasons why people haven't heard it.

Perhaps they haven't heard it because they have not come into contact with people who reflect the loving, compassionate and forgiving Christ.

We bear a heavy responsibility for this failure.

Largely, I suspect, simply because we are reticent when it comes to our religion, or, perhaps don't feel knowledgeable enough.

And yet.

And yet, we have been chosen by God to be his own people.

And the baptism of Jesus – something he didn't need to undergo – is our baptism too.

As God was *well-pleased* with Jesus, so he is with us.

Yes, confidence ebbs, faith fades.

And that's why we are given fresh revelations of God's love.

So today we are put in mind of our baptism.

But also, in the way the liturgy has of making events present, this is a fresh outpouring for us of God's love and forgiveness.

As Jesus was sinless and in no need of repentance, so God treats us as forgiven, so that we can take heart. To take into ourselves the realization that we are forgiven and accepted by God is the beginning of our mission.

Once we recognize and keep on recognizing that the Christian faith is good news, then we shall be able to draw others into the Church.

Faith fades.

Well, it would if God would let it.

The Christian liturgy is not pantomime or mere pageant.

It is an arena for the living God in his Christ, active among his people.

Last week we were there with the Magi, on pilgrimage to find the Lord who had already found us.

Today the grace of Christ's baptism passes on to us again.

We constantly move on from one new beginning to another.

Through the Church year we are drawn into an ever-intensifying sense of the presence and activity of the God of love.

And at every eucharistic celebration the presence of the ever-loving Christ graces us in the consecrated bread and wine.

The Saviour, who took flesh in Mary's womb twenty centuries ago continues to offer himself to humanity as the source of divine life.

If this is so we have nothing to fear.

His baptism is a sign to us of Christ's promise never to leave us.

It was a promise fulfilled when his resurrection became a reality.

And it continues to be fulfilled every time we gather for this sacred assembly.

To hold on to what sustains us and to enter ever more deeply into the relationship with himself that God has made a reality is the best possible preparation we can have for this mission.

And we can be confident that the relationship itself will be sign enough to those we meet of the reality and seriousness of our faith.

We are sent out from this supper table to be what we are through our baptism: living members of the ever-present body of the Word made flesh.

Birth and Death at Christmas

GORDON GILES

Gordon Giles, 34, is the Succentor of St Paul's Cathedral in London, and is married to Jessica, who is a Law Reporter. They were married at St Paul's in September. As one of the Minor Canons, he is involved in singing and leading the regular worship there.

Before moving to St Paul's in 1998, Gordon was a curate in Cambridge, where he had also trained for the ministry at Ridley Hall. He began an academic career by studying music and aesthetics at Lancaster University, and then moved to Cambridge where he wrote a thesis on the philosophy of authentic musical performance.

'Music has always been a major part of my life, and working at St Paul's Cathedral is a tremendous privilege because of the very high musical standards which are maintained by the choir and organists. Many people come to the Cathedral specifically to hear the music, and it is important that they are not disappointed. But it is also important that Choral Evensongs, or Orchestral Eucharists are not performed or treated as concerts. They are not presented as such, because there is something unique and special about singing God's praises in such a splendid and awesome building, and hopefully the congregation feel this too.'

Preaching has a prominent place in Cathedral worship – at each of the four main Sunday Services a sermon or address is given, and preachers are invited from all over the world.

'This actually means that I don't get to preach anything like as frequently as I used to in the parish, but also that the quality of preaching experienced by anyone who attends regularly, is very high. It also means that even if people have "only come for the music", there is a good chance they will be able to take some words away with them too. Many come from abroad and may be with us only for one day, so we only get one chance.'

Gordon is interested and involved in other arts too. He paints watercolours, and has had poetry published.

'It seems to me that we have moved beyond denying a place for music or imagery in worship and restricting our teaching to lengthy treatises. The iconoclastic days of history are largely behind us now, but so are the days of extended prognostication. Cranmer was once told that if he preached for more than two hours, he would annoy the King! Today we are rediscovering how to draw inspiration from other sources, among them music and paint-

116

ing. The famously successful "Seeing Salvation" exhibition put on at the National Gallery proved that there is a public attraction to Christian art, and to imaginative explanations of the meanings of religious paintings.

'In the north transept of St Paul's Cathedral hangs the large version of William Holman Hunt's "The Light of the World". This image of Christ toured the world in the nineteenth century, drawing crowds of admirers who were inspired and moved by it, and with the National Gallery's millennial exhibition interest in Christian art has revived. And in the same way that people may be drawn to worship through wanting to hear good music, so too they may encounter Christ through paintings. Paintings, and music can speak words of their own.'

But art can never take the place of preaching.

'Many hold preaching to be an art form, and indeed, a sermon has its own rhythms, tone, structure and even melodies and counter-melodies. Some composers, notably Bach or Messiaen, composed what we may call "sermons in sound" – musical works which are based upon, and which in some sense express theological truths and values. In a complementary way, a sermon can be a symphony of words, with themes, developments and recapitulations that give a satisfaction beyond their mere content. Although, having said that, there is no substitute for a good tune, nor for having something interesting to say!

'Just as there will always be a market for good music played well, and indeed in its proper liturgical context, there will also continue to be a market for good preaching, and for Christian comment on the events happening around us. As I write, Concorde has just crashed in France. We need to make sense of events like this, and if we try, we can be enriched, and humbled.

'Last year there was a massacre at Columbine High School in Colorado, and a young Christian, Cassie Bernall was brutally murdered. A story soon circulated that she had died confessing the name of Christ. I told this story on Whitsunday in a brief address at Choral Mattins. A fortnight later I had a letter from Cassie's grandparents, saying they had heard about what had been said, and asking for a copy. They were so grateful that her story had crossed the Atlantic. I was amazed, of course, and felt very honoured and humbled to have become involved, even so slightly, with such a significant and terrible event, which had resonated around the globe. For as long as a sermon can strike chords like this, preachers will continue to be crucial players in the midst of the cacophony that makes up our modern life.'

His home page is at: http://homepages.enterprise.net/gjg

W HEN ST PAUL'S CATHEDRAL was burned to the ground in the Great Fire of London in September 1666, the tomb of Sir Anthony Van Dyck was destroyed in the flames. Erected by King Charles I, it was a very splendid tomb and it described Van Dyck as a 'Genius of Painting'. One of his pictures, painted in 1624, is of the Stoning of St Stephen – St Stephen, whose martyrdom we commemorate today. Stephen who spoke up, and spoke out – Stephen who was chosen by the first disciples to be one of the seven deacons whose express task it was to minister to the poor and neglected.

Van Dyck portrays Stephen dressed in the martyr's red, wearing a deacon's dalmatic robe, and gazing heavenward as five men raise stones against him. In the picture they have yet to strike – we are spared the bloodstained reality. Above the saint hover two cherubs, ready to receive him as he forgives those who are about to kill him – 'Lord do not hold this sin against them'. In the middle ground of the painting we see Saul, later known as St Paul, standing on the martyr's clothes, explaining to another onlooker what is happening.

And yet, glorious and beautifully depicted as the painting is, there is something unsatisfactory about it. Something unrealistic – something which makes us forget what is actually happening as these five boulder-wielding thugs set upon a man who has done little more than deliver a sermon.

Perhaps the art causes us to see through what is going on, to a greater glory – a depiction of a certain serenity as Stephen goes to his maker. An attempt even to suggest how sweet and decorous it is, to die for one's faith. But the reality of death is withheld – we are protected from it, as the moment is frozen in an almost idyllic scene.

Idyllic like another of Van Dyck's paintings, of the Adoration of the Shepherds at the birth of Christ. There is the same style, the same heavenward gazing, the same cherubs in the sky watching over as the coarse shepherds pay homage to a splendidly-dressed Madonna displaying her clean white baby. Paintings such as this find their way on to our Christmas cards and Christmas pudding labels. And in one sense, rightly so, for they are masterpieces – there is no question as to their value as works of art, nor of their status as objects of devotion, nor of the authenticity of the artist's intentions.

And yet, paintings that depict the mother and child in pastoral elegance, with rich robes and a clean stable floor are in some sense, unrealistic. Convention can disguise the truth. These splendid images can determine *our* picture, helping us to forget the reality of the events portrayed. Cake-tin depictions of martyrdom veil us from the realities of thuggery, intolerance and bigotry. Or veil us from the pain, fear and danger of natural birth in a first-century Middle Eastern cow shed, with all the lack of hygiene and disease that that might bring. Some music and poetry are capable of the same with their sweet words and honeyed melody.

In the world of art, which mirrors the imaginations of our own hearts, we are more than content to witness a cosy martyrdom, or believe in a pale and gentle-skinned Madonna cradling a clean and sleeping baby. But of course, it wasn't like that. There was a lot of blood, dirt and pain on those occasions, and likely more besides.

And yet, we must have our art – we must have our painters, com-

posers and poets who show us the heavens and depict a greater significance. We need interpretations and descriptions, that point us beyond
the surface facts to deeper truths. We need artists who can *show* us that
this baby is the Saviour of the world, artists who can *show* us that
Stephen was not just a victim of just another street lynching. We need
our storytellers to tell us the stories and point us beyond the facts, to
the Truth.

St Luke, that great story-teller, who gives us the most extended
account of Jesus' birth, is also the one who writes, in Acts, of Stephen's
death. Both stories appeal to our imagination and our emotions. But
we must not succumb too easily. There are realities of birth, of life and
of death that we must face. Realities, not only of who we are and how
we act, but also of how we relate to these overfamiliar events.

It's so easy in that carol by Christina Rosetti, 'In the Bleak Midwin-
ter', to sing, 'if I were a wise man, I would do my part'. But would you?
Could you? Dare you?

It takes some conviction to follow a call. To follow a call to a dingy
animal shed to greet a divine child. And courage still to speak out
against those who would harm you for it. Sadly, St Stephen was the first
in a very long line, and it is quite deliberate that we commemorate him
on this first day after Christmas.

Dietrich Bonhoeffer, who was also killed for his beliefs and actions,
wrote in a book entitled *The Cost of Discipleship*, that Christ calls us to
come and die. Christ calls us to take up our Cross, and die for his sake.
This was the cost for Stephen, as it was for Bonhoeffer himself.

'When Christians are exposed to public insult,' he wrote, 'when they
suffer and die for his sake, Christ takes on visible form in his Church.'
(p. 273). For Bonhoeffer, the only true form of witness – the only way
to show that the message of Christmas actually matters, is to be prepared to pay the ultimate price.

Most of us are never asked to do this. So the question as to whether
we would be prepared to, is not often asked. And when it does get
asked, as it might do on St Stephen's day, it is too easy to hide behind a
pretty picture of red robes and angels singing as a worthy soul is carried
to heaven. It can be so easy to fantasize about martyrdom, just as it can
be so easy to fantasize about Christmas.

But fantasy needs reality – reality is fantasy's food. Fantasy covers a
bloodstained dirty baby in pure white linen, and a martyr in red silk.
Fantasy talks of good will, and peace on earth – but at no cost. And
Bonhoeffer would call that cheap grace. Salvation bought cheap. Suffering ignored.

Reality covered in candy, and sold for pennies.

Another Christmas carol, 'Away in a Manger', assures us that after
little Jesus has laid down his sweet head, 'no crying he makes'. The
notion that the baby Jesus never cried, is unreal. And I understand

there are moves afoot now to remove any mention of Jesus from this carol, so it can be sung in politically-correct contexts where a reference to Christ could be construed as offensive. That would not so much be a cheap Christmas – but a free Christmas – a Christ-free Christmas.

And there *is* an offensiveness of the Gospel – the idea that God takes on vulnerable human flesh in order to take on the sin of the world is indeed offensive to those who suspect that all this talk of sin and death is a load of old rot, but quite nice for the children. The true message of Christmas *is* offensive, even if you wipe away the blood and the tears.

It's offensive, and it's expensive – it costs lives, from day one. Birth and death, in quick succession. And all of this involves us – it is *for* us. If we really buy into Christmas, we become involved. We involve ourselves in the birth at Bethlehem, and we watch in real horror as a man whose job is to help the poor is slaughtered by persecuting fanatics. And we can become involved, because these events happen around us today, as well as in the past. We've all enjoyed sharing with families who have had a new baby. And we've all been moved by violent stories in our news media. Pray God that we do not lose our ability to celebrate new birth and be horrified at killing, every single time.

When Old St Paul's was burned down in 1666 another creative genius' tomb was also damaged. He was the Dean, and was also a remarkable poet of both worldly and spiritual insight. In words that you may recognize, John Donne wrote:

> Any man's death diminishes me, because I am involved in Mankind; and therefore, never send to know for whom the bell tolls – it tolls for thee.

We are all diminished by suffering, and by any refusal to engage with the truth. Part of John Donne's tomb was saved, and it now stands in the Dean's aisle of St Paul's. His words also remain, and speak of the shared cost of discipleship yesterday and today. And Van Dyck's portrait of St Stephen also remains, and it may yet remind us of how easy it is to gloss over the true suffering of martyrdom.

And above all, we still have the Christmas story – the greatest story ever told, wrought by the creator-genius God. The story of a birth, not of a death, the story of one whose tomb was not destroyed, but abandoned. The fantastic salvation-story the facts of which we all know, and the truth of which we must never ignore.

Note
Quote: Dietrich Bonhoeffer, from *The Cost of Discipleship*, translated by R. H. Fuller (SCM Press, 1959).

A Sermon on Depression

John Young

Canon John Young, 63, has a roving brief in the York diocese where he goes by the official title of Diocesan Evangelist. Married to Isabel with two children, Debbie and Kate, and three grandchildren he has now had a sermon published in four of the six Times *books of best sermons.*

His father was a Welsh miner who went to London looking for work, where he met his mother, the barmaid at the Lion and Lamb in Hounslow, Middlesex, when he popped in for a drink.

Before his ordination in 1964, Canon Young did two years' National Service and also worked as a physical education teacher. He became a committed Christian as a student at Loughborough, when he was 21. 'Two things brought this about. One was the friendship of a Christian man. The second was when he invited me to a Christian weekend where the speaker was Dr Donald English, who went on to become twice the President of the Methodist Conference. Before that, although I went to Sunday School like most children of my generation, I was not an active Christian.' Soon after this, he began to think about ordination.

Canon Young preaches every week in a different church, not always Anglican, in the diocese. He also chairs an ecumenical organization, One Voice, which links some 200 churches from many denominations including the Salvation Army, the Methodist Church and the Roman Catholic Church.

He has had some varied preaching experiences.

'Only once have I preached in St Paul's Cathedral, and on that occasion I stood in the great pulpit, opened my mouth, and 30 people walked out. I like to think they were tourists who didn't understand English! Once, as a reward for preaching at a lifeboat service, I was taken for a ride in the boat. One mile out from shore I was told they needed some hands-on practice, and I was thrown overboard! Luckily, after ten minutes they came to reclaim me. I'm not sure if this was them commenting on my sermon or not.

'Preaching is not a lecture, although obviously they have something in common', he says. 'Like a lecture, there needs to be a structure and a clarity. Good sermons can change people, they can really help with the stuff of life by giving people encouragement about their faith. I hope we have all had the experience of sitting through a sermon and feeling a cloud of difficulties lift as we see our problems in the perspective of the love of God. Or we have sat there and thought, yes, tomorrow I must write that letter of reconciliation, or

send off that cheque. Preaching sets our lives within the context of the love of God, which is encouraging, but it has to be shared, which is challenging. When I am in the pulpit, I hope to get through to people, to encourage and to challenge – to inspire, even. It is not me and them, it is us.'

His work as a preacher is supplemented by his work as a writer. He has written a dozen books, most published by Hodder. Some of these books have been translated into ten or more languages, including Chinese and Russian. More recently, he co-founded 'York Courses', Lent courses material which has been used by, he estimates, 30–40,000 people over the past two or three years.

Choir and Congregation sing 'O worship the Lord in the beauty of holiness'.

'MORNINGS OF JOY, give for evenings of tearfulness, Trust for our trembling – and hope for our fear.' I can identify with the first part of that sentence from John Monsell's fine hymn for, normally, I am a morning person – eager to welcome all the possibilities of a new day. But one morning a few summers ago I woke up feeling quite unable to get up and get going. All I wanted to do – *felt* able to do – was to stay in bed and nurse a lead ball which continued to grow in my stomach. The morning post went unopened, phone calls required a heroic effort and the prospect of standing up in front of a group of people was pretty well impossible. In my fifties I was experiencing my first bout of depression.

In this Service we're considering a personal journey of faith encountering depression. That journey is mine. In one sense I feel a fraud. Some people battle with depression year in year out. In a very real way they wrestle with a giant and are aware that the outcome is uncertain. My depression was short and nasty – but it lifted within a few weeks. True, it did return some months later, but after another period of blackness it disappeared over the horizon. So far – thank God – the storm clouds have not gathered again. But perhaps describing my experience will be useful, because around 30 per cent of people in Britain are likely to share it. For most of these, depression will not be an ongoing condition. It is more likely to be a debilitating but relatively short illness, which may return from time to time.

When asked to describe their experience, people use a range of images. A tidal wave engulfing them, a heavy weight pressing down, endless darkness or greyness, walking through treacle, a ball of lead in their stomach (my own experience) or Winston Churchill's famous 'black dog'. What took me completely by surprise was just how *physical* it was. Depression may be a mental illness but it affects the body. I usually enjoy high energy levels but once I had made the heroic effort to get up, I would look longingly at the bed and count the hours until I would be horizontal and inactive again.

Christians sometimes feel guilty about depression. Surely its a failure of faith? What do the Scriptures say about that?

The Bible announces 'glad tidings of great joy' with its emphasis on resurrection, the love of God, new life in Christ and glory to come. But it caters for all moods and conditions and there is another side. Indeed, the Scriptures contain quite a lot of material about, and by, people suffering from depression. The fiery prophet Elijah for example. Having triumphed fearlessly over a host of prophets of Baal, he ran away in fear and eventually lay down utterly exhausted, longing only for the release of death. This gives rise to the gentle, moving story of the way in which God met his physical needs. This is in our reading, from 1 Kings 19:3–9:

> Then he was afraid; he got up and fled for his life, and came to Beersheba, which belongs to Judah; he left his servant there. But he himself went a day's journey into the wilderness, and came and sat down under a solitary broom tree. He asked that he might die: 'It is enough; now, O Lord, take away my life, for I am no better than my ancestors.' Then he lay down under the broom tree and fell asleep. Suddenly an angel touched him and said to him, 'Get up and eat.' He looked, and there at his head was a cake baked on hot stones, and a jar of water. He ate and drank, and lay down again. The angel of the Lord came a second time, touched him, and said, 'Get up and eat, otherwise the journey will be too much for you.' He got up, and ate and drank; then he went in the strength of that food forty days and forty nights to Horeb the mount of God. At that place he came to a cave, and spent the night there. Then the word of the Lord came to him, saying, 'What are you doing here, Elijah?'

'He came to a broom tree, sat down under it and prayed that he might die.' Several Bible passages speak the same language of bewilderment and distress – which often gives way to quiet faith or praise. Quiet faith is certainly a characteristic of Psalm 62 with its gentle refrain: 'On God alone I wait silently, God my deliverer, God my strong tower.'

The New Testament also brings encouragement to those wrestling with depression, for it shows with great honesty the way in which some of its leading figures grapple with despair and darkness. The most celebrated example is Jesus in the garden of Gethsemane – perhaps the most solemn episode in the entire Gospel story. The whole passage is heavy with dread and desolation: 'My soul is overwhelmed with sorrow . . . Abba, Father, take this cup from me. Yet not what I will but what you will.'

Significantly, the whole mood stands in surprising and stark contrast to the way in which the martyrs faced death. The female slave Blandina for example who, reported Eusebius, went to her death as to a marriage feast. Or Polycarp, Bishop of Smyrna, who as an old man stood in a pagan arena in 156 AD. He was offered his life in exchange for denying Christ, to which he answered: 'I have been his servant for 86 years and he has never done me any wrong. How then can I blaspheme my king, who saved me?' He was burned to death.

Neither Blandina nor Polycarp showed dread in the face of death. Indeed, both drew strength from their faith in Jesus Christ, despite the fact that he shrank from the cross. In pondering this great mystery theologians have found a profound answer. Jesus shrank from death for he was, in the words of John the Baptist, 'The Lamb of God who takes away the sin of the world.' In doing this, he suffered spiritual suffocation – a unique and terrible experience which set his followers free from fear and filled them with hope and faith.

Another example of faith facing depression can be found in the Second Letter to the Corinthians. St Paul is trying to establish his credentials as a leader and an apostle. He is remarkably frank. For he speaks not only of victory and triumph but of 'fightings without and fears within' – taking an enormous risk in exposing his vulnerability to a church which seemed to want strength, buoyancy and charisma in its leaders. (2 Cor 7:5–7)

From the New Testament we know a fair bit about the life of St Paul and might expect him to go on to say that God comforted him by a dream, a vision or an in-filling of the Holy Spirit. Something dramatic. In fact he completes his sentence rather lamely. 'But God who comforts the downcast, comforted us by the coming of Titus.' His friend turned up, bringing good news from the other churches and this was a turning point for the apostle.

What might help you or me if we find ourselves struggling with depression? Medication almost certainly. And gentle exercise. I didn't much want to walk but always found it beneficial. Reading novels too was a great help, as in my imagination I could escape to another place and enter into other lives. And like Paul the Apostle I discovered afresh the importance of friendship and good listening. I'm grateful to God for those who let me set the pace and who, in today's jargon, 'were there for me'.

That's not always easy, especially for close members of the family. One writer on depression has suggested that depression is catching. It certainly affects the mood of every home, family and workplace which experiences it.

That same writer also reminds us that depression is a dangerous disease. I love life and have never given a thought to ending it. During my period of depression, suicide didn't become a big issue for me, but I do recall sitting in a traffic jam and looking longingly at the exhaust pipe in front of me.

I got a tiny glimpse into the frame of mind which drives people to suicide – the desperate desire to end it all and to escape from the oppressive life-draining darkness. Not, I suspect, to escape from the circumstances of their lives – however desperate and tangled they might be. Rather, the need to escape from the depression itself. From the greyness,the weight pressing down, the lead ball within or whatever the image might be for them.

Where does depression come from? Sometimes the causes are clear. Loss, perhaps. Or deep disappointment or frustration. A disastrous decision maybe. Exhaustion and overwork. Abuse in childhood. Or an important relationship which turns sour. This weekend, the papers are full of greetings from Pooh Bear to Tigger and Bunnykins to Honeysuckle. St Valentine's love can be the source of the greatest joy, but when it goes wrong, it can plunge us beneath deep dark waters.

Sometimes, of course, we simply cannot discern a reason. It comes unheralded, from the deep recesses of our lives where it has been waiting, lurking, barely awake. But I am anxious to introduce a positive note. Many people in depression feel that they are in a dark tunnel which has no end. But most do come through the tunnel and out into the glorious sunlight. This was certainly true of the Psalmist, for even those Psalms with the most despairing opening, end with an affirmation of faith and sometimes of joy – a mood which is carried even more strongly in the New Testament.

And so to the most difficult question of all. Why does God allow such apparently unproductive suffering? The ministry of Jesus is full of healing miracles – sometimes for people whose faith was no bigger than a mustard seed. I don't doubt that the same Lord heals people today. Perhaps it is the prayers of my friends which have kept my own depression at bay.

But the New Testament outlines other experiences too. Some of the most famous prayers have been answered with a 'No'. Jesus in Gethsemane . . . And Paul's persistent prayer for the removal of his 'thorn in the flesh'. We can't be sure what that was. Eye problems perhaps. Epilepsy maybe. Or depression. Who knows?

What we do know for certain is that Paul longed to be rid of it. It blighted his life and hindered his ministry. Try travelling vast distances in modern Turkey (his Asia Minor) on foot or pony and you'll soon see that you need to be in excellent health.

God's answer to Paul's urgent prayer was 'No'. But there was a rider. Paul needed to learn this great truth. 'God's strength is made perfect in weakness.'

At the heart of the Christian faith are two great miracles: incarnation and resurrection.The incarnation is caught wonderfully by St John. 'The Word was made flesh and dwelt among us, full of grace and truth'. Jesus came among us as one of us – and he suffered for us and for our salvation. It is not surprising therefore, that Jesus calls his followers to identify closely with a world in anguish. So – hard as it is – I believe that he calls members of his church to suffer the full range of human miseries – from unemployment to bereavement; from cancer to depression. It is a tough message. But when it is heard in humble obedience it can be wonderfully inspiring. Here, for example is an extract from a letter from a friend – a deputy head – who learned that she had multiple sclerosis.

'I've had to give up driving. The fatigue is rotten, but not such a worry now that I've stopped working. The blurred and double/triple vision is a nuisance, but curiously interesting. For example, the Cathedral has had two spires for a couple of years; there are three moons in the sky and an awful lot of eight-legged cats about! I am quite used to it now and it's not a worry. I've made no retirement plans, confident that something will emerge for me, when the time is right.'

I think too of a conversation with a mother, following the death of her child. She told me that a particular verse brought her great comfort. Which one, I asked, expecting her to quote from the resurrection narratives. The words of Jesus on the cross, she replied: 'My God, my God, why have you forsaken me?' She drew strength from the knowledge that Jesus was with her in her sorrow – and that he understood and shared her desolation. And so we end with a hymn by Charles Wesley, which catches and mingles the twin themes of confidence in the love of God and realism about the storms of life. Verse 2 reads like this:

> Other refuge have I none,
> Hangs my helpless soul on thee;
> Leave, ah, leave me not alone,
> Still support and comfort me.
> All my trust on thee is stayed,
> All my help from thee I bring;
> Cover my defenceless head
> With the shadow of thy wing.

(*Hymns and Psalms*, 'Jesu Lover of My Soul', Methodist Publishing House, 1983)

How to Hold On to Hope

JAYNE OZANNE

Jayne Ozanne, 31, is a freelance strategic consultant, primarily helping Christian charities with various organizational, change management and marketing issues. She has had an interesting and varied international business career, ranging from overseeing brands such as Fairy Liquid, Kleenex and BBC1 to launching a large multinational company into Central and Eastern Europe.

After graduating from St John's College, Cambridge in mathematics she was recruited by Procter & Gamble. Here she oversaw several major marketing initiatives before moving to Kimberly Clark as a European Brand Manager. She was relocated to Paris where she was given the chance to help lead the company into Central and Eastern Europe – working on the merger, acquisition and integration of several Central European companies. Following an extensive international marketing career, involving some of Europe's best-known brands, she was asked by the BBC to help set up a new marketing department within BBC television.

In 1998 she began work as a freelance consultant in order to help facilitate her appointment to the Archbishops' Council, the new management and policy body at the heart of the Church of England. Her faith has always been an integral part of her life, and she gives much voluntary time to advising the Church on many strategic and communication issues. She is actively involved in a lay leadership role within her church, St Paul's Anglican Fellowship, in central London. She is a keen musician and sings with St John's Smith Square Choir. Her other hobbies include sailing and scubadiving.

Her faith is strong. 'I have been fortunate enough to have known the Lord Jesus Christ most of my life. I remember that I first accepted the Good News of the gospel at the age of five on a Beach Mission in Guernsey, and then later at the age of twelve I remember becoming really aware one evening that Jesus had died for ME, and that this was personal! I have had a very broad church background – I was baptized in the Anglican church, confirmed in the Methodist church and baptized (on my request) in the Baptist church. I have sung in a formal cathedral style choir and helped form a House church. Over the years I have worshipped in both large university congregations and small rural parishes. In 1998 I was given the immense privilege of being able to serve the church by being appointed to the Archbishops' Council.'

127

Life has not been without its ups and downs, including of course its many doubts. 'In 1997, following a severe period of illness, I came to a much deeper understanding of what a life committed to Jesus Christ was all about. Instead of presenting Him with a shopping list of my hopes and dreams, I started to "get real" and tell Him exactly how I was feeling! I decided to "let go of the control pedal" of my own life and asked Jesus to guide and direct me wherever He wanted me to go. The result? A roller-coaster ride into the unknown, which I can only describe as being the most exhilarating and exciting journey I have ever known!'

This sermon arose from a request by her Vicar that she preach on the subject 'How to hold on to Hope' as part of a series the church was doing on 1 Timothy. 'He knew that this was something I had had a lot of personal experience of, and felt that I might therefore be able to help others. "Hope" is something we all need to hang on to as it is easily lost!'

She believes people respond to and need to hear about vulnerability. 'For too long we have put our leaders on pedestals, and expected them to be perfect. The truth is that we are all broken human beings, and that it is through our own life experiences we are able to learn, grow and support others. Sermons therefore work best, I believe, when they are based on the personal witness of the person involved. As a society we are repulsed by "being told" what we "should do", but respond openly to hearing about how others have struggled and doubted.'

She believes the sermon should come at a time when people are most receptive to hearing what God has to say to them as individuals. 'I believe that this means it should follow a time of worshipping God, a time of repenting before Him and leaving Him with all our baggage (prayer), and a time of preparation (listening to His word).'

She believes that the sermon published here was the first she ever preached. 'I hope it shows that we all have something to offer, and that the only credentials we need are that we root ourselves in prayer and listen to what the Holy Spirit wants us to say!

'In preparing for this sermon I asked various friends how they went about writing their sermons. I received various pieces of really helpful advice, but I think by far the most valuable was this: "That I should pray for my congregation and ask that God would speak to them no matter what I said!" This did, along with the prayer I always pray whenever I speak in public: "That people will be able to sense the love of God when I speak – no matter what I say!"

'The result? Well, when I had finished speaking and came down off the podium, I buried my head in my hands and asked that God would touch at least one person – or just one person – with what I had said. You see, we normally have a time of ministry for anyone who feels they would like prayer after a service, and I believed that there were going to be several people there who would want this – and had said so publicly. So I kept my head down and prayed. When I looked up, I could hardly believe my eyes, people were queu-

*ing to come to the front! Nearly three quarters of the church came forward
that night – which is a complete work of God's grace!*

*This story I believe is summed up completely in 1 Cor 1: 26–31: "Brothers,
think of what you were before you were called. Not many of you were wise by
human standards; not many were influential; not many were of noble birth.
But God chose the foolish things of the world to shame the wise; God chose
the weak things of the world to shame the strong. He chose the lowly things
of this world and the despised things – and the things that are not – to nulli-
fy the things that are, so that no man may boast before him. It is because of
him that you are in Christ Jesus, who has become for us wisdom from God –
that is, our righteousness, holiness and redemption. Therefore, as it is written: 'Let him who boasts boast in the Lord'."'*

Text: 1 Timothy 1:12–20.

I'VE JUST COME BACK from three wonderful weeks in Scotland,
which I spent with an elderly Christian couple in their seventies,
who took me sailing up the west coast of Scotland! Rosanne is probably one of the most spiritual and humble Christians I've ever met. The
Lord has blessed and used her in many ways – she's been instrumental
in the lives of many key Christians across the world – and currently one
of her priorities has been to set up prayer support for the work that God
is doing in Eastern Europe and the Middle East. Last Monday afternoon, in a tiny village in the middle of nowhere, I had the privilege of
meeting and praying with a young couple who had come to her to tell
her what was happening in their particular mission field. This couple
had an amazing story – Jonathon had trained as a lawyer in Glasgow,
and just as he had qualified he had felt called to Turkey. There he struggled to learn the language and then put himself through university
again – this time to do a Turkish law degree. Due to his Christian ethics
he has become known and respected as one of the most reliable and
trustworthy lawyers in Turkey – and has had as a result – access to some
of the most senior men in Turkey. With his wife, who has a real heart
for working with children, they have seen God beginning to work in
mighty ways out there. So we all prayed, we shared, we gave them
words of encouragement, and then they left. You can imagine our horror when just over twelve hours later we heard the news of the earthquake!

Watching the news that evening I think I, like all of us, was stunned
by the pictures of all those buildings, homes to hundreds of people,
folded in like packs of cards – knowing that in all probability there were
many people trapped inside them. I was deeply struck by the statement
given by the Turkish government – pleading for help and pledging to
continue the search for survivors until (and I quote) 'all hope was lost'.
Slowly, as the week passed, the pictures of the lucky few being pulled

free from their graves were rapidly replaced with pictures of women sitting alone with their few possessions staring blankly into space. You know, I think TV is beginning to make us numb to the impact of these catastrophes – we've seen so many. These women had lost everything – for most this included their husbands, their children, their home and with it all any hope for a meaningful future. We rang Jonathon (luckily he hadn't left Scotland yet) for any news. He hadn't been able to talk to anybody – all the lines were down. He was adamant he wanted to get back there as soon as possible to encourage the Christians to hang on in there – to hang on to their hope!

Nearly 2000 years previously Timothy had travelled with Paul very close to this region. I don't say this to be flippant, but to try and put this passage into perspective as I know that, for myself at least, New Testament places can seem as if they belong to another 'Alice in Wonderland' world. Actually, in Acts 16 it says that Paul and his companions travelled throughout the region of Asia but were kept by the Holy Spirit from preaching the word there. In verse 7 of that chapter it says that when they came to the border of Mysia (just where the epicentre of the quake was), they tried to enter but the Spirit of Jesus would not allow them in! An interesting verse, which we'll never really understand the reason for – but I think what we can safely say is that the gospel had not been widely shared in this region.

Timothy spent much time assisting Paul on his travels – shadowing him and learning from him, in Paul's words 'as a Son with his Father'. I suppose that's really what I was doing with Rosanne this summer – I listened to her, I watched her, I learnt from her – and I was ministered to by her. Once Paul felt he was ready, Timothy became a follow-up man or troubleshooter, and in fact by the time we find him in Ephesus he has already spent time in the churches in Thessalonica, Philippi and Corinth. Although we know that Timothy was greatly spoken of by Paul, we also know from Paul that Timothy was quite timid and shy, with a bit of a 'weak constitution'. On the surface of it, he was the last sort of man that you would expect Paul to send to one of the most rapidly growing churches in the area, facing one of its most difficult times.

Acts 19 records that God had done extraordinary miracles through Paul in Ephesus – even handkerchiefs that had touched him were taken to the sick, and they were healed and evil spirits left them. Those who had been practising sorcery came and publicly burnt their scrolls – all in all this would have been a pretty hard pair of shoes for Timothy to fit into. Ephesus was also the commercial and political centre for Western Asia, and as such had some pretty strong and dominating characters around. Men skilled in political rancouring – who could probably tear our front benches to shreds – and self-made millionaires who felt that their wealth gave them the right to throw their weight around.

Not much different from today – but again, not really the place were a shy young man, who wasn't good at speaking out would have had much impact, or even respect – that is, in his own strength! However, when Paul had last been in the region he had put certain elders who had been teaching false doctrines out of the church and had commissioned Timothy to 'sort it all out'.

I'm personally convinced that Timothy would have been desperate for a letter from Paul freeing him from this assignment and/or saying he was going to send in the big guns – like John or Silas. Can you imagine Timothy receiving at long last a letter addressed personally to him (not the whole church), tearing it open (or whatever you do with a scroll) and skim-reading it frantically – hoping against hope to see if he was finally being sent for? Unfortunately, he didn't have to go very far to find his answer – right up front in verse 3 Paul writes 'as I urged you stay there in Ephesus', and then just in case he began to doubt the reason why Paul wanted him to stay, he read in verse 18 'Timothy, my son, I give you this instruction in keeping with the prophecies made about you . . .'. You know, just the fondness of the phrase 'Timothy, my son' says to me that Paul really did understand the impact on Timothy of what he was asking him to do, and yet he wasn't going to change the order.

Instead, what he does do is to write this paragraph 12–20 as an encouragement to him. On first glance it may seem like Paul is going off on one of his many tangents – getting sidetracked from his core message. But I believe it has been purposely placed here, upfront at the start of the letter to encourage Timothy and GIVE HIM HOPE – even after receiving the worst piece of news he could have hoped for, so that he could hear the rest of the letter.

As a friend trying to help his hurting brother he does three practical things:

Firstly, he does what he tells everyone to do in every situation – he PRAISES GOD (v. 12). In particular he praises God for the fact that he has been appointed to his service. This would have been something, like it or not, that Timothy would have also had to resonate with. Timothy had been commissioned by the laying-on of hands by the elders and had received a gift through a prophetic message (1 Tim 4:14; 2 Tim 1:6). One of the many things I learnt from Rosanne was to praise God in *every* situation – particularly the toughest ones, as this is when the devil most wants us to turn our eyes off Jesus and start doubting God's authority. This is a topic for a sermon in itself, but I would really urge you to look at your reaction to painful circumstances and try praising as Paul sets out in 1 Thes 5:18 – 'give thanks in all circumstances'.

Secondly, Paul SHARES HIS OWN TESTIMONY (vss. 13–14) of how hopeless his own situation was before he was saved by grace. Paul freely admits he had committed three of what, under Jewish law, were the most 'deadly sins' – blasphemy (3rd commandment), murder (6th commandment), and persecution of the godly (God clearly states in his 2nd commandment that he will punish to the 3rd and 4th generation those who hate him). In the eyes of the false teachers that Timothy was trying to keep in order, Paul would have been classed as a 'no hoper'. Of his own volition he 'was the worst of all sinners' (v. 15) – and yet Jesus saved him, not by anything he had done, but by grace, to show his unlimited PATIENCE (v. 16). Gosh, how those words must have stung a bit. 'If Jesus has shown so much patience with you,' implies Paul, 'surely you can hold out a little bit'.

Finally Paul reminds Timothy of the prophecies made about him. These, as I like to call them, are 'personalized God promises' which Timothy was to hold on to in order to help him through the ups and downs of his own faith journey. 'Fight the good fight' (v. 18) implies that the going was not going to be a cinch – Jesus himself warned us that 'in this world you will have trouble' (John 16:33). I think sometimes we need to remember this – all too often we expect life to be nice and smooth once we become Christians, and are really knocked for six when hard times hit us.

A couple of years ago I went through one of the worst times of my life. In fact, I have often said that I wouldn't wish my experience even on my worst enemy. Without going into too much of the details, I can say that what happened was that I was stripped of all the props and masks that I had used to create me – Jayne Ozanne, one of THE most successful highfliers of the 90s – whose identity was all mixed up in a fast car and a job which many would have given their eye teeth for. I was stripped completely bare, and almost overnight found myself at that place which, for those of you who have been there, will know has No Name. It has nothing, absolutely nothing – just a dark void of deep despair and pain. You can't go on, you can't go back and you can't opt out. You're trapped. And it's there you have to make decisions.

It's a difficult place to describe. I tried to paint it, and yet all I ever seemed to paint was a crack of light coming through the darkness. No matter how dark and deep my hole, I could always see a crack of light piercing the dark – I realize now that that tiny faint line of light was hope. I began painting it for other friends going through the same trouble and gradually, over time, I found myself being pieced back together again – this time with God in the driving seat, moulding me the way he wanted.

So how DO we hold on to hope? Let's look again at the passage, and with the benefit of a little hindsight from someone who nearly lost all hope I'd like to pull out a few more key points.

Firstly, let's look at v. 12 – 'I thank Christ Jesus our Lord, who has given me strength'.When I was praying about this passage I had a very vivid picture of a businessman hanging on to a cliff by his fingernails.

This wasn't a Sylvester Stallone character who was going to pull himself up with one easy jerk, but a chap who really was hanging in there by the ends of his fingertips. As I meditated on this picture, I began to see his face more clearly – it was contorted with the pain and the strain of using every ounce of energy to just 'hang on'. Panic was beginning to set in as the awful realization of 'there's no hope – I'm going to fall' began to dawn. And then, just as I too began to really fear for the safety of this man I saw the full picture. Jesus was bent down, on his knees and was holding the man by his wrists. I saw Jesus weeping – not because of the strain of holding on to him. Not at all! This was no effort at all for him, but more because this poor chap could not see how safe he really was – in the arms of Jesus.

We aren't expected to hang on in there in our own strength – but in the strength we are given by grace:

- 2 Samuel 22:33 – It is God who arms me with strength and makes my way perfect.
- Psalm 46:1 – God is our refuge and our strength, an ever present help in times of trouble.
- Philippians 4:13 – I can do all things through Christ who gives me strength. (Actually, this is one of the Archbishop's key verses – which he has had printed on cards and gives out to people.)

In fact, God particularly chooses the weak things of the world so that he can give them strength – 1 Corinthians 1· 27 'God chose the weak things of this world to shame the strong'. Timothy knew this so well and I must admit that I know it for myself. God has catapulted me into the very centre of the Church of England – me, a broken, young female (which frankly is about as low as you can get in church) and has used me in the most outrageous of circumstances. Only the other day was I sat in my car outside the offices of a very senior Christian businessman, crying to the Lord that he'd chosen the wrong person because I didn't know anything about the topic I was to go and talk to this man about. It was at that point that I felt God say, 'but that's when you're most useful, Jayne'. 'That's all very well,' you say, 'but he never shows up when I really need him'. And that's certainly how I felt, although I must admit that I couldn't see or recognize the loving help he had sent me in the form of many good Christian friends when I was so ill. The main reason – because I was relying almost completely on MY strength – and to experience HIS strength we have to let go – of everything!

Look at verse 17 – Paul's rapturous explosion of praise. 'Now to the King, eternal, immortal, The ONLY God . . .' It's CHRIST JESUS who gives him strength – no one else. The main problem that Timothy was having to confront was that the false teachers were still trying to teach that salvation came through the LAW. However, hanging on to this was not going to save them. Some of the false teachers were also preaching that godliness was a means to financial gain (1 Tim 5:5). They were hanging on to money. In fact Paul had to spell it out later in 5:17 (have a look – turn the page). 'Command those who are rich in this present world not to be arrogant nor to put their hope in wealth, which is so uncertain, but to put their hope in God, who richly provides us with everything for our enjoyment'.

You know, perhaps I should start my story a little further back. About three years ago, I remember being really challenged here one Sunday evening as to just how much I was prepared to let God control my life. I remember praying then that I wanted God to use me, to take over everything – except my car, because that was my pride and joy, my means of 'enjoyment' and my job, as that was what gave me my identity. Within a month I had lost my car, and within six months I was too ill to be doing my job. A lot has happened since then – major surgery for the most part. However, since last October when I heard I had been appointed to the Archbishops' Council – a miraculous story in its own right – I knew God was calling me for a short time at least to live by faith. This is not something that everyone is called to by any means, but sometimes it's exactly what God wants in order to teach us complete dependence on him. I went from living on a very good salary to almost nothing over night. It's certainly not been easy, but God really has provided – and I now realize He can give us major goodies too. I really needed a holiday this summer, and he provided the perfect one. A week's houseparty in the Quantocks followed by three weeks in Scotland, incorporating ten perfect sailing days around the Western Isles – all beyond my wildest dreams!

So where is your hope? In your savings, in your partner, in your career prospects or in God? You can only have one – there is no plan B or safety plan with God. Your hope must be in Him and nothing else. You see, for half of this year I was relying on my savings as a sort of 'back-up plan' to see me through – and then they ran out. And that's when the real crunch time came – my only hope was in God!

But we've said that God doesn't leave us to fend for ourselves. He gives us strength and HE GIVES US PROMISES – both personally and through his word. As I've already said, Paul reminds Timothy of the prophecies made about him as an individual. Personal prophecies are SO important. If you ever receive any, I really urge you to write them down and keep them in a safe place. They become of most use when you're doubting and under attack – that's when you need to have faith in your calling more than ever. I know this for a fact, and I thank God that he gave me words from people I knew and trusted before I found myself in the position I'm now in. Now when I doubt, my friends can remind me of these words.

In verse 15, Paul states one of the ETERNAL PROMISES – 'Christ Jesus came into the world to save sinners' – there's no qualification, no exceptions – just a statement of truth. Similarly, the Bible is packed full of promises for us to hold on to. Here are just a few from God himself, that we as Christians can ALWAYS claim:

'Call to me and I will answer you and tell you great and unsearchable things you do not know'. (Jer 33:3)

'Do not fear for I am with you, do not be dismayed for I am your God. I will strengthen you and help you, I will uphold you with my righteous hand'. (Isaiah 41:10)

'They will call to me and I will answer them'. (Zech 13:9)

Jesus said: 'If you remain in me, ask whatever you wish and it will be given to you'. (John 15:7)

These promises HAVE to be true as God never lies! However, a word of caution – just because God doesn't do the specific thing you asked immediately doesn't mean that he has broken his promise. God's timing is perfect – and he knows far better than we do what we need. So claim the promise and hold on!

Finally, let's look back at this phrase 'fight the good fight' in verse 18. What I believe Paul is urging Timothy to do is to ENDURE. To carry on. To not give up.

On my desk at home I've pinned up this sheet that I received some time ago through my weekly Monday Manna – an Internet service to the world's business community. It's entitled 'Don't Give Up' and says:

Calvin Coolidge once said, 'Nothing in the world can take the place of persistence. Talent will not; nothing is more common than unsuccessful men with talent. Genius will not; unrewarded genius is almost a proverb. Education will not; the world is full of educated derelicts. Persistence and determination alone are omnipotent.'

Great people are just ordinary people with an extraordinary amount of determination. They simply don't know how to quit. They just keep on *'keeping on.'*

The writer believes that a person's greatness is not determined by his or her fame, position, or wealth; but rather, what it takes to discourage that person. You can tell a lot about someone by watching how they respond to criticism or failure. It reveals character.

What does it take to discourage you?

Things not going your way?

Expectations not being met?

Someone disapproving of how you did something?

The Bible says this: 'Let us not get tired of doing what is right, for after a while we will reap a harvest of blessing, if we don't get discouraged and give up' (Galatians 6:9).

Things that last usually require more time and determination

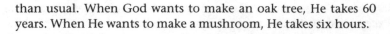

than usual. When God wants to make an oak tree, He takes 60 years. When He wants to make a mushroom, He takes six hours.

To 'fight the good fight' is not a one-off battle that will be won once and for all – it's a lifetime of endurance. Paul often likens life to running a race, a race that must be run with perseverance (Heb 12:1). We must always continue with the battle, never giving up otherwise we run the risk of becoming (in Paul's words) shipwrecked like the two men he handed over to Satan.

So, in summary, how do we hold on to hope? I've covered a lot this evening – perhaps too much. But the thing is that when I received this title and I was praying about what to say, I felt God saying that the points to make would be in the letters H-O-P-E. So, looking back, what we've covered is:

H   was for HELP – remember, we're not expected to do this in our own strength, He's there holding us.
O   was for ONLY. We must put our hope ONLY in God, not in money or in people but in Him alone.
P   was for PROMISES, both personal and those in His word.
E   was for ENDURANCE. We must fight the good fight, persevering until the last!

The great news for us, as Christians, is that we have a hope that is STEADFAST AND CERTAIN. There's absolutely no probability or chance about it. Unlike the situation in Turkey our hope can NEVER be lost – unlike those poor women who had seen the lifeless forms of their loved ones and in doing so have lost all hope, we will NEVER have to look on the lifeless form of Jesus. He HAS conquered death and has set us free. He is alive, and in him we have our hope, a hope of a glorious new life. All we have to do is to believe, let go and let him hold on to us!

The Holocaust and
Divine Suffering

DAN COHN-SHERBOK

Dan Cohn-Sherbok, 55, Professor of Judaism at the University of Wales, Lampeter is married to Lavinia, formerly headmistress of West Heath School. They have two cats, Herod and Dido. Educated at Williams College in Williamstown, Massachusetts, he was ordained a Reform rabbi at the Hebrew Union College-Jewish Institute of Religion in America where he received a Doctorate in Divinity. He has also gained a Doctorate in Philosophy from Cambridge University. He went on to work as a rabbi in England, Australia and South Africa, and in 1975 moved to England permanently, becoming lecturer in theology at the University of Kent at Canterbury where he stayed until 1997. During this period he spent six years in the 1990s as the Director of the university's Centre for the Study of Religion and Society. He has also served as rabbi on the QE2.

He has written and edited over sixty books on various aspects of Jewish life and thought, including: Understanding the Holocaust, Holocaust Theology, *and* The Crucified Jew: Twenty Centuries of Christian Anti-Semitism.

Ever since he ws a little boy, Professor Cohn-Sherbok wanted to be a congregational rabbi. Growing up in a Jewish home in the leafy suburbs of Denver, he imagined himself preaching to a hushed congregation in the Midwest, and leading his people. However, it didn't turn out that way. To his chagrin he discovered that most of the congregants in the synagogues he served were more interested in social life rather than his sermons. 'I tried being a rabbi in Jasper, Alabama; Harrisburg, Pennsylvania; Denver, Colorado; Galesburg, Illinois; Johannesburg, South Africa; Melbourne, Australia; and London. But it was always the same – I was a disaster. They never listened to anything I had to say!

'In one synagogue hardly anyone came to services on the Sabbath. But there were literally hundreds on bingo night. Each week the synagogoue held a bingo evening, and there was a gigantic sign outside which dwarfed the synagogue sign. My job was to announce the winner at bingo for which I received a tumultuous applause, and once I had to dress up for a ladies fashion show. But hardly anyone came to my adult education classes.' Eventually he came to the conclusion that being a rabbi is not a job for a nice Jewish boy – the title of an autobiographical novel he wrote about his experiences.

'In 1975, I was appointed to teach Jewish theology at the University of

Kent, and I have been happy ever since. Unlike my congregants, my students listen with rapt attention to whatever I say. They write everything down. It's all most gratifying . . . but of course I know they are preparing for exams. If only I could have set exams for my congregants in the context of sermons!'

Despite such discouragement in the rabbinate, Professor Cohn-Sherbok believes that the sermon has a central role in Judaism. 'It is the high point of the service, and possibly more than anything else, can profoundly influence people's lives.'

Although he believes that sermons are of crucial significance, Professor Cohn-Sherbok feels that the context of preaching should undergo significant change. 'When I was a rabbi in London, I encouraged congregants to stay behind after services. I wanted to hear what they thought of what I said. Not everyone remained, but those that did often challenged my views. This, I believe, is healthy and important. Sermons should not be monologues – they can provide a basis for discussion and debate.'

His sermon here addresses a subject, the Holocaust, that has eclipsed contemporary Jewish life. 'Jews are perplexed how to make sense of God's seeming inactivity. In my sermon I seek to wrestle with the religious implications of the Nazi onslaught. How could God have brought about, or allowed, millions of innocent individuals to die in the most horrific circumstances? I know that not everyone will agree with my views, but I hope some might find what I have to say to be of some consolation.' His aim here is to provide a means of coming to terms with the horrors of the concentration camps. 'It is a sermon for both Jews and Christians and draws on both traditions. Congregants are deeply concerned about the religious implications of the Holocaust, and in synagogues wish to gain some understanding of God's nature and actions.'

He believes the sermon is still vital today. 'It is an opportunity for Jews to gain some understanding of the significance of religion in the modern world. It should be the centrepiece of the liturgy, possibly placed after the Torah reading. But wherever it is located it should provide a focus. Ideally congregants should have an opportunity to ask questions after the service.' His interests outside religion include cats, drawing cartoons, and, drawing on his own experiences he has written a novel about becoming and being a rabbi: Not a job for a Nice Jewish boy.

THE DAVID IRVING TRIAL has focused attention on Nazi atrocities during the Second World War. But the events of the Second World War also raise the perplexing issue of God's seeming absence during the Holocaust. Where was God when six million died? The twentieth century has never had a more serious question, and over the past fifty years it has haunted thinkers from all the branches of Judaism. From the traditional side a number of Jewish theologians have sought to defend God. In their view it is not God who is responsible for the horrors of the Holocaust, but human beings. Other more radical thinkers, however, contend that our views about God's nature must be modified after Auschwitz. Some Jewish death-of-God theologians even go so far as to argue that we must abandon our belief in God altogether.

Yet, among these varied theological positions, there is one writer who has provided an answer to the problem of the Holocaust which can serve to draw Jews and Christians together in a quest to understand God's action in the world. The novelist and concentration camp survivor Elie Wiesel in his autobiographical novel *Night* relates how one day the SS guards hanged two Jewish men and a young boy in front of the entire camp. The men died quickly, but the child did not. Describing this scene, Wiesel wrote that he heard someone ask: 'Where is God? Where is He?' For more than an hour the child stayed there, dying in slow agony. Wiesel continued: I heard the same man asking: 'Where is God now?' And I heard a voice within me answer him: Where is He? Here he is – he is hanging here on the gallows.'

For Wiesel, God is not an impassive presence in the universe. Rather, he suffers when his people endure misery and death. As a compassionate and consoling God, he weeps for the Jewish people in their distress and rejoices in the faith of those who hold steadfast to him despite their agony. In a later work, *Ani Maamin* ('I believe'), Wiesel elaborates this view. The setting of this play is a dialogue between Abraham, Isaac, and Jacob who have the responsibility of directing God's attention to Israel's suffering. As they witness the Holocaust they turn to God who does not listen to their plea.

Abraham beseeches on Israel's behalf, but to no avail. Abraham refuses to be silenced. He argues that if he had the right to appeal for the people of Sodom, he has the same responsibility to speak for one million innocent children. A voice replies:

God knows
What he is doing –
For man
That must suffice.

Abraham continues his plea and extracts the promise of salvation, but this does not silence him. He asks:

But what kind of Messiah
Is a Messiah
Who demands
Six million dead
Before he reveals himself?

A voice answers:

God wills
That is enough
God takes
And God gives back,
That is enough.
God breaks
And God consoles,
That is enough.

Yet Abraham is not persuaded. Joined by Isaac and Jacob, he contends that the events of modern Jewish history – the establishment of the state of Israel, the return from exile, the reunion with Jerusalem, the armies and flags – are no consolation for the Holocaust. Instead of defending God, the voice attacks human beings for what they have made of God's creation. Again, the patriarchs are not convinced. They are led to even greater despair, and the narrator states: 'What is the use of shouting that the future corrects nothing? That it is powerless to change the past? What is the use of pleading? The judge is avenger. There is no hope.'

Together the patriarchs resolve to inform humanity that there is no justice and that God does not reveal himself in history. They leave heaven to visit earth. As Abraham sees mothers and children being slaughtered, a little girl facing death proclaims: 'I believe in you'. The narrator comments that, unknown to Abraham, a tear clouds God's eyes. Isaac also witnesses the slaughter of the community, yet its rabbi proclaims his belief in God and the Messiah. Again, God is moved by this display of faith. Jacob observes a Passover celebration in a concentration camp. The narrator relates that, unknown to Jacob, 'God surprised by his people, weeps for the third time – and this time without restraint, and with – yes – love. He weeps over his creation – and perhaps over much more than his creation.' Despite God's inaction, the patriarchs were struck by the faith of these Jews. Abraham praises Israel; Isaac blesses her for such faith in human beings despite the cruelty she endured; Jacob blesses Israel for her loyalty despite both humanity and God. God does not remain silent. He leaves heaven and accompanies the patriarchs without their knowledge, weeping, smiling. The play concludes with a celebration of Israel's faith in human beings and God.

For Wiesel, God is not an impassive presence in the universe. Rather, he suffers when his people endure misery and death. As a compassionate and consoling God, he weeps for the Jewish people in their distress and rejoices in the faith of those who hold steadfast to him despite their agony. Here in Wiesel's vision of a suffering God is a response to those who maintain that religious faith has been eclipsed by the Holocaust. If the God of Israel is a God of love, such love must be both costly and sacrificial. It must embrace and share in the suffering of those who are loved.

The Hebrew Scriptures speak most acutely of such divine suffering. According to the biblical prophets, God is in pain when his people go astray. As Jeremiah put it: 'As often as I turn my back on him (Israel), I still remember him, and so my heart yearns for him' (Jer. 31:20). Such suffering is central to God's love. He is not a detached being who stands aloof from human affairs. Instead God is with his people in their trials and tribulations. In the death camps, the God of Israel was the hidden God, who was with his loved ones as they went to their deaths. Those Jews who died in the camps with God's name on their lips glimpsed his anguish in their anguish. In some mysterious way his absence amid the horrors of the death camps was an affirmation of his abiding presence. Obviously this was not true for everyone. For many, Auschwitz was the final confirmation that there is no God. But for others is was in the depth of the darkness that God was to be found.

Today we are faced with natural disasters and conflicts in many parts of the world. How should we respond to the pictures of suffering every day in newspapers? At the very least we may be confident that God does not abandon his creatures. Even in the Gehenna of the Holocaust, he can be found. As the contemporary theologian Jürgen Moltmann remarked, 'there would be no theology after Auschwitz . . . had there been no theology in Auschwitz'. This theology gives us a glimpse of the love of God, a glimpse of his compassion. It is an extraordinary mystery but we believe that our God is the one who enters the depths of degradation with us and is there always sharing our suffering.

Jesus' Last Words:
Hope in Times of Despair

KEN PATERSON

Kenneth Paterson, 77, a lay preacher and an elder in Highfield United Reformed Church, Birkenhead, Merseyside, is married to Beryl, a retired teacher of handicapped children. They have two grown-up children, Rachel and Alastair. He began by studying architecture at university but in 1944 stopped his studies to train as a mechanical engineer for the Royal Electrical and Mechanical Engineers. At this time he also became a lay preacher. After service in Egypt, where he attained the rank of Captain, he completed his training in architecture and town planning and during the 1950s was heavily involved in the post-war reconstruction of Liverpool. In 1958 he set up in private practice with two other architects, working throughout Wales and the North-West. He was responsible for the design of 30 churches of various denominations, including the St Martin's Anglican Church in Suez Road, Cambridge, and retired in 1988 'after a happy and fulfilling career'. His interests include gardening and walking, and he featured in the BBC's Gardeners' World magazine.

'My father was minister of our church, Highfield Congregational Church in Birkenhead, for 30 years. He was ably supported by my mother and together they led me and many other young people into faith in the Lord Jesus Christ. I had no sudden conversion, but slowly and doubtfully came to a deeper faith supported and encouraged by many and varied good people within our church.'

His own slow climb to faith is mirrored, he believes, in the experiences of the disciples. 'They didn't, I feel, really understand what Jesus was teaching until Pentecost. Many of our own congregation are at the same stage and my object was to encourage people to move on in their spiritual lives.'

He often splits his sermons into two or three sections, divided by illustrative hymns, with the aim of retaining interest and attention. 'I also often put a hymn, prayer, hymn and benediction after the sermon. Preaching is and must be still relevant when so much of the Bible is seen by many as irrelevant and diffcult.'

He recalls one occasion when his congregation was asked to consider what they would give up for Lent, as an exercise in Christian discipline. Without hesitation one young lad called out: 'Cabbage!' On another occasion, a week or two before the wedding of a church member, a horrible smell pervaded the Church. 'Toilet sprays didn't work; the gas man found no leaks. Eventually with two days to spare, I was deputed to go under the church floor, where a poor dead cat was found. It had entered through a ventilator and got lost in the darkness. It was given a decent burial in the church grounds and I was awarded the DCM (dead cat medal). It made a children's talk!'

Text: Mark 15:34.

My God, My God why hast thou forsaken me?

ALTHOUGH IT WAS MIDDAY, the sky was black, the sun had disappeared and the watching crowd fell silent. They had been there since the early hours of the morning fascinated as the drama unfolded. The three men under heavy guard had come stumbling up the hill accompanied by their heavy crosses. With the crosses laid flat on the ground, the men were forced to lie upon them naked whilst the crude iron nails were driven, blow after blow through their wrists and feet. The crowd winced at each blow but could not avert their eyes. Each cross in turn was lifted upright and dropped with a sickening thud into its prepared hole – the flesh ripped and the blood poured. Then they had waited for death under the hot sun – a slow tortured death in agony. They all heard 'Father, forgive them for they know not what they do' and 'Today you will be with me in paradise.'

Some of the crowd felt cheated – they had been so certain that Jesus was going to lead an uprising against the Romans – he had said he was going to establish a 'new Kingdom' – but he'd backed out and let them down. Perhaps even now he could win the day – perform yet another miracle and come down from the cross in triumph. They had waited with bated breath for something to happen – but it didn't and they were cheated. 'Save yourself if you are God's Son! Come on down from the cross!' Others jeered, 'He saved others but he cannot save himself.'

Then the darkness had come and they had all fallen silent as the hours went by. Suddenly Jesus in a loud and terrible voice called out, 'Eloi, Eloi, lama sabachthani; – my God, my God why hast thou forsaken me?' – then he gave a loud cry and breathed his last.

The centurion in charge who had seen many men die and witnessed more carnage than he cared to remember said in a quiet voice that penetrated to the furthest watcher, 'Truly this was the Son of God' – then even he fell silent whilst the prisoners' clothes which his men had diced for lay in a heap on the ground.

Of all things which Jesus said during his lifetime, that final sentence must be the most poignant and heartrending. My God, My God, why hast thou forsaken me? In some of our most traumatic periods – when we feel alone and distressed and abandoned, we say to ourselves – My God, My God why hast thou forsaken me? and no answer comes and the sky is dark and forbidding.

But there is an answer as Jesus knew well, for the words which expressed human hopelessness so well are, in fact, the opening words of Psalm 22. Let me read some of its verses.

My God, My God, why have you abandoned me?
I have cried desperately for help but still it does not come. During the day I call to you, my God, but you do not answer; I call at night but get no rest.

So pitiful, so human – so like our own experience. But now there come a few verses of hope – a faint hope admittedly:

But you are enthroned as the Holy One – the one whom Israel praises. Our ancestors put their trust in you – they trusted you and you saved them.
They called to you and escaped from danger, They trusted you and were not disappointed.

It happened in the past – O God our help in ages past – but a vain hope, apparently, at present – for the psalmist goes on – (how apt and meaningful for Jesus in agony on the cross).

But I am no longer a man; I am a worm, despised and scorned by everyone!
All who see me jeer at me;
They stick out their tongues and shake their heads. 'you relied on the Lord,' they say.
Why doesn't he save you?
If the Lord likes you, why doesn't he help you?

Now the psalmist's thoughts turn to his own past life – how God has cared for him right through to this awful present. So must Jesus' thoughts have turned to his own childhood as he remembered all the words learnt by rote at his mother's knee.

It was you God who brought me safely through birth, and when I was a baby, you kept me safe.
I have relied on you since the day I was born and you have always been my God.
Do not stay away from me! Trouble is near and there is no one to help.

How often have we prayed for help and there comes no answer. We have been brought up to pray and our lives have been blessed with much care and love – but now, when we most need help, none comes. My God, My God why hast thou forsaken me!

The psalmist's words were written several hundred years before the crucifixion but listen to this:

My strength is gone, gone like water spilt on the ground.

All my bones are out of joint, my heart is like melted wax; my throat is as dry as dust and my tongue sticks to the roof of my mouth. You have left me for dead in the dust. All my bones can be seen. My enemies look at me and stare. They gamble for my clothes and divide them amongst themselves.

Now, suddenly and without explanation, the whole tenor of the psalm changes. The prayer is answered, triumph replaces despair. A whole vision of a future for God's people suddenly comes into view – the personal tragedy disappears in the wonder of the greatness of God.

I will tell my people what you have done;
I will praise you in their assembly:
Praise him, you servants of the Lord!
Honour him, you descendants of Jacob!
Worship him, you people of Israel!
He does not neglect the poor or ignore their suffering;
He does not turn away from them but answers when they call for help.

What it was that changed things for the psalmist we shall never know. But for Jesus at the very point of death it meant the most earth-shattering event – the very conquest of death. It was necessary to come through the torture, the abandonment, the apparent desertion by God to achieve what had never happened before in the history of the world.

The psalmist concludes: –

All nations will remember the Lord.
From every part of the world they will turn to him;
All races will worship him. The Lord is King and he rules the nations.
All proud men will bow down to him;
All mortal men will bow down before him.
Future generations will serve him; men will speak of the Lord to the coming generation.
People not yet born will be told, 'The Lord saved his people.'

'The Lord saved his people.'

The great final triumphant words of the psalm were to be fulfilled three days later after Jesus had been gently taken down from the cross and buried in the cave-tomb of Joseph of Arimathea. The rumours spread like wildfire through all Jerusalem and the country round about – Jesus is risen – Jesus the crucified is risen, he is alive – he's been seen and talked with. It can't be true – it can't be true – but it is, we've seen him He *did* come down from the cross after all, he did not let us down. Now he *will* save his people.

For 2000 years Christians have recognized the death of Jesus Christ on the cruel cross and his resurrection as the very root and cause of this belief. The central Christian belief is that Christ's death has somehow put us right with God and given us a fresh start. A good many theories have been held as to how it works – what all Christians are agreed on is that it does work. We are always looking for explanations but in this we must be satisfied to accept a mystery – something inexplicable but which has been found to work in the lives of millions of Christians down the ages – they all witness to the fact that 'The Lord saved his people.'

Now how can all this help us who are living our lives near 2000 years later. It tells us that (if we put our trust in Jesus's God) nothing, but nothing should distress or frighten us. The key words are 'Everything passes.' Whatever threatens you – be it the frightening prospect of a visit to the dentist, some desperate family upset, the passing of some dear friend, husband or wife, parent of grandparent – or the discovery of some life-threatening disease, Everything passes – there is hope and new life beyond it if we place our hand into the hand of God.

> Hell may assail you,
> It cannot move you;
> Sorrows may grieve you,
> faith may be tried.
> Though you have nothing,
> he is your treasure:
> Who God possesses
> needs naught beside.

(Hymn 'Nothing Distress You', written by St Teresa of Avila, from *Nada Te Turbe*, translated by Colin Thompson, copyright C. P. Thompson.)

Jesus has led the way, he has conquered death and we shall not be afraid. Like Moses before him, he leads his people including you and me into a new promised land – the Kingdom of Heaven which gives us a transformed life here and now *and* the knowledge that he has triumphed over death – turning death itself from a full stop into a comma

– a pause between stages of existence. Life is changed – it is not taken away.

So, when you are inclined to cry out 'My God, My God, why hast thou forsaken me?' remember that you are part of a great company of Christians past, present and to come who glory in the conquest of death and in the empty cross and that 'From earth's wide bounds, from ocean's farthest coast, Through gates of pearl stream in the countless host, Singing to Father, Son and Holy Ghost – Alleluia, Alleluia.'

Enough of Stunned Silence

HUGH-NIGEL SHEEHAN

Hugh-Nigel Sheehan, 56, has been Minister of Winchmore Hill Methodist Church and Oakwood Methodist Church, Enfield, London, for the last two years and Minister of Ealing Green Methodist and United Reformed Church for five years. Married to Tina Engel-Sheehan, a legal executive, he has four stepchildren: Natascha, Stephanie, Nina and Fridolin.

He is a gifted musician, and that was where his professional life began. He studied music and singing at the Royal Academy of Music, London, and at the Vienna Academy of Music in Austria. His many scholarships and prizes include the Kathleen Ferrier Memorial Scholarship and the Richard Tauber Scholarship. He became Principal Bass-Baritone with the Royal Opera at Covent Garden and was also Principal Bass-Baritone in European opera houses including Germany, Holland, Belgium, Austria, Switzerland, Italy and a guest soloist in the United States. But as his vocation emerged he signed up to study Theology and Religious Studies at Kent University and then went to Wesley House, Cambridge. He studied at Cambridge University, at the Federation of Theological Colleges, Cambridge and The Humboldt University, Berlin, gaining First Class Honours in Theology, History of Art and Pure Art as well as a Master of Philosophy degree and a Cambridge University Diploma in Theology and Mission. He was finally ordained at St John's Church, Glastonbury, 1995.

'My faith came by giving a nominal assent to the teaching of the Christian Church, regular church attendance and trying to live as a follower of Jesus in my daily life, and keeping going, even through failure and doubt. At some time on my Christian pilgrimage, my nominal assent became a positive assent to Jesus Christ and the doctrines and teaching of the Christian Faith. I have never had a 'Damascus Road Experience' like that of Paul; faith has come and grown through countless 'conversion experiences' through my life in the Church, in my first career, failures, successes, doubts, and interaction with other human beings, but primarily through the grace of God working in and through all aspects of my life. My pilgrimage continues!'

In spite of the many disappointments, frustrations and irritations that his vocation has brought him, his 'call' to the full-time presbyteral ministry has never lost its power. 'Over the years, however, I have come less and less to see my call purely in denominational terms and much more as a call to be a full-time Minister and Preacher in the Universal Church. I see our denom-

inationalism as a scandal at the beginning of a new millennium and would be more than prepared to see the Methodist Church, if it be God's will, cease to be a denomination and Methodism to return to what it has always been throughout the Church's history, a movement of the Holy Spirit towards spiritual holiness and renewal, a Society or Order within the Universal Church.'

The sermon published here came from his own personal experiences coming together with a contemporaneous controversy and court case verdict that had dominated the headlines and news reports over the previous week. 'I fused this with my own understanding of history, and the ethics, morality and teaching of the scriptures and Jesus Christ. Also I felt that this was a contemporary news item that demanded to be taken seriously and had so much to say to us when seen in the light of the Gospel, the Kingdom of God, and, indeed, religious belief and teaching generally.'

He believes there is no 'right' place for the sermon in a service and that it should be governed by the week-by-week preparation of the whole service and the thorough working through of the theme in hymns and prayers. 'Usually the sermon is placed after the Adoration and Confession and the Readings from the Scriptures.'

His vocation began as a specific call to be a Methodist Preacher. 'I still have the conviction that preaching has a central significance in the Church's life. The first five books of the New Testament are words that were heard to begin with, many having been preached, and only later written to be read. Thus every preacher has a commission to preach that goes back to Jesus and the first Disciples.' He quotes Charles Silvester Horne. Let every village preacher who climbs into a rude rostrum, to give out a text and preach a sermon to a meagre handful of somewhat stolid hearers, remember to what majestic Fraternity he belongs and what romantic tradition he inherits. He says, 'Christian preaching is a transaction between God and those who live and move in the same tradition and anybody who is prepared to stop and listen. The aim of preaching is to inform, strengthen or change attitudes in the light of God's Word, Revelation and love of all mankind. Like all words, preaching is a medium of change, personally or collectively, and should lead to the word of God operating in men and women obedient to that word in the entirety of their lives. It is also an integral part of worship, as preaching should give a sense of the transcendence that evokes adoration, confession, absolution and praise. Preaching in the Christian tradition is "a manifestation of the Incarnate Word, from the Written Word, by the spoken word" [Bernard Manning]. Thus, Christian preaching is telling and retelling of the story, ministry and teaching of Jesus, and as Jesus is the Reigning Christ, it should always be solidly set in the contemporary life and realities of the individual, society and the world. When I look at history, and having lived in Northern Ireland, I can see, and have experienced how dangerous the spoken word and preaching can be. Thus, all interpretation and Christian preaching must be authenticated by the life, preaching and gospel of Jesus Christ. Yes, preaching is relevant to *today's worship environment, as it is about relating Christ's presence in the midst of the world, to the world as it really is. It is to do with the Christian engagement in political and social action. In this sense the Church sanctuary, the House of God, is not a place apart from the world, but is the symbol of the world, as God is in the midst of both. It is in the sanctuary and the world that the Word is both proclaimed and met.'*

He describes preaching at a Methodist Church in South London, where the membership is almost entirely African Caribbean in origin. 'I sensed that the congregation, having had their natural joy and spontaneity stifled over the years, needed "permission" to free themselves from the chains of Victorian non-conformity. I invited the congregation to "sing in the spirit" by singing well-known hymns and choruses. Thus, the congregation could "gather", relax and become focused on why they were there. As if in answer to a prayer, just as I gave the formal "Call to Worship", a very large woman, who in a less politically-correct age would be called "A big black Mama, with enveloping bosoms, and a hat to match", called out: "Thank you Jeeeesus for sending us this man!". Instantly, I replied: "Say it again, sister!". She cried even louder: "Thank you Jeeeesus, thank you, for sending us this man." The congregation now knew that they could relax and offer their praise, freely and spontaneously.'

He continues to sing as often as he can, but also loves painting and drawing and attends art galleries, special exhibitions and museums as often as possible.

'Often it is when the Preacher is most prone to doubting his own ability and even doubting the value of preaching, that he will experience the truth of Colin Morris' words: "The promise is the assurance that no word spoken in the name of Jesus is a mere beating of the air – it has its place, however modest, in God's scheme of salvation." Someone will come, often a least expected someone, with those most wonderful words of grace for a Preacher. "Thank you, your words spoke to me. They were words I needed to hear. I have been ministered to." Thanks be to God!'

Text: Revelation 3:15–16.

I know all your ways; you are neither hot nor cold. I wish you were either hot or cold! But because you are lukewarm, neither hot nor cold, I will spit you out of my mouth.

IN SPITE OF ALL THE RAZZMATAZZ, for many this new century began with a refreshing mood of optimism. The old was past! The century of so much suffering, so much death, of scarred lives and scarred earth, was over. Good riddance!

Now we had learned the lessons of the last hundred years we could look serenely with confidence to the future. Now there could be a new beginning, a new optimism, a new hope and perhaps, at last, a New

Earth. And yet, almost before the world's new resolution had died upon our lips, it was business as usual for those whom the Apostle Paul calls 'the principalities and powers of this world'.

Not six months into the new century, front pages and television news reports have been dominated by images of a certain Mr David Irving, one of the arch-priests of what is called 'Holocaust denial'. In the face of all the evidence, he has spent the last twenty years advancing the absurd thesis that the mass extermination of Jews in the Third Reich did not take place.

Thankfully, Irving lost his libel lawsuit against Deborah Lipstadt and her publisher, Penguin Books. However, we dare not fool ourselves that this victory over falsehood and those still active powers that spawned National Socialism is final. Irving, though discredited and vilified in England, is touring the United States where he has become the new 'poster boy' for the extreme right and Holocaust denial. After Jesus had been tempted in the wilderness 'the devil departed, biding his time.' One day a more eloquent mouthpiece will emerge to serve the Holocaust deniers' conspiracy and their obsessive evil quest to rob those who survived the killing machine of their suffering and history. Someone, somewhere, will put the revisionist case again. The tempter may have departed for the time being, but, as throughout history, he is biding his tune.

And what of those of us who are of the monotheistic households of faith – Christianity, Judaism and Islam. How do we stay awake to the big truths that have to be defended and the big lies that have to be repudiated, again and again? How do we stay awake to the evils of our own day in the face of the horrors perpetrated in Cambodia, the former Yugoslavia, Sierra Leone, and so many other places since the end of the Second World War? How do we keep awake to the horrors that are taking place even now as I speak?

On a quiet day in November, I visited Sachsenhausen, a former concentration camp in the very midst of a quiet Berlin suburb. It was *Busstag*, the day of repentance, and as I walked around the camp, the site of the incarceration, torture and murder of so many, I was numb and stunned into silence.

There were no bodies, no smell, no filth, no excrement, no screams. I tried to imagine what it must have been like when in that very place prisoners were tortured, forced to become subjects of mutilating medical experiments and killed. I tried to feel something other than just a dull numbing of my senses. I wanted to experience something more than numbness. Numbness seemed too close to indifference. Something that would convince me that I would not be an indifferent bystander in the face of the terrible evils of my own day, even if I had been in the past.

As I stood on the parade ground where the roll-call and inspection had taken place, where a gallows once stood and young and old were executed for the slightest infringement of the rules, I wanted to feel real emotional passion, an intense fervour of moral outrage. I could not lie to myself. I knew that I had often remained formal, restrained and dispassionate in my response to man's inhumanity to man. I too had in the past been 'neither hot nor cold' in my response to evil. I too must accept my share of responsibility. None of us have completely clean hands. As Sophocles said in *Oedipus*:

> In vain do you deny that you are accountable, in vain do you proclaim that you have striven against these evil designs. You are guilty, nevertheless; for you could not stifle them; they still survive unconsciously in you.

As a human being I must share in that sense of total moral failure that the Holocaust represents in the history of humankind. As a Christian I share in the guilt for the hostility of Christianity towards Judaism and the anti-Semitism throughout the history of the Church, anti-Semitism that so directly contributed to the events that led to the Holocaust. Vile and active anti-Semitism that is still with us in Holocaust denial.

Those who were incarcerated in death camps could have been pardoned for asking how God came to deal so harshly with his creatures as to provide them with such a home. Inside the walls they could be excused for thinking that our world was a desert place. Nevertheless, the reality was that Auschwitz in spring is surrounded by hedgerows full of lilac and wild flowers, while other camps were situated in some of the most beautiful countryside in all Europe. All that was required to show the inmates that the world was not a desert place was to open the gates, both literally and metaphorically. Why did this not happen?

It did not happen because of the evil and the extreme repression of Nazi totalitarianism and the complicity of the German military, civil service, police and legal institutions. But also, it did not happen because of the acquiescence, resignation and indifference of so many ordinary men and women to the evil that was happening in their very midst.

Within the context of the utter depravity that this former concentration camp represented, there was something missing in my response to this brutal place – call it what you like – passionate emotion, indignation or anger.

What then was missing? Was it a real moral passion; a passionate indignation, a passionate anger, instead of a stunned silence? There has been enough stunned silence in the last century. As we look around our world six months into a new millennium, there is just as much indifference to evil today as there was in 1943; indeed we have become even more immune to injustice, violence and dead bodies through the daily diet of horror on our television screens.

If this new century is not to see a repetition of the horrors of the last, there must be an end to the indifference, passivity and deafening silence of so many of the people of faith in the face of the continuing evils of today. In a world bursting at its seams with all the good gifts of God's creation, millions still starve. In a world where drugs costing a few pounds can cure, men and women are still left to rot.

Could it not be that our passivity in the face of evil, our lack of moral ardour and indifference, are themselves among evil's crowning works, as without them so much evil could not, would not, exist? As a Christian I am certain of one thing. If I resign myself to my own passivity and indifference, I betray the one that I claim to follow. It is not until men and women of faith feel for the victims of evil in the depths of our beings that we will have the moral passion to defeat it.

At the beginning of this new century the world doesn't need men and women who show greater moderation in their moral principles and ethical ideals, but men and women who are overflowing with moral indignation and a burning zeal for justice and what is right. Not the moral indignation that condemns those who have fallen short of moral laws, such as that shown by those who would have stoned the woman taken in adultery'. But, the intensity of righteous indignation for social justice that burned in Jesus' heart when faced by the exploitation of helpless men and women, leading to his cleansing of the Temple: 'My house will be a house of prayer but you have made it a den of robbers.' As William Barclay in his commentary on this passage so perfectly expresses it: 'The courage of the Christian should match the courage of the Lord. He left us an example that we should never be ashamed to show whose we are and whom we serve.'[1]

Until men and women of faith are aflame with moral passion and indignation when confronted with the evils of injustice, violence and bigotry, we stand condemned by all those who throughout history have taken the rugged 'Avenue of the Righteous' and have had the active and engaged courage to publicly and loudly cry, 'NO!'.

In a real sense we all stand under the judgement of those who did not stand idly by while men and women were slaughtered, but in their words and deeds protested. As a Christian I must learn from those authentic Christians who not only said 'No!', but paid for saying it with imprisonment, suffering, and even death.

These men and women must be our inspiration and essential examples of the nature and requirement of faith in this new century, as indifference can never be part of the nature of authentic faith.

The Russian mystic, Alexander Yelchaninov, wrote: 'The indifference of believers is something more dreadful than the fact that unbelievers exist.'[2]

Perhaps in the eyes of God the indifference to evil of those who claim to be of the household of faith, is more dreadful than the fact of evil itself. Could that be the meaning behind the words of our text in the Book of Revelation?:' I know all your ways; you are neither hot nor cold. I wish you were either hot or cold! But because you are lukewarm, neither hot nor cold, I will spit you out of my mouth'.

Jesus wept over Jerusalem, a city today sacred to Christianity, Judaism and Islam. Jerusalem, the city that God intended to be a centre of justice and a light to all nations. His words 'Would that you knew the things that make for peace' echo down the centuries in a city divided, disunited and fragmented. In a sense Jerusalem is really a microcosm of the world, a world torn apart by hatred and hostility because it does not know the things that make for its peace.

Jesus still weeps! The world has had enough of stunned silence. Let us cry out against everything that makes this world seem like a desert place to so many. Let us open the gates to peace, justice and freedom and let the prisoners free.

Do not lose the faith that God will restore that which is battered and broken. God has his own plan to bring to fulfilment the things that make for peace. Take heart as we hear one of the most triumphant passages of all scripture at the close of the Book of Revelation. Yes, take heart! The great cosmic battle between good and evil is over and the legions of death have been defeated. The tempter, Satan, has been completely crushed and God's righteous age has begun.

> Then I saw a new Heaven and a new earth, for the first heaven and the first earth had vanished, and there was no longer any sea. I saw the Holy City, new Jerusalem, coming down out of heaven from God, made ready like a bride adorned for her husband. I heard a loud voice proclaiming from the throne: Now at last God has his dwelling place among men! He will dwell among them and they shall be his people, and God himself will be with them. He will wipe every tear from their eyes; there shall be an end to death, and to mourning and crying and pain; for the old order has passed away.

Notes

[1] William Barclay, *The Daily Study Bible (Revised Edition) The Gospel of Luke*, Edinburgh: The Saint Andrew Press, 1975, p. 242.

[2] Alexander Yelchanivov, from his Diary published after his death, *Dreams and Regrets – Selections from Russian Mystics – Mysticism and Modern Man*, ed. Catherine Hughes, New York and London: Sheed and Ward, 1973, p. 31.

To Light, or Not to Light?

Jonathan Wittenberg

Rabbi Jonathan Wittenberg, 43, is Minister of the New North London Marorti Synagogue based at the Sternberg Centre in north London. He is married to Nicola Solomon, a solicitor and deputy district judge, and they have three children: Mossy, Libbi and Kadya. He says they suffer growing up in a rabbinic household with good grace. 'Is that a serm you're working on?' said Mossy when he was little. Another time when Kadya overheard Nicky speaking about trust and distrust with someone on the phone, she said 'That's right. Trust in God.'

He comes from a rabbinic family on both sides. 'My mother's father, Rabbi Dr Georg Salzberger was a rabbi in Frankfurt-am-Main until he was mercifully able to escape from Nazi Germany with the family after a period of internment in Dachau concentration camp. My father's mother was the daughter of a noted line of orthodox rabbis. I inherited a love of literature and read English at Cambridge, then trained to be a teacher before rabbinic work caught up with me. It was in my blood. My grandfather is a particular role model and I think about him frequently.'

He became a Masorti rabbi having increasingly developed a love of traditional Jewish practice but never having believed in the literal understanding of the origins of the Torah that has come to characterize orthodoxy. 'I was fortunate in being in the right place at the right time, as the daughter community of Rabbi Dr Louis Jacobs synagogue was beginning to develop. They took me on first as a teacher, then as student rabbi and for the last thirteen years as full-time minister. Staying with the same congregation over a considerable period of time means that strong ties of affection can be formed.'

He and his wife Nicky share a love of plants, animals and people. 'We adore our dog Safi who always comes to synagogue. (He is most particular about the rule of walking there!) We love gardening, walking, reading and Scotland, and find contact with nature spiritually restorative. I sometimes feel that inner city living is a form of spiritual deprivation.'

He does not believe that there is any ultimate and absolute proof of God's existence. 'When we were staying near Loch Ness last year I once complained a bit too loudly about all the money being made out of the Loch Ness Monster, which nobody is really sure exists. "So what do you do for a living?", came the comment from someone sitting nearby. But I find much testament about faith in the lives of people, in human tenderness, love and courage. For this reason my work in the multi-faith chaplaincy of the North London Hospice means a lot to me. I am moved by the faith and wisdom with which people encounter their death, and by the devotion and understanding of the staff.'

The sermon offered here was sent in by a member of his community and was not actually intended to be part of the Preacher of the Year competition when he delivered it. Like many of the preachers in the book this year, he would never have volunteered himself for the award, and was nominated by a member of his congregation.

'I consider the sermon to have an important role in community life. Though a sermon is generally spoken by just one person, I see it as a dialogue. A sermon is a response to the concerns and needs of a community and is at best the fruit of much listening.'

For during those days the Menorah burnt by virtue of the miracle of the very small quantity of oil that they had; there is such a very small point in every person even now which belongs to God.

The Sefat Emet, Rebbe Yehudah Aryeh-Lev of Ger

IF ONE LIGHTS the kind of oil the Maccabees lit, it will be sure to burn for longer than one day. For it contains the secret of inspiration and its radiance is God's light in the world.

The Maccabees were fighters. The early Maccabean leaders rose in revolt against the Seleucid tyranny and its Jewish collaborators who were turning Jerusalem into a Greek city. But the later leaders were no less power-seeking and corrupt than those whom their elders had made their reputation by defeating. For this and other reasons they were little loved by the rabbis who accorded their victories hardly any space at all in the vast literature of the Talmud. But there remain three achievements to their credit. They had the vision to fight an impossible war and the courage to win. Once they had regained the Temple precincts they had the persistence to search them until they found a vessel marked with the High Priest's seal. Then, although the oil they found was really far too little, they filled the lamps on the Menorah and set them alight, trusting in whatever would be. These three acts represent the essential stages of leadership and inspiration.

The Temple was defiled; Jerusalem, ruled by renegades, was in the grip of a foreign and antagonistic culture. But what the Maccabees saw was not defeat; they beheld the Temple as it would be – rebuilt. Look at the world in any age, in any place, and one has the same choice. One can either see only destruction and misery, all the unending testimony of disappointment. Or one can see, together with and in defiance of it, striving, courage and compassion, an ineradicable humanity in the humbling endeavour of transforming defeat into new hope. One can see only the ruins of the Temple. Or one can see the rebuilding as well.

My friend, who works with victims of torture and persecution, shared with me a moving example of just this endeavour. An old peasant and a young man whose family had been killed for their political beliefs were in prison together. One day the elderly man was brutally beaten. The young man comforted him, telling him that he would teach him to read, an opportunity his harsh fortunes had until now denied him. This, he said, would be their victory. In studying reading together they would be making an affirmation of their common humanity which no amount of force could ever take away

It must have been a similar faith which led a more famous victim of persecution to write in her diary in July 1944:

> It's really a wonder that I haven't dropped all my ideals because they seem so absurd and impossible to carry out. Yet, I keep them, because in spite of everything I still believe that people are really good at heart . . . I see the world gradually being turned into a wilderness, I hear the ever-approaching thunder, which will destroy us too, I can feel the sufferings of millions and yet, if I look up into the heavens I think it will all come right, that this cruelty too will end, and that peace and tranquillity will return again.

Every moment of life presents us with a choice in how we perceive; do we see disappointment and defeat or opportunity and hope? I am filled with wonder by what people have managed to achieve. In situations of conflict it is often women who lead the way back to the appreciation that the enemy are people too. There are mothers who use e-mail to find mothers on the other side who have also lost a husband, father, child, because they believe that the common humanity they discover will transcend the power of war and hatred. There are teachers who work in peacetime to develop the abilities of sick or maltreated children, because they believe in the power of love to awaken the intrinsic creativity that lies within us all. There are carers who work with the dying because they trust that beyond pain and physical humiliation may lie comfort and reconciliation. None of these people see only the ruins; what they perceive is a temple rebuilt.

Behind this lies an earlier question; what is it that gives us the capacity to look at the world in this way? Where is the oil that burns with the light that enables us to see the sacred everywhere? For, as Rebbe Yehudah Aryeh Lev, the Sefat Emet of Ger, taught over a century ago, 'There is such a very small point in every person which even now belongs to God'. There is a vessel within each of us the contents of which are simply not susceptible to contamination; there is a part of us which remains eternally pure. It is there that we must go to seek the oil that burns with a pure and sacred flame. The difficulty is to find it. That is the inner meaning of the Maccabees' search among the ruins of the

Temple for the one jar that was still intact, sealed with the High Priest's seal.

The Talmud, in recounting the brief story of how the Maccabees found and lit the oil, makes it clear that there were other jars. But they were not pure; the High Priest's seal was broken. In the same way there are in our lives many kinds of thing that burn. Anger burns. Of course, righteous anger sometimes leads us to oppose what is wrong. But even justified anger often simply consumes us as its victim. I have sometimes had to say to people who came to talk to me about how angry they feel that they may indeed be right they have been exceedingly badly treated. But who has become the main victim of the anger if not themselves? It will devour them, a second kind of suffering, and affect the person who has wronged them not at all. Greed also burns; in our society its flames are constantly being fuelled. We are lured by countless incitements into the heat of our own desires. We do not see clearly by the light of such fires.

I believe that like the Maccabees we too must constantly search the precincts of our inner self for what lies buried there. Then we may come to know by the testimony of our own heart and soul that there is a part of us which nothing can contaminate, that we have a certain purity of being that cannot be sullied. Light it and it burns with a sacred radiance. Just as Midas' touch turns everything to gold, so the spirit has the power to reveal the spirit in everything that lives. But every day we have to struggle to find the flame; it is far more often lost than found. In silence, in beauty, in prayer, in the example of good people, we rediscover it and may be consoled by the reminder that, though hidden, it is never utterly or irretrievably lost.

Once they had regained the temple and found their jar of oil, there remained for the Maccabees one more issue: to light, or not to light? It cannot have been a simple decision. They knew, after all, that it would take eight days to replenish their supply and that the contents of the single flask they had with the High Priest's seal of purity would provide for only one day. Should they light it, or should they wait? Perhaps they should wait. Until this point it was not exactly their fault that the Menorah had been extinguished; it was for this that they had fought. But if they were to light it now and then let it go out wouldn't they be responsible? After all the flame, once burning, had to be *Tammid*, constant. The Maccabees lit the oil.

And light it one must. This is the essence of faith. We never know how long the flame that results from our deeds will last. But if the oil is pure, we have to find the courage to use it. It is natural to think that we won't have the energy to see our plans through, to worry that our courage might not last, that our confidence, or our spirits, or our love or our faith may fail. These concerns are only human and reveal a modesty in our knowledge of ourselves. But it would be wrong if they were to prevent us from using what oil we have. We must trust that what we begin in truth we and others will be given the strength to continue. If we must first know how everything will finish, we will never undertake anything and our oil will go to waste.

But perhaps, it might be argued, the Maccabees were lucky. After all, God ordained a miracle and a single day's supply of fuel burnt for eight. But that, I believe, is to misunderstand the nature of such miracles. For that reason I prefer the word 'wonder'. For it is a wonder, but true, that such oil always burns more brightly and for longer than one had thought. Start something with real spirit, with good intent and inspiration, and though you may not have enough energy to see it through, others will come and replenish the fire and restore the flame. Thus one person's vision becomes the heartfelt task of many. Or sometimes it is the spirit itself, God, if I can say so, who nurtures us. Then it is as if by some invisible pipette our hope and courage and energy are replenished night by night and we enter our day restored by powers we ourselves do not understand.

For where, whatever our vision, whatever our inner searching, whatever our courage to light the light, did the first fire come from, if not from God? Who formed the spirit within us and who made all life sacred, if only we could see?

Note
Quote from *The Diary of Anne Frank* (pp. 218–19, Pan Macmillan).

Fearful Symmetry

Neil Fairlamb

The Revd Neil Fairlamb, 50, is vicar of five parishes in Merioneth in Wales.

His childhood was spent in North Wales and he went on to read history and English at the University of Wales in Bangor, graduating with a first class honours degree in 1971. After research at Oxford on 17th-century sermons, which gained him a BPhil in 1973, he went to Cambridge for teacher training and then taught for 21 years at Dulwich College, south London. But his vocation was also emerging. He qualified as a lay reader in the Southwark Diocese from 1982 and after three years on the Southwark ordination course was deaconed in 1993 and priested in 1994. Although accepted for full-time ministry, no curacy was found, so he reduced his teaching to part-time and served a title as a non-stipendiary minister, working one day a week in his parish, his local hospital and Brixton prison, which he still visits. Then in 1995, out of the blue, he was invited to Wales to be a vicar of four parishes around Aberystwyth. 'This involved brushing up, to say the least, on my forgotten childhood Welsh, learned not as a native speaker.'

In 1998 he moved and married Yvonne. 'We decided it was best to start together in a new place and moved further up the Welsh coast to a benefice of five churches in Merioneth.' He completed a theology master's degree with the Theological College in Aberystwyth and still pursues research on faith and reason in the late seventeenth century. He helps also with the teaching of lay readers in the diocese.

His faith was strong from childhood and he was confirmed at thirteen. 'I must have been an odd boy, going often on my own to church, occasionally with mother to Evensong. I liked order, ceremony, dignity. I also liked preaching and sermon-tasted widely at Oxford. I was not very keen on the liberal soft centre I seemed to see often in the 1970s. I was a dormant and critically aloof observer until I realized something should be offered from inside as well; a tolerant vicar and PCC let me train as a reader and I relished preaching and felt there was a vocation to bring a wider range of experience to bear on texts than I had heard: this experience was, it must be said, literary and historical but teaching in a very busy school brought plenty of social experience to bear as well. I was happy to be a reader, and felt it gave freedom to speak out in a way clergy didn't; I also wasn't very keen to be involved in building maintenance and parish minutiae in which clergy I observed seemed to be preoccupied. However, looking back, I suppose the vocation to the priest-

*hood was developing all the time, though the church turned me down at first
– I still didn't like the Southwark ethos.' When a post at Dulwich fell vacant
and there were over 80 well-qualified candidates he realized full-time ministry in the church was beckoning. 'I felt a strong need to widen my experience
outside education and without a doubt the deepening of my faith and ministry took place, and takes place, in Brixton prison, which I asked to go to;
there, I feel the urgency and reality of the Christian ministry more strongly
than anywhere else – in the befriending and listening role as well as in showing the message. There the reality of life after various kinds of death is daily
possible. In the texture of parish life, of course, the Christian thread is spun
more slowly but the possibility of a changed life, renewed and redirected, is
behind much of what I attempt.'*

*The sermon he sent was not typical of the eight-to-ten minute pastoral
message of the Parish Communion, repeated with variations, including variations of language, each Sunday in Wales 'An invitation to preach at a Cambridge college was an occasion to offer a more old-fashioned sermon,
perhaps, with a range of reference that might connect with an academic congregation. Worth doing occasionally! Alas, poetry in the parish sermon rarely
works.'*

*Most of his services are Eucharists and the sermon follows the gospel on
which it is based. They take ten minutes at most, otherwise he feels the balance of the service is distorted. 'But once a month I offer a different service,
some form of morning prayer with an extended sermon: I find it better to do
this straight after the second reading as the scripture passage is soon forgotten otherwise. I acknowledge how short people's attention spans seem to have
become but with a variety of story, some personal notes, and an unobtrusive
sense of structure, 15–20 minutes is still possible for most congregations. I
rarely get feedback but then remember a Methodist preacher advising us not
to worry. How few sermons can we recall well ourselves? But then, if we
remember in detail very few of 1000 sermons, we can probably not remember
many of the 1000 sausages we must have eaten in life. Nevertheless, they fed
us at the time. Preaching can still be the means to energize the rest of the service and can still make the prayers and the liturgy come alive. Entertainment? – well, yes, and why not? There isn't enough serious fun in sermons.'*

*He is a great believer in wearing a dog-collar and walking about. 'Parish
visiting seems on the decline but the contacts one makes by simply being seen
are invaluable. Otherwise I'd never have met an old lady by the bus stop:*

"Are you Cof E?" she asked sharply.

"Yes?"

*"I'm so glad. I read a prayer book service at home I can't find anyone to do
it . . . My name is Stoy. Think of Tolstoy and take away the Tol." This indicated her world. This led to a two-year contact with a richly blessed life, in
the sharing of which, both of us were blessed, even if she was rather naughty
when I secured her a ticket for a school service with the Archbishop of Canterbury and she sat on the nave end of a pew, insisting I introduce her to Dr*

Carey – how could I not? – so that she could impress on him that a relation of hers had served long enough in a Falkland Islands chaplaincy and could now be brought home.'

He also describes a hospital visit. 'There were curtains round a bed I was to visit. Out peered an elderly head, "Can you come in a minute? . . . You are C of E aren't you? . . . It's my husband, he's going to pass away. I just need someone to sit here with me." After about twenty minutes, he died peacefully – a nurse and a doctor came round and went, and we sat on. She brightened a bit and became chatty. I attempted the standard remark, "You must look back on a long marriage together."

"Oh no," she said crisply, "We were married the day before yesterday, here by special licence."

"But you said 'My husband' so firmly!"

"Well yes, we've been together for years and he always wanted me to marry him but I wouldn't – he was an alcoholic, you see, and I told him I wouldn't marry him until he gave up. But he never did. Until this last month in hospital when he couldn't get any – he proposed last week and I couldn't refuse him could I?".'

In prison, he remembers the senior chaplain advising him when he first assisted at Communion, 'Now Neil, I don't care whether you're High Church or Low Church, but when you give the wine – don't let go of the chalice.' He met a bespectacled, neat and tidy prisoner. 'I'm very glad to see a minister,' he started. 'He was a Jehovah's Witness, he said, and was very sorry he was in for fraud – he worked for a pharmaceutical company and had got into debt, couldn't manage and had fiddled. No, he didn't want to see someone from the Witnesses – he had dishonoured them, had resigned but might seek to rejoin when released. Could I get him a book? . . . I knew he wasn't being truthful. He was in solitary, unlikely for a fraud case. I looked him up but it wasn't until after the fifth visit that he felt able to tell me the truth; he had been abusing little girls and had done so for years, including his granddaughter. Why the lie – to protect himself in prison, to get by with a "respectable" crime, to deceive even himself. The following week he was moved to another prison without notice, but I felt that at least in being able to share his horror prison ministry was worthwhile.'

His other interests include walking, opera, wine appreciation.

IF YOU COULD KEEP only one verse of the Bible which would you choose? To rip out just one page to keep might seem a desperate measure; for Sir Ernest Shackleton on his second Antarctic expedition it was a matter of life and death. His ship, *Endurance*, was trapped and being crushed by ice; lifeboats had to be lowered and dragged across the ice before they could be sailed to Elephant Island. There they were turned upside down and used for months as winter shelter before, in the southern hemisphere spring, they could be launched again for the perilous 800-mile journey to South Georgia where, on a later expedition, Shackleton died and was buried. In abandoning all inessentials from *Endurance* to equip the lifeboats Shackleton had to throw out a huge leather-bound, gold-clasped bible, presented to him by Queen Alexandra, wife of Edward VII: it was beautiful but too heavy. However, in the act of throwing it out Shackleton decided to tear out and keep a page: remarkably, for he was no sort of orthodox Christian, he chose the passage from Job 38 which we heard as our first lesson tonight and for the sake of the lines which spoke directly to his situation: 'Does the rain have a father . . . a mother from whose womb comes the ice? Who gives birth to the frost from the heavens above when the waters become hard as stone, when the surface of the deep is frozen?'

In the extremity of his physical situation, Shackleton affirmed his faith that if there is a God he must be responsible for all of his creation, snow and ice no less than sun and balmy breezes. The choice was his and is ours: *either* you agree with Richard Dawkins that the cheetah is superbly designed to kill antelopes and that antelopes are equally impressively designed to survive and cause starvation among cheetahs, so that if there is a skill of a great designer to admire it is that of a sadist who takes special delight in blood sports; *or* you make the venture of faith that the God who made the lamb and the tiger created a 'fearful symmetry' and found it good for his purposes for the world and his people. For each verse is inclusive: the female imagery of the womb balances the male imagery of the rain, perhaps the semen of the storm god. Balance is all. Turner said that if you want to understand his pictures you must put them all together, side by side. And when you do, they seem to fall into two groups. There are those about the sea, about its storm and fury – you'll remember how he got the sailors to lash him to the mast in a great and terrrible storm to experience what it was like from the inside and so be able to show it to others. And then there are his skies – those wonderful dawns and sunsets, and the magic of the sunlit clouds. Light and dark, the tension of opposites: it is in the living out of this tension that our Christian journey is made. Here are the great themes of Paul's letters: he dwells on the suffering of Christ which we are called to share that we may share his resurrection and about the storm of human agony but his letters are also about the Christ whose glory fills the skies, the one who embodies the divine purpose to the end of time, the one in whom all the universe is held together.

It is never easy to live that tension. The Victorians, for example, seemed reluctant to do so; when Millais painted Christ in the carpenter's workshop *The Times* critic found the association of the holy family with the details of trade 'with no conceivable omission of misery, of dirt or even of disease . . . disgusting'. Tennyson, who came up to this university in the same year as Darwin, found the downside of creation too hard to integrate into his picture of God:

I . . . who trusted God was love indeed
And love creations final law –
Though nature, red in tooth and claw
With ravine, shrieked against his creed.

I prefer the wisdom of earlier ages: of Milton for example, a son of Christ's College, who defended the freedom of the press in 1644 on the grounds that the knowledge of vice was necessary to the constituting of virtue – 'that which purifies us is trial and trial is by what is contrary'. Or, indeed, the wisdom of the Jews who have never baulked at admitting the perversity of their god – 'Of course our dietary laws are unreasonable,' argued an Orthodox friend, 'whoever expected God to be reasonable?' To Kierkegaard, Abraham was in just such a situation of crisis as Shackleton when he was asked to sacrifice his son Isaac – against all common sense, against morality even, he had to float on twenty thousand fathoms of water and be unafraid. Here is the wisdom of that great heretic Blake in seeing the fearful symmetry which sees 'joy and woe woven fine / in the fabric of the soul divine'.

For the tension of 'fearful symmetry' includes preserving the lightness of serious things and the weightiness of comedy. Joy, as C. S. Lewis affirmed, is the serious business of heaven. Two months ago I took the funeral of a young man killed in South Africa in a banal traffic accident who had lived with danger all his life: he had spent himself recklessly in England but had found in whale-watching in Port Elizabeth, at the eleventh hour, the vocation to which his whole life had moved and in whose balance of fun and danger he had found himself. Michael Ramsey pointed out that in an hour on your knees it is only in the sixtieth minute that you are really praying. James cared about whale conservation, he respected their awesome mystery; yet he also would play with whales – as a chat-up line to girlfriends, 'come and stroke my whales' takes some beating. And, astonishingly, this mixture of seriousness and lightness is also in the Book of Job: whether Leviathan was a crocodile or a whale doesn't matter but God sees both the fun and the seriousness of living with whales:

Will you play with him as a bird? Will you bind him with strings for your maidens?

and

Or will you fill his skin with harpoons and his head with fish spears?

So might also our Lord's life. For the God who gets himself dirty in the carpenter's shop, the God with calloused hands, the God whose birth amongst muck and whose death saw the dribble of spit from cursing opponents course down his face is also the God who invites us to his feast of life, who ate and drank with sinners, who sat lightly to the serious things of this world but who also gives great weight to the mustard seed and the fall of a sparrow.

There was a coda to Shackelton's safe arrival on South Georgia. Trudging to the Norwegian whaling station he felt a fourth presence was beside him; there were only three of them but he felt constantly a fourth man was there. The story inspired T. S. Eliot's line in *The Waste Land* about 'the one who walks always beside you' and in this Easter season it reinforces the message of the experience on the road to Emmaus. Let us pray with Augustine that God may restore to health the eye of the heart whereby He may be seen.

The Death of God

SIR ALAN GOODISON, KCMG, CVO

Sir Alan Goodison, 74, who with his late wife, Rosemary, has three children and four grandchildren, joined the Foreign Office in 1949 where he learned Arabic. Half of his career was spent in, or dealing with, the Middle East, and half in or on Western Europe. 'My career went backwards and forwards between working in the Foreign Office in London advising ministers, and working in embassies abroad,' he says. He was deputy ambassador in Rome from 1976 to 1980. In 1983 he went to Dublin as ambassador where he was engaged in the negotiations the Anglo-Irish agreement of 1985. He retired in 1986 and became director of the Wates Foundation for five years. His responsiblity was to help to distribute up to £1.5 million a year in grants to young people who were disabled, homeless, who missed out on an education or who were disadvantaged in other ways. After stepping down from that he began to study theology seriously and gained an MA in systematic theology from King's, London, in 1997.

However, he has been a Reader in the Anglican Church for 41 years. The son of a bank official, he was brought up in a Methodist church and went to Colfe's Grammar School in Lewisham. He became an Anglican when he got married.

When he was an undergraduate at Trinity, Cambridge, studying German, he did not attend church regularly. 'It was getting married that had an important effect on me, and having a family. But I have never been what used to be called "an enthusiast". My church in Hampstead is mainstream. The priest wears vestments and we have occasional incense.'

He began as an Anglican Reader in Lisbon, Portugal, when the vicar fell ill and there was no one else to take the service. 'They appointed me Reader because I had done a lot of preaching in the Methodist Church,' he says. 'I took the services every Sunday for six months'. Since then he has been a Reader in Anglican parishes and dioceses worldwide, including Jerusalem. He recalls once preaching in Dublin on baptism. 'The main point of the sermon was to reassure people that God looked after babies, whether they were baptized or not. As I was coming out of the church, a woman thanked me for emphasizing how essential it was to have babies baptized as early as possible. She had heard the opposite of what I said! When I preached at St Patrick's Cathedral in Dublin, the Dean said to me: "Whatever you do, don't preach to the people. Preach to the microphone."'

His church has been without a vicar for a year, which has increased his preaching commitments.

Almighty Father, look with mercy on this your family for which our Lord Jesus Christ was content to be betrayed and given up into the hands of sinners and to suffer death upon the cross; who is alive and glorified with you and the Holy Spirit, one God, now and for ever. Amen.

Text: 2 Corinthians 5:19.

. . . in Christ, God was reconciling the world unto himself.

WE ARE GOING TO BEGIN our Three Hours Devotion today by talking about the Death of Jesus under various headings. So we shall talk about this death, as the death of God, of a Man, of a Leader, and of a Friend, and we begin with the death of God.

Some of you will remember how fashionable 'The Death of God' was as a slogan thirty years ago. It was, of course borrowed from that poor old boy Nietzsche: more than a hundred years ago he felt an imperative to defy the culture of the nineteenth century and God with it. His imitators thought it rather clever to invoke the crucifixion as evidence that God was dead and done for.

I am glad to say that they had got it all wrong. If the story of the Passion is authentic, then it does not involve an account of the passing away of God; it is about God's self-affirmation in death. Of course, in Christ, God died, in the one-dimensional movement which we experience as time. But in the multicoloured scope of eternity the Trinity continued to rule. The crucifixion is the supreme occasion on which the Father opened a window into eternity and showed himself to human beings, suffering for our sake. '. . . in Christ, God was reconciling the world unto himself'. The cross is an occasion of revelation. Make no mistake about it, what God is in his saving activity is what God is in the divine being itself. This is how we know what God is like: this is how we know God loves us. One of our tasks today is to trace the outlines of God's face in the story of Christ's suffering. Just as the events of Easter form the climax of the earthly life of Jesus of Nazareth, so they present the most important features of God's self-expression, of his incarnate Word. The cross is a photograph in time of the life of the Trinity. Note, it is one snapshot. I do not assert that it tells us everything we need to know about God. The incarnation and the life and preaching of Jesus, together with our own direct experience of his love and the testimony of scripture, of his saints, and of his Church, give us further information. Above all, we must look at the cross in the perspective of the resurrection, and vice versa. But at this time of the year it is natural and desirable that we should study them separately, and we will not talk about the Resurrection today.

The first and last thing to say about the death of God on the cross was that it was an act of love. Death is one of God's good gifts to humanity. Death is not a failure but a fulfilment. This world is not the whole of his creation, and Jesus taught us that there were many abodes under his Father's care apart from this one. We need to accept that our life here is only a stage in the experience of God's goodness, that there is more to come, and that it is right for us to move on out of this world into the next. Just as we must live conscious that God, in the person of Jesus of Nazareth, has lived a human life, and thereby consecrated it, so Jesus showed us how to die under God by dying with us. 'Only a suffering God could help.'

But in many other senses, too, the death of God on the cross was an act of love: God's acts always have many meanings and many effects. The Trinity knew all along that Jesus Christ would have to die when he brought his humanity into time, and he knew that he would be killed by his fellow human beings. I don't mean to say I think that when Jesus of Nazareth was small he could already foresee the cross, as some sentimental painters have suggested. I don't even mean that the only purpose in the incarnation was, as Leo the Great declared, that Jesus should die. I mean that the basic contradiction between God's nature and the will of human beings made a clash inevitable in due course, and that Jesus of Nazareth grew up realizing more and more clearly that this was so and that he was to endure this clash. This did not deter the Trinity from an intervention which was bound to be necessary from the moment of the Big Bang, when life was set to form the human race, and nor did it deter Jesus from the hill of Calvary. Why not? Because God loves us. That is why he made us in the first place, forming an object for his affection out of nothing, and that is why he was ready to die for us. Because God loves us, he made us in the image of his Son, free to choose our own way of life, free to choose our Maker or to prefer ourselves. Because God loves us, he came down in his human form to rescue us from the consequences of our choice and rebellion against the life we were designed to lead, from our frequent refusal to choose His kind of love, either in our relations with him or with one another. 'God was in Christ reconciling the world unto himself.' Note, Paul does not say, as some would have it, that Jesus was reconciling an angry and punitive God to us: it was the other way round. He was reconciling self-assertive human beings to God. Because God loves us, Jesus accepted that he must die for us. For us, as the Creed says: *etiam pro nobis*. But not just for all human beings. Not even just for all creation.

One of Luther's greatest insights was that Jesus Christ died *pro me*, for me, that is for each one of us as an individual person, though nevertheless at the same time for all, pouring out his love with his blood. The cross is a vehicle of revelation, yes, but a revelation to each individual human being that God cares, cares personally for her or for him. What happened on the cross happened to God as a person and is a message of love to persons too. It is to *me*. We must not run away from the challenge of the cross, or leave it to others: it is directed to each one of us as a claim we are called to acknowledge whenever we become aware of it.

I do not, of course, forget that Paul saw it also as a universal revitalizing impulse, affecting in a mysterious way not simply those who never hear or accept the message of the cross, but the whole of creation, those parts we call inanimate, from animals to the universe itself, glowing with the divine fire and hurtling forwards with the wind of the Holy Spirit. We must not ignore the significance of today as the commemoration of a cosmic event, the death of Him through whom all that is, in time and space, was created, 'for without him was not anything made that was made.' The message of the cross is not a message directed only to humankind: it is about God's irruption into time and space.

But it is a message *pro me*. It is a revelation of God to each human being: we are called to be the kind of person God had in mind when he thought it worthwhile to die for us. This thought implies standards of being that we may not have contemplated: not merely standards of selfless love, but a preoccupation with the things of God and the welfare of others that we have hardly brought into question. We have to ask ourselves whether we ever thought that this is why God died for us. This message, if we really accept it, is rather shattering.

And it is not just a message. Too often, I think, preachers have interpreted God's act of love on the cross as if it were a picture for us to look at, be moved by, and respond to, but only if we think fit. Perhaps this is partly the result of the wonderful achievements of the great painters who have portrayed the cross. But we devalue both their achievements and the cross if we regard it merely as a spectacle, dependent for its effect on our response. Theologians describe it as the work of Christ: it is not our work, our reaction, which is of the first importance; what Jesus achieved on the cross was an eternal rearrangement of reality. It was a victory over sin, death, and evil.

These are categories which were familiar thought-forms to previous generations and which no longer arouse those immediate echoes in the third millennium. We so often think and speak of sin in church, but as if it were a disease afflicting others, not ourselves, no doubt partly because we fail to acknowledge any sin that is not sensual. We deplore the death of others, but are reluctant to contemplate or prepare for our own, as if we were exempt from the ordinary fate of humanity: indeed, too often we complain bitterly that we or our loved ones should be subject to what everyone else must undergo. As for evil, we have no difficulty in recognizing its effect on the Six O'Clock News, and yet we cannot see that our own lives are distorted by it. I have no wish to revive the nineteenth-century preachers' gloating emphasis on individual guilt and shame: I am not even prepared to proclaim eternal punishment for anyone, but I am concerned to emphasize that human error, human guilt, brought Jesus to the cross and meant that God had to die. It is the confrontation between the world and Him by whom it was made.

It is the self-assertion of the world over against God. Yes, one can see that Pilate tried to be just, but was the prisoner of the system. Yes, one can see that the Sanhedrin was pious in its way, cultivating a god after its own image of exclusive respectability. But the world had developed rules, even by then, which left no room for God as he really is. They failed to recognize God when he came to them because they were determined to assert themselves: their beliefs, their ideas, their obligations. The paradox is that God had given human beings the glory of selfhood, and they did not see how to assert it except in opposition to the Trinity, while the whole nature of the Trinity is the exercise of selfhood in communion with one another. It is a sharing in being. The three persons are distinct, and yet each shares in the life and nature of the other, co-inhering, so that we can speak, without confusing the three persons, of the death of God on the cross. The point surely is that God is love, and human beings were made to find their essential personhood in relationships. But we have become far too selfish to love one another as he loves, except occasionally, and then usually in a sexual context. The consequence is that we do not live the life he intended, and, faced with the incarnate Godhead, human beings turn him out of their lives, as in this case, by condemning him to death. We might almost say that it was not surprising: given their sin, facing God, they were bound to react badly. God seeks a dialogue with us, but we deny him an answer. Jesus found that it was like this, and he refused to say much to Pilate or his accusers. What is there for God to say to people who do not want him, except : 'I love you!' So, given that human beings are far too inclined to reject such a statement as sentimental, Jesus was bound to die, and, in dying, to affirm his love for us all, and thereby conquer the hostility he had faced.

Another victory of Jesus was over death itself. We talk so little of death these days that this does not, perhaps, appear to us as the most significant thing about the cross. In former times, when the problems of dying were not concealed, more or less, by the antibiotics and analgesics of the National Health Service, death often bore a more terrifying face, and the death of Jesus was portrayed by painters such as Grünewald in repulsive detail. Today death is a more private occasion, and people often face it alone without the family weeping by the bed. This has the effect of protecting the healthy from serious thought. I think it is very important for us to remember today that God in Christ has experienced death, in whatever form, and that death is not, therefore, unknown to him. When death comes to meet us, however alone we are, we can know that our prayers, whatever we ask for, whether to go or to stay, will be understood by someone who has been through the same experience.

Good Friday, therefore, is not a day of mourning, however much the life-denying traditions of the fifteenth-century Western church may weigh on us. Whatever God wills is good, and today especially, Good Friday, we should rejoice that 'God was in Christ, reconciling the world unto himself.' Today, God came to rescue us from the consequences of our self-love. Today, God opened up the future to a life lived with him in accordance with his love. Today, we can be confident that whatever happens, God is with us and will look after us.

There is a great deal more to be said about the cross, and we can only hope to touch on these topics. Meanwhile let us pray that we may find comfort, for whatever ails us, in contemplating the death of God on the cross and find in him a resting-place for our souls, however troubled. What I most want to assert is that 'God was in Christ reconciling the world to himself' and that it was on the cross that he did so. May we all respond as we ought to this manifestation of His love!

Amen.

Erev Rosh Hashanah

SHEILA SHULMAN
(BEIT KLAI YISRAEL)

Rabbi Sheila Shulman, 63, founded a community/congregation, BKY, with a group of friends in London which has just celebrated its tenth anniversary. She is also working as half-time Associate Rabbi for the Finchley Reform Synagogue, and teaches at Leo Baeck College. A lesbian, she has no spouse and no children.

She was a late entrant to the Rabbinate, after a career as an academic and also having worked in publishing as an editor. She spent many years as an activist working in the women's liberation movement. She worked with Only-women Press, earning her living as a printer in a quick-print shop. 'The decision to study for the Rabbinate came rather late in life; it was, and continues to be, a surprise.'

In order to discuss her faith and vocation properly, she prises these terms loose from their implicitly Christian context. 'Faith and vocation are words I use only tentatively, and diffidently. A rabbi is just a teacher. I didn't become a rabbi because I "had faith" or because I felt "called" in any sense. I had questions; I felt in some indescribable way "nagged". I was in love with Jewish learning, though I'd only just begun to discover it, despite (and for me it was a big 'despite') the huge load of patriarchal freight in Judaism. That freight is of course no heavier in Judaism than in any of the other major religions; it's just my freight.

'As I moved, slowly, from being a "secular" Jew to engaging with Judaism in all its richness and complexity, I kept being moved in unexpected ways, by a liturgical tune, by a phrase in a service, by a bit of biblical text. I was at a point in my life when I was looking for what I can only call "more life", and I kept finding it. I found a religious tradition that was tough, and ironical, and funny; it answered both my need for sophistication and my longing for simplicity. I still have no answers, but that's OK; I only ever promised to engage with the questions. And religious certainty is so often an unedifying spectacle, not to mention dangerous.'

She gives a moving account of her journey to the Rabbinate. In the early 1980s she was busy being a Jewish Lesbian Feminist, part of a group of (she thought) like-minded women. 'I realized at some point that I knew almost nothing about Judaism, religiously speaking. When I don't know about something, I start to read. I read, almost at random, but I have a pretty good nose for good and/or important books, or at least books that will lead me somewhere. In this case I was led to the author of one of the books I'd been reading, and he was kind enough to see me. I explained that I didn't know what I was doing in his office; I'd hardly talked to a man in ten years, let alone a rabbi. He said, "So what brought you here?" At which point I wept.'

He put several rabbis in touch with her. 'As a consequence of meeting with them, and especially with Rabbi Prof Jonathan Magonet, I went as an occasional, visiting student to Leo Baeck College, auditing those courses that were in English (I had no Hebrew.) Soon several of the teachers suggested I apply for the rabbinic course. Initially I thought they were mad. But I was at a turning point in my life.'

At the same time, during these years, she made friends with a Benedictine nun, the then guest mistress at Stanbrook Abbey, where she had gone, because it didn't cost much, to try to sort herself out. 'Sr Jane was a formidable woman, utterly astringent and very loving. Our initial conversations were unimaginable to me, even as they happened. I found myself sitting opposite this elderly person in a full habit, talking about being a lesbian, and a feminist, and politics, and I don't know what all else, with entire ease. I'd never met a nun in my life. She told me I was in a prophetic position. It took me a minute before I realized that she had not said "pathetic". That conversation stayed with me.

'Later on I went to talk with her about this to me preposterous idea of studying to be a rabbi. She said I was a teacher, I was passionately Jewish, and whether I knew it or not, I was a religious person. But that in making any decision, I should coldly weigh up the pros and cons. I have to admit that one of the biggest "pros" was that a student bursary came with the rabbinic course. Someone was going to pay me to study? The biggest "con", of course, was what, if any, employment possibilities awaited me should I ever be ordained.'

She discussed it at length and in depth with her then partner. She talked with her friends, who were bemused. 'They asked me (a) Had I lost my marbles?; (b) Was I hearing voices?; (c) Did I have all the answers now? The answer to all the above was of course "No", and that thinking the way I was thinking meant more trouble, more questions, not less trouble or fewer questions.'

She decided, eventually, in the interests of 'more life,' and because, however implausible, and maybe even because it was so implausible, that she might be headed in a fruitful direction, and that she would apply to Leo Baeck College. 'I said somewhere in the lengthy application that I was a lesbian and a feminist. I figured that if that was clear, and they still accepted me, perhaps that "meant" something. I think I had some notion of a kind of gamble with God. Eventually I was accepted, though not without difficulty, and I said to myself I would go until I hit a brick wall. Though I worked very hard (I was after all starting practically from scratch) I never for a moment believed that I would be ordained.'

But she was ordained in 1989. 'I have yet to hit the brick wall, though it's been right in my face on a number of occasions. Being a woman rabbi, much *less a lesbian, is no easier than being either of those in a Christian context. However, much as I from time to time think I'm crazy, being a rabbi contin-ues to feel right, and I don't know what else to trust. Except that my work, in quiet ways, seems to prosper – so far, anyway. None of that is or has been easy, but much of it is and has been fruitful, and I don't think that would be the case had I made the wrong decision.'*

The subject of her sermon is on one level her only subject. 'In Isaiah Berlin's terms, I'm a hedgehog. I want my community to be real, and for me being real means finding what ground we really do have in common in and through being clear and explicit about conflicts, divisions, real differences. I am sick to death of cheap rhetoric, of psychobabble, of pious mouthings about "community". And I want everyone that is part of the one we are build-ing to know that it isn't easy to build; it requires attention, pain, and the exer-tion of critical intelligence. So I try to reflect that, as best I can.'

The sermon is not, and ought not be, the centrepiece of a Jewish service, she says. 'If there is a "centrepiece", it should be the reading from the Torah, and possibly the "drash", the exposition of that reading. Congregants want ser-mons because they've grown up in a largely Christian culture, where sermons are de rigueur. *Traditionally a Rabbi preached twice a year (at length, to be sure, but still . . .), on the Shabbat before Pesach, and on the Shabbat between Rosh Hashanah and Yom Kippur. For me, sermons are for occasions when there are too many people present to have a discussion, which is what I usually do, or if some issue is really burning. I try very hard never to think of myself as "preaching", but rather as articulating one facet of an ongoing con-versation, the rest of which will follow sooner or later from the people to whom, or rather with whom, I'm speaking.'*

Outside the synagogue, she reads omnivorously. She walks and talks with her friends. She dotes on cartoons from the New Yorker. *She spends time looking at small flowers and big trees. 'This summer, in New Mexico, I dis-covered cottonwoods.'*

THIS IS THE TIME OF YEAR when we are asked to consider, in a more concentrated way than usual, our relationship to 'the other,' that is, those who are not us. 'The other,' in the context of this time of year, can be understood as those who inhabit the world with us, close-ly or distantly. 'The other' can be understood as those within our own community or those in other communities with whom we hope to forge connections. For some of us, 'the other' is also God, Whom we cannot separate from our thinking about other 'others'. I want to talk to you about all that, because I want you to know what kind of think-ing and feeling animates and informs my work with you, what goes into my understanding of the kind of entity BKY is, and what ground we need to stake out, or go on creating, as we enter our second decade.

When I was a child, my favourite stories, and the substance of end-less fantasies, were the legends of Robin Hood. Naturally, in all these fantasies, I was Robin Hood, not Maid Marian. Robin Hood and his band were a community, pledged to each other, though open to others who were willing to do the same. They were outcasts, outlaws, even. They had suffered injustice but were not victims; they were fighting back. It was very clear who their enemies were: the rich, the powerful, the exploiters, the malevolent institutions of state and church. Historical reality, whatever it may have been, did not, could not, impinge on my child's consciousness. A long time passed before the irony of a Jewish child identifying with the defenders of a crusader king came home to me.

Somewhere at the centre of myself, I've neither changed nor 'grown up'. I don't want to do either, really. I cherish the simplicity of that fantasy, the sharp, clear perception of injustice, the certainty that the way to fight it is to take to the greenwood with a band of comrades and begin to make the world you wanted to live in. Never mind that Robert of Locksley had his estates restored when the king came home. That part always annoyed me. It didn't fit with the rest. The important part was the anarchic, but far from unholy, band in the greenwood. The important part was knowing who was 'us,' who was 'them,' and what was wrong. The boundary, though, was always permeable. One of 'them' could, in good faith, always become one of 'us', either because they too fell foul of the powers that be, or because they chose in conscience to join 'us'. And there were always a few people, caught in their various situations, who were neither 'us' nor 'them', but helped.

Time has passed. Half a century has passed, and more than half a peculiar, unsettled, difficult lifetime, a lot of it lived on various kinds of margins. Here I am now, still to my surprise, a rabbi for ten years, balancing uneasily between the demands of that simple child's heart and a necessarily complicated consciousness, trying to talk to you about what it is to 'encounter the other'.

I don't think any of us would be here unless we wanted our life with others to be in a Jewish context, but one that was open rather than closed. We presume we have a lot in common, and often, we do. At the same time, it would not be wise to count too much on that presumption. There are serious differences: political, ideological, cultural, sociological, even spiritual and temperamental. No matter what the level of good will, and I know it is considerable, the potential for collision is always present, as much between individuals as between different groups of us. I only know one way to minimize that potential, and that is to be as explicit as possible. For me, part of that explicitness is to situate myself as clearly as possible for you. Unless we know how different we all really are, and how those differences affect us, we are not likely to discover how we can meet. We've gone some way toward doing that, among ourselves, but not far enough, and we haven't even begun to consider what I think one of our next tasks will be: to make connections with other, analogous groups from different communities.

I hope what I say will find echoes among you. I believe my perspective to be saturatedly Jewish, but because I am also a woman of my generation, a lesbian and a radical feminist, that perspective is neither typical, nor representative, nor exemplary, and I do not speak for anyone but myself. I speak out of the matrix of my own experience, my own longings, my own failures, my own fragmentary and evasive hopes, my own struggle to understand this business of 'the other'.

My experience, on the whole, is of being 'other', in several ways which are mutually resonant and often compound each other. That experience, and the kind of consciousness that stems from it, has often been painful, but it has taught me at least two things. I learned them very early on, but have lived through different versions. I learned a sense of solidarity (much more easily imagined than lived) with other 'others'. I may have nothing else in common with them but my version of being perceived as 'other', an understanding of the iniquities of institutional power, and a shared sense of injustice. That sense of solidarity may not go very far if each of us perceives the other as implicated in particular, different, contradictory injustices, but it's there, and it's a beginning.

I also learned that my place, my home, is so to speak in the greenwood, on the margins, with other people who have chosen to be there with me and with each other. There we are, I hope, building and not destroying, though we are also, however metaphorically, fighting against the patent injustices that surround us. So, for me, both as a model and as a felt sense, there are 'others' who are 'us', and 'others' who are 'them', though as I said before the boundary is permeable. Within that constellation, there is myself, and my nearest 'other', should I be so lucky. At the centre is God, Who is as 'other' as you can get, and God encompasses it all. I reiterate, that's *my* model and *a* Jewish model, not *the* model. For a long time, from my perspective, God did not come into it, certainly not in any explicit way. Then I had to think again, hard.

That engagement, begun nearly twenty years ago, has brought me to where I am today. The shape it took was an encounter with Judaism. I had never been anything but a Jew, culturally at any rate, though I'd not paid much attention to it for years. But it began to feel intellectually dishonest to go on not engaging with the religious dimension of being a Jew. Also the hole created by a sort of spiritual hunger in myself had, I suspected, a Jewish shape. There were shreds, fragments, echoes somewhere in my consciousness that resonated out of all proportion to their attenuated nature.

At the heart of Judaism, for me, is precisely this question of the one and the other, how they are inextricably bound up together yet always and invariably separate, how reality does not inhere either in the one or the other but is created in what Martin Buber memorably called 'the between-world'. That is, reality itself is relational; it is created, it exists, between us. There is something else. In Judaism, neither the one nor the other is abstract, or general, or even generic. Both are particular and unique. There is no route to anything we might call 'the universal' except in and through the particular and the unique. We (Jews) arrive at our understanding of how we (human beings) are all connected and the same through our understanding of how we (human beings) are each, all of us, distinct and unique.

Consider the first line of the *Shema*, that call of the one to the other which we should say twice each day, and which, while not a prayer, has probably always been part of the liturgy, and is the closest we have to a *Credo*. Except it is not a *credo*; it is a call to attention. *Shema yisrael Adonai Eloheynu Adonai echad*. It is flatly impossible to translate. The usual 'Hear O Israel, the Lord is your God, the Lord is One' is worse than crude. 'Hear' could and probably should be 'listen'. As for 'the Lord', I hardly know where to begin. It is the unsayable, unspeakable 'name' of God, and is an archaic, continuous form of the verb 'to be'. And 'One' in Hebrew carries a whole cluster of meanings: 'one', 'singular', 'unique'. There is a related word with the same root letters meaning 'closed up' or 'mysterious', and also 'joined' or 'united'. So perhaps we could say, 'Listen Israel, YHVH is your God, YHVH, to Whom you are bound in covenantal love, is indivisible, unique, mysterious.'

As a kind of commentary to this, there is an *aggada*, a rabbinic story which, read carefully (or, to be exact, read the way I think it should be read) ends with God as it were saying: 'You [the people Israel] have made Me a beloved unique in the world, and I shall make you [the people Israel] a beloved unique in the world.' (TB Ber. 6a) The whole emphasis is on particularity (both of God and of Israel), reciprocity, choice, and making, as if that quality of beloved uniqueness were contingent upon recognition, perception, decision.

All anti-Semites, many people who are ignorant or misinformed, and, unfortunately, some Jews as well, are convinced that this language necessarily embodies a hierarchy, with Jews, so to speak, at the top next to God and everyone else lower down and further away. I certainly don't see it that way, and I don't believe it is so intended. For me, in fact, the true force of the language of covenantal love between God and Israel is quite the reverse. For me, that language provides a way of thinking about others, any others, that is *least* likely to violate their integrity, or their own centre of self, not to mention their life. If I think that way, if I believe that way, if I feel that way, then with any luck I may possibly speak and act that way. Let me try to explain.

First of all, what I have called the language of covenantal love between God and Israel insists upon the respective uniqueness both of the one and of the other, whether the other is God or the person next to you. Second, the necessity for continually re-affirmed reciprocal recognition and choice is built in. Twice each day, we are called upon, and call upon each other, to acknowledge that necessity.

Third, that language, which I could describe as a metaphor become a model, does not exist in isolation. In the rabbinic tradition of setting one text beside another in order to consider them together, I'll set the first line of the *Shema* beside the following *aggada*:

> Only one single person was created in the world, to teach that, if we (any one) cause a single soul to perish, it is as if we have caused a whole world to perish, and if we save alive a single soul, it is as if we had saved a whole world . . . Again, only one single person was created to proclaim the greatness of God, for an emperor will stamp many coins with one die, and it will always show his own face, but God has stamped every person with the die of the first person, (who was made in God's image), yet each one of us is unique. Therefore, everyone must say, 'For my sake the world was created.'

'A single soul' and 'everyone' in this text does not mean 'Jews'; it clearly means 'every human being'. (Though I do wonder if, in its original context, it ever meant 'women'. I, and other women like me, have decided it had damn well better mean 'women' too.) Anyway, this is the context in which the particularist language of the love between God and Israel makes sense to me, and the point from which such language can begin to illuminate the question of my relation to 'the other', any 'other'.

This *aggada* articulates how we are connected and alike, since each of us carries the stamp of God's image, and how we are distant and radically different from each other, since each of us is unique. Most of us would feel odd (I certainly would) saying 'for my sake the world was created'. But, since we each encounter the world with our unique self, it takes a more strenuous imaginative effort than we usually realize to overcome our sense of being the centre of the world, which is after all also partly true. It is not only in science fiction that worlds collide.

It seems to me that the biblical and rabbinic language of an intense, particular love between God and Israel is on the one hand a powerful metaphor for illuminating one facet of the relation between the human and the Divine, and on the other hand, especially in the context of the *aggada* about the coins, it is severely, and deliberately, self-limiting. 'This,' it says, 'this particular love is what we have seen. This is what we know. This is how it is for us. There are other perceptions, other ways. What we have is *our* truth, not *the* truth. God, being God, is radically Other, unencompassable by any single, unique vision.

If this is how you see it too, if this metaphor, this model, this way of apprehending, is real for you, then join us. You are welcome. If not, not.'

There is no claim to exclusivity, to universality. Precisely that particularist language is the strongest acknowledgement, the strongest validation I know that there are others in the world, also unique and precious and beloved, for whom the relation between the human and the Divine is understood differently, or yet others for whom, in the most honourable way, there is no such relation.

It is on one level easy to read that *aggada* and say, 'Oh, sure, of course, I know that.' It is something else again to try to realize it, to live it out, even in relation to someone we care about, never mind a stranger, never mind an 'enemy'. Remember that the sense of 'realize' is 'to make real'. There is a passage in *Middlemarch*, by George Eliot, which describes with poignant clarity exactly what the difficulty of our task is. I could describe that task as the need to fully apprehend the depth, the density, the extent, the intricacy of worlds that are not our own, the need to apprehend the otherness of the other, and to take that as our starting point for meeting.

The heroine of *Middlemarch* is a romantic, idealistic young woman who, in her search for a life that would engage her fully, has convinced herself that she loves, and should marry, a much older, wizened, burrowing scholar/pastor, because, provincial innocent that she is, she mistakes his trickle of exhausted scholarship for a torrent of knowledge and wisdom. He was, after all, the first man to cross her path who appeared to be involved with the life of the mind. In this scene, they are on their honeymoon, in Rome. He buries himself in archives. She does not know what to do with herself. He is utterly self-absorbed but determined to behave 'correctly' to his young wife. She is all pent up and full of ardour. They are utterly at cross purposes. At this point they have had something refinedly approaching a quarrel, and then she realizes something.

We are all of us born in moral stupidity, taking the world as an udder to feed our supreme selves: Dorothea had early begun to emerge from that stupidity, but yet it had been easier to her to imagine how she would devote herself to Mr. Casaubon, and become wise and strong in his strength and wisdom, than to conceive with that distinctness which is no longer reflection but feeling – an idea wrought back to the directness of sense, like the solidity of objects – that he had an equivalent centre of self, whence the lights and shadows must always fall with a certain difference. (225)

For me, that passage has become a sort of parable about all our encounters with each other. If I could, I would post it on billboards, have it up in sky-writing or neon lights, make it visible everywhere people talk with each other. That the 'other' in front of you is truly other, with 'an equivalent centre of self' is the easiest thing in the world to forget or ignore, whether in love, in incipient friendship, in political confrontation, in intellectual argument, in moments of irritation or exasperation, or in the merest brush with the other.

While I continually try to arrive at that 'distinctness' of realization in relation to others that Eliot talks about, and that I believe is inherent in texts like the *Shema*, or our *aggada*, and while I firmly believe that is what we should all be doing in relation to each other, there is another factor to consider: the workings of political, or institutional, power.

Each of us is embedded somewhere in the complex web of power relations that makes up the world we inhabit together. In that world there most certainly are hegemonies, and we would be fools not to take account of their existence and of how we are situated in relation to them. The lights and shadows fall with a certain difference not only upon each of our separate selves, but upon the construct each of us makes of our common world. And it is not only a question of constructs.

The weight and pressure of the various hegemonies in the world we inhabit together affect some of us more than others of us, and those of us who are affected are affected differently. So while, as I said, part of me not only longs for but lives in the simplicities of the greenwood, where I know who is 'us' and who is 'them' and what is wrong, the rest of me knows it is never so simple, and that in order to apprehend reality as fully as possible I'd better go on trying to develop a consciousness like a fly's eye, which as you all know has hundreds of facets.

What we're trying to do in BKY isn't easy. I hope that what I am saying will at least make it more possible. Even if some of what we do is a kind of shouting across vast distances, or conversely, being irritated out of all reason at the thorn sticking in our own shirt, or, worse yet, talking to the walls, it's better than not trying at all. And sometimes, in my memory invariably, we will be surprised into real meeting, often where we least expect it.

From long and complex experience of being, and being perceived as, 'other', I know what it is to be stereotyped, to have assumptions made about me and my life, and even to be rendered invisible precisely by not being seen as different. I know what it is to have my world, my reality, my identity, either grossly misperceived or cancelled out altogether. That is why I am and always will be more at home in the greenwood, on the margins, not a victim, but building and fighting back, with others. At the same time I'm part of the Anglo-Jewish establishment, and consent to go on being so, even if I do so almost always from a critical position. It is a position that a feminist writer called being 'an inside outsider.' 'Inside outsiders', she said, engage with the world 'on its own turf, but never on its own terms.' It is my strongest hope for BKY as a community that we continue to live precisely there, continue to find our strength there, and grow because we live there, real and in the world, but on our own terms.

As such an 'inside outsider' my relation to our tradition and our institutions is necessarily one which the Yiddish Socialists would have called 'in *gerangl*,' in struggle. But since that was how they signed their letters to each other, instead of 'with love', I take the phase to mean 'in loving struggle'. So, just as I hope my controversies with Judaism will always be 'for the sake of heaven', so I hope our controversies with each other (and there will be controversies) will also be 'for the sake of heaven'. I wish you a good and sweet New Year.

Note
Quote, George Eliot, *Middlemarch* (p. 225, Oxford University Press).

Sacrifice

RONALD CREIGHTON-JOBE

Fr Ronald Creighton-Jobe, 55, a Roman Catholic priest at the London Orato-
ry, entered the novitiate in 1968 after gaining an honours degree in English
Literature at King's College, London. He continued his studies, gaining a BD
in theology at Heythrop and was ordained priest in 1973. The offices he has
held at the Oratory include Prefect of Ceremonies and Prefect of the Sacristy.
He is currently Librarian and Archivist. For 20 years he was chaplain to the
Royal Brompton Hospital and for 12 years he served as Ecumenical Officer of
central London for the Archdiocese of Westminster. For six years he was
chairman of the Kensington Council of Churches. He is also Chaplain of the
Sovereign Military Order of Malta.

'My parents were non-baptized, non-practising Christians,' he says.
'Through reading I became Catholic at the age of twelve. The initial inspir-
ation was my first attendance at a Catholic Mass. Hence the subject of my
sermon. The continuing presence of Christ in His Church, through the sacra-
ments and through prayer, has always been central to my understanding of
faith and how it bears fruit in the love of neighbours.' The Oratory, founded
by St Philip Neri in sixteenth-century Rome and brought to England by
Cardinal John Henry Newman, has provided an ideal environment for his
vocation. 'The Oratory has enabled me to serve God in an active apostolic life
while at the same time giving time for prayer and study within the context of
a stable community life.'

The sermon published here was inspired by a conviction regarding the
place of the Eucharist in Church life which has grown out of his ecumenical
work over many years. 'I became more and more convinced that the challenge
of Christian Unity must lie in the presentation of the centrality of the
Eucharist in the life of the Church. The sermon submitted is an expression of
this conviction. Preaching presents the Word of God as it reflects on His abid-
ing presence in the Scriptures. The Mass realizes that presence by inserting us
into His passion, death and resurrection.'

He believes the ideal context for a sermon is within the Eucharist, imme-
diately after the reading of the Gospel. 'This is so that the ordained priest may
bring the people to a deeper understanding of faith in order to lead lives more
and more modelled on the example of Our Lord. In our fragile world this is
more than ever necessary.'

He recently preached at the funeral of a close friend, the celebrity cook

Jennifer Paterson. 'I remember when I was first ordained, 27 years ago, and taking my role as a priest very seriously. She picked me up in one of her bear-hugs and twirled me round. It was difficult to take oneself seriously after that.' Outside religion, he is actively interested in art, history, music and architecture.

IN TIMES OF GREAT MOMENT in the history of Israel, God's people were summoned to observe a year of special import, a Jubilee, summoned by the deep, resounding notes of the *shofar*, but above all, summoned by the Word of God to reaffirm their fidelity to the sacred covenant established by God between Himself and His people: 'Hear, O Israel.' The Word of God is not an object; it is the means whereby the Lord who rules His people dwells amongst them. It is the covenant that expresses the reality that is at the heart of our understanding of God's abiding love for His people.

It is difficult for us to really understand man's relationship with 'the other' before revelation. It was dominated by fear, the deified forces of nature must be kept away; the gods must be propitiated at all cost. Sacrifice was essential, even of one's first-born.

And then came the momentous change. The God who creates man, chose, out of no other motive than love, to reveal Himself. He enters into a loving relationship with His creatures. He establishes the covenant.

Abraham sets out from all he gives him, security and identity, impelled by the conviction that God has spoken to him, that He has made a promise and given His word: 'I will give you a land. I will make your descendants as the sands on the shore of the sea.' He goes out into the desert on a journey, summoned by the Word of God.

To His servant Moses he reveals His name, invites him into living intimacy with Him; even more he opens to him the mystery of His very nature. 'I am who I am. Tell them I AM has sent you'. And he delivered His people from bondage. He liberates his chosen ones and the sign of this is the blood of the lamb – freedom, redemption. As the psalmist proclaims: 'He saved us because he loves us.' The lamb is slain instead of the first-born of Israel.

The sacrifices continue in the life and rhythm of the temple, but the prophets deepen the concept; the sacrifice most acceptable to God is a pure heart, a heart at peace with God.

We know the fulfilment of this long process. The last of the prophets cries out in ecstatic greeting: 'Behold the Lamb of God who takes away the sins of the world.'

Jesus comes to initiate and seal a new covenant. He does so with His own blood. The first-born becomes the Lamb who is slain. We remember this wonder in the great eucharistic discourses of St John: 'I am the living bread which has come down from heaven. Unless a man eat my flesh and drink my blood, he can have no life in him.' He eats the Passover with His disciples, the first Mass with the new Israel. 'Do this is remembrance of me.' The drama is not completed until the cup of consummation is drained on Calvary, and He cries out in triumph: 'It is finished; it is accomplished.'

This divine action continues in His mystical body, the Church, where he continues to realize His presence until He comes again. In the Church, His body, the Word of God is not merely proclaimed, it is also made effective through the Holy Spirit who presides over the sacramental life of the New Israel and is the life of the individual believer.

This indissoluble bond between the Word and the Church must never be seen as something which reduces the sacraments which realize this link to mere images. That is the classic Protestant understanding. If we were to limit the presence of the Word only to its manifestation in the scriptures, as indeed the Reformers did, then, in the end, the Word is deprived of its very content. The Word of God is always an action in which Someone is giving Himself to someone – and this giving involves a true revelation of the very nature of Him who is the giver – in this case the Eternal Word of God Himself, made flesh for our sake, living and active in the Church with those who have been incorporated into His life through baptism.

It is the Church, founded on the rock of the apostles, and chief amongst them the rock of Peter, that the Lord, risen and glorious continues to give Himself, is made present and continues to speak to us.

In the Mass, quite naturally, we proceed from the mystery proclaimed to the mystery revealed and made present. The things of this world, bread and wine, are brought to the altar, and then, in a miracle beyond imagining, they are changed into His very self. In Holy Communion He feeds us and transforms us into Himself and we take Him to others to share in His love for all His creatures. We are literally Christ-bearers, accepting His command to love one another. The Mass is our source of union with God and with our fellow men.

One cannot separate the Body of Christ present on our altars from His abiding presence in each and every one of us. This should transform and illumine the whole challenge of love of neighbour. In our fellow Christians, we find realized, the presence of our Saviour whom we adore in the sacramental presence in the sacrifice of the Mass. Today, in this Mass, celebrated in its most solemn form by a successor of the apostles, in a Holy Year of Jubilee, at the beginning of a new century and new millennium, we are summoned by the Word of God to enter more deeply into the mystery of His passion, death and glorious resurrection. We are challenged to grow in love, to renew our fidelity to Christ and His Church in a world which seems so often unaware of His loving presence. And we are commanded to love one another, even as He loved us, and continues to offer Himself for us in this, the greatest of His gifts.

Pentecost

DAVID HATTON

David Hatton, 81, of Clare, Suffolk, is a retired lecturer in religious studies, and former Methodist minister. He is married to Joan, has a daughter, Susan, and had a son, Peter, who died in 1998. His first occupation was as a local-government clerk. He served in the National Fire Service during the war, then trained for the Methodist ministry at Richmond College and worked in that ministry until 1962. He then became a secondary school RE teacher until 1970, when he became a lecturer.

'My faith grew from parents and a church with excellent ministers and Sunday School teachers (Kensal Rise Methodist). It was challenged, but not negated, by the onset of war, and has remained since despite a number of ups and downs in life.

'My sense of vocation took a change of direction after unfortunate experiences a couple of times in the Methodist ministry, but continued to find fulfilment in seeking to encourage students to explore religion – first youngsters in their teens, and then those of normal college age through to mature students in their middle years.

'For as long as I can remember my approach has been a questioning one, encouraging thinking rather than blind acceptance. I find it striking that in his great commandment about serving God and neighbour, Jesus added "and all your mind" to the original words in Deuteronomy. As a school teacher, I preferred that the outcome of teaching should be a thoughtful atheist rather than an unthinking Christian (though a thinking Christian was better still!) and was gratified when pupils spoke of the difference between their questing RE lessons and the indoctrination attempts of an anti-Christian history teacher. Another expression of my approach has been in the series of booklets I wrote for the Methodist Publishing House entitled "The Questioning Christian", in which I attempt to suggest lines of thought for those who, while sympathetic to Christian ideas, cannot fully accept traditional approaches to subjects such as the Bible, doctrine, prayer, suffering , other religions and death.

'Thus my sense of vocation has found expression through different channels, and I count it a privilege that my whole working life involved constant face-to-face encounters with people rather than machines.'

His choice of subject for this sermon was dictated by the fact that it was to be delivered at Pentecost. 'Knowing of people who often yearn for the spectacular and are disappointed or disillusioned when they don't find it, I feel there is a need to point out that God's Spirit is no less active in small, quiet ways. Our God is as much a god of the ordinary as of the extra-ordinary.

'I believe the sermon is still very relevant to today's worship environment. That is not to say there is no place for services without sermons, for they can certainly induce that sense of reverence which should be the heart of all acts of worship. But I cannot foresee a time when relevant, worshipful preaching will be outgrown, despite all we are told about the need for short soundbites and visual aids. Perhaps it reflects my age, but I still favour a sermon towards the end of a service, followed by not-too-verbose prayers which tie in with the theme of the service, and a closing hymn – often a short sharp one!'

He can recall a number of amusing and moving experiences from different phases of his life. 'At my first church, in the Welsh valleys, one member of the congregation was enthusiastic in his shouts of "True, brother, true" during the sermon – which was unfortunate when I had said something in order to repudiate it.' On another occasion, when he said, 'Jesus points the way to God', a little child called out, 'It's rude to point.' He also describes how, when supervising student teachers on school practice, he was once observing a lesson where a young child was being very disruptive. 'Afterwards I glowered down at him from my great height and said "I've been watching you!" He, from about two feet above ground level, smiled up at me towering above, and said "And I've been watching you." One evening service which has always stuck in my mind was when there was a complete failure of lights just before the sermon. Fortunately I knew what I wanted to say, and church officers eventually found a couple of candles, which added to the atmosphere. The singing of the final hymn "When I survey the wondrous cross", made possible because the words were so well-known, helped produce what to me was one of the most moving of services.'

In spite of retirement, he has found that there is all too little spare time for various interests. 'I have always enjoyed photography, and still carry a camera with me on walks in the nearby Priory grounds and Clare Castle country park, where swans pose beautifully to be photographed once more, robins cry out from nearby branches to be "taken" yet again, and leaves and wild flowers grow more beautiful year by year. I enjoy writing, and in addition to the booklets already mentioned and occasional letters to the press, politicians and so on, have written four lengthy books on our little town, its church, and its Augustinian Priory which was the first in the English-speaking world, and is still going strong. Occasionally I am asked to show visitors around the main features of the town – always a pleasure. I enjoy reading worthwhile books including poetry, and toy with writing poetry myself. And I like the dance band music of the thirties – but that memory of the distant past warns me it is time to stop.'

IS THIS PENTECOST or Whitsun? Pentecost is a Jewish festival held fifty days after Passover which later became also a celebration of the giving of the Law to Moses, so was taken as the birthday of the Hebrew religion. Whitsun recalls what happened one particular Pentecost, and is treated as the birth of the Christian Church. It became known as Whit or White Sunday because it was a time favoured for baptism, when participants dressed in white. I like the fact that we now seem more likely to use the word Pentecost, which has a Jewish origin, instead of Whitsun, which is specifically Christian, because it reminds us of the links with our mother religion, the religion of Jesus throughout His life.

Today Christians think of the story in Acts chapter two. The followers of Jesus had seen their master die. Then they had come to feel he was still with them. At the Ascension – a vision? – they came to believe that the man of Galilee was now 'at God's right hand', an assertion that he was at the seat of power behind the universe. Now, as they waited in prayer, they experienced something they likened to a strong wind and flames of fire, and felt the power of the Spirit of God. They went out and preached 'in tongues' . A spectacular occurrence!

And it has sometimes been celebrated spectacularly. At St Paul's Cathedral in pre-Reformation days a massive censer was swung from the roof giving off huge sparks and great clouds of billowing smoke, and a flock of doves was released to symbolize the descent of the Holy Spirit.

But we should remember that the Spirit of God was already there in what Christians call the Old Testament. The Genesis story says the creation of the world came about by the Spirit of God moving upon the face of the waters. Samson's growth in strength was said to come when God's Spirit came upon him. The artists' crafts at the building of the Temple were said to come through the Spirit of God, as did the words of the prophets. And it is interesting that a wind and flashes of fire had come into Ezekiel's vision earlier, while later, in the Talmud, rabbis spoke of the Holy Spirit coming in rushing wind or blazing fire.

One trouble with such images is that they may be thought to imply that the coming of the Holy Spirit is only associated with the spectacular. One Pentecost a few years ago the church at Clare's Augustinian Priory was packed for an inter-denominational service. During a shared prayer someone spoke excitedly of feeling the wind of God's Spirit coming among them. Afterwards the prior of the time confided to me it was a draught caused by his opening the door to relieve the heat! Some expected the spectacular, and found it. But even if the explanation was more mundane, it doesn't prove God's Spirit was not present. Acts only says 'LIKE wind and flames': the Bible's writers frequently told their truths in poetic language – a point we too often fail to grasp.

Of course exceptional things happened the first Whitsun. Men had a great experience, and were changed. No longer a group in hiding, but a company speaking in tongues, with power, and confronting the world.

We still sometimes look for – yearn for? – spectacular happenings. whether in the experience itself, like wind and fire: or in the consequences, like speaking in tongues, miraculous healings, or even rolling in the aisles.

I suggest it is wrong to set the spectacular and the ordinary against each other.

First, consider the experience of God's coming to mankind – the 'winds and flames' part of the Pentecost scene.

True, Moses encountered God – and, in speaking of Divine comings, whatever doctrinists may say, I cannot myself separate the coming of God's Holy Spirit from any other comings of the one, even though triune, God – true. I say, that Moses encountered God in the thunder and lightning and smoke of Mt Sinai. But he also found God in a bush which appeared to burn yet was not consumed – a quieter experience, perhaps open to a 'natural' explanation. And it was not in the earthquake, wind or fire, that Elijah heard God speak, but in a still small voice. To assume God is just in the spectacular may mean we imagine He is not in the ordinary – and this is manifestly wrong. There are stories of Him appearing in quiet ways, as well as spectacular.

But are these stories, whether dramatic or quiet, to remain just stories? Sometimes what starts off as a story turns into something more. A year or so ago I heard on the radio of a yacht capsized in the Solent, and of a body washed ashore. It was just a story in the news. Later I saw the name, that of a world-renowned doctor – which was also a name I knew. He had played at our house when a toddler, the son of a neighbour. That yachting tragedy was no longer just a news story, but a sad experience my wife and I felt deep within ourselves.

And the 'wind and fire' and the 'burning bush' are not to remain 'just stories' , but should lead to something we feel deeply within ourselves – whether soul shattering, or quieter as ordinary events become sacraments, ways through which the Spirit of God comes to us.

I have had my ' burning bushes'. A sunrise behind a roadside bush while driving over the Pennines. Autumn at Clare Priory when the Virginia creeper covers the walls of the former cloister and monastic church. Frost on a tree, so beautiful that it demands a photograph. Leaves unfolding like hands extended in prayer. The beautiful plumage in the head of an ordinary duck, or body of a common starling. The sacred hush when sitting in the garden in early morning:

Still, still with thee, when purple morning breaketh.
When the bird waketh, and the shadows flee . . .
Alone with Thee, amid the mystic shadows,
The solemn hush of nature newly born.
(Methodist Hymn Book, 474)

These are some of my 'burning bushes' – and doubtless you have yours. Sights, experiences, which make you say to yourself 'Lo, God is here . . . Take off your shoes for this is holy ground'.

Our daily, commonplace, situation can be holy ground. The disciples of Ignatius Loyola, 16th-century founder of the Jesuits, said

We often saw how even the smallest things could make his spirit soar upwards to God who even in the smallest things is the greatest. At the sight of a little plant, an insignificant worm or a tiny animal, Ignatius could soar free, above the heavens, and reach through things which lie beyond the senses.

The old story says God walked with Adam in a garden. St Augustine was in a garden when he heard a child's voice which led to his finding the presence of God.

But not only in the garden. The encounter can be anywhere, not least, of course, in church. It can in be in an ordinary service on an ordinary Sunday, not just in TV spectaculars, that we find something magic, a sense of mystery and awe – a realization of the presence of God, Creator of the universe. I have felt it in liturgical services at the parish church, perhaps with a distant choir of mischievous urchins temporarily become angels: in a Quaker meeting house: in a nonconformist chapel even if only a handful are gathered and perhaps without an official preacher – for such experiences are not dependent on great scholarship or musical ability; they can come through those who in the world's eyes are very ordinary people, for the spirit of God has been poured on ALL flesh.

I am not decrying the great occasions – when a Saul of Tarsus is stopped in his tracks, or a John Wesley feels his heart strangely warmed. I am saying 'Don't only look there for the moving in of God's Spirit'.

And after such an experience? Evelyn Underhill wrote of the Holy Spirit:

Softer than dew.
But when the morning wind
Blows down the world, O Spirit! show thy power:
Quicken the dreams within the languid mind
And bring thy seed to flower!

With the Spirit come gifts which we call charismata. The group in Acts burst into speaking with tongues and working wonders. The word charisma is often linked to spectacular events and the oomph which rare leaders reveal. But are we to think only of those who speak in tongues, or of whom miraculous cures are told, when we speak of charismata?

The gifts of the Spirit are not restricted to the abnormal and world-shaking. St Paul's list in 1 Corinthians reads: wisdom, knowledge, faith, the ability to heal, to work miracles, to prophesy, to interpret prophecy, and – yes – to speak in tongues and to interpret such speaking. Some of these qualities ARE spectacular, but most of them are ones which the most ordinary person may possess.

Is wisdom only to be found in the really brilliant people such as St Augustine at the Fall of Rome, or some scintillating modern mind on radio or TV – or have we not sometimes found it in humble parents and friends? Is faith only to be found in a character such as St Francis, or have we not found it in some workaday person who encouraged us more than did the famous? Is healing only to be found in the 'incurable' and spectacular? An ordinary person's healing of another's broken heart is no less wonderful. Is 'working miracles' only to be seen in walking across water – 'walk across my swimming pool', as 'Godspell', or was it 'Jesus Christ, Superstar', expressed it? What about when somebody works wonders for a poor mother in a desperate situation?

Don't be overwhelmed by claims of the spectacular – these other actions which are of infinite value in our daily personal lives, are no less charismata, gifts of the Holy Spirit.

Again I'm not speaking against the great and mighty people and their accomplishments. The world would be infinitely poorer without the Nelson Mandelas, Martin Luther Kings, and Mother Teresas we have known – the people of great charisma.

But greatness of the same order can be found in 'little' people. I spent some weeks in pre-war Nazi Germany with a family which did not approve of Hitler. When, after some revolutionary talk, I foolishly began playing the 'Internationale' on their piano, they had to shoosh me because they knew the walls had ears. Later they were warned that their failure to hang out a swastika flag on national days had been noted. My friend's mother felt compelled to show one, but made it a tiny one, the size of a pocket handkerchief, which cocked a snoop at the huge flags of their neighbours. She wasn't among those who became famous for their resistance to Nazism, but she was of their spirit. Norah, the first person I received into church membership when I was a minister, a teenager with a terminal illness, wanted us to say together at her reception service in her bedroom the words of the hymn 'I give Thee back the life I owe'. She was of no less worthy a spirit than the famous Father Damien who faced a lingering death in a leper colony.

St Paul, after listing specatacular acts goes on to ask 'Are ALL workers of miracles? Have ALL gifts of healing? Do ALL speak with tongues? Desire earnestly the greater gifts . . . A still more excellent way I show you', and proceeds with that great chapter on love, ending by saying that love is the greatest gift of all. The Holy Spirit's coming is revealed in loving actions, no matter how small: tending the old and infirm and cantankerous: relieving the carers, or babysitting to relieve harrassed parents: chauffeuring people to church or – even better? – in one case I know, taking men from their nursing home to a local pub, when they preferred that: doing a bit of baking for someone. The greatest gift of the Holy Spirit is love, and every one of us can exercise that gift every day: simple everyday things that the doers of such actions hardly think of. To borrow a thought from Tagore, a great Indian of a hundred years ago, 'There are some who leave no trace of wings in the air – but have passed that way'.

One other thought, an essential part of my own thinking about Pentecost, but different from my main point so I'll be brief.

Joel spoke of the coming of God's Spirit on all flesh. Just to the people of that area? Or dare we apply the thought more widely? John's Gospel has Jesus saying 'The wind blows where it wills . . . ' The Greek word means both 'wind' and 'spirit'; dare we interpret this 'The Spirit blows where it wills . . . ', perhaps more widely than we sometimes suppose? The longer I live the more convinced I am that Christians should be less exclusive and should acknowledge the working of the Holy Spirit elsewhere. God did not leave Himself without witness in the rest of the world. The enlightenment which came through Gotama, the Buddha, led not only to inner peace for oneself, but also to the *bodhisattva* concept, characters who give up their own salvation for the sake of enlightening others. It also led to a great empire based on justice and non-violence in the 3rd century BC. The Hindu *Bhagavad Gita* has passages which are similar to the Beatitudes of Jesus. St Paul told the Galatians that love, kindness, gentleness, self-control and the rest, were the fruit of the Holy Spirit: are they not fruit of the same Spirit when they have been revealed through Buddhist, Hindu, or other, thinkers and writers? I believe that if we are prepared to look, we will find that the Spirit of God has been poured on many cultures beyond our own.

But that really calls for further thought, so back to my main theme. God's Spirit coming through miraculous winds and supernatural fires? The consequences – mighty miracles and speaking in tongues? The Holy Spirit also means God's coming to us and working through us quietly, breaking into everyday life, touching and working through ordinary people whose offerings, again in the words of Tagore 'are not for the temple at the end of the road, but for the wayside shrines at every bend'. The God of the ordinary – no, the God IN the ordinary –

the Holy Spirit of God the Almighty, Creator of everything, 'poured upon all flesh' – upon little you and me.

Note

Quotes. Evelyn Underhill, 'The Holy Spirit' from *The Lion Christian Poetry Collection* compiled by Mary Batchelor (Lion, 1995). 'Ignatius of Loyola from *Ignatius the Theologian* by Hugo Rahner SJ, translated by Michael Barry.

CONTENTMENT

Lessons in Contentment

Harry Young

*The Revd Harry Young, 80, a teacher, was ordained as a Baptist minister in
1970, ten years before he retired from education. Married to Joyce, they have
three children, Christopher, Philip and Martyn, and six grandchildren. Born
in Cumbria, he entered teacher training college in 1938 and from 1940
served in the Royal Army Pay Corps. He was appointed a Lay Pastor in 1947,
which he did alongside his work as a teacher in primary and secondary
schools.*

*'I was born, a twin, of Christian parents, and became a Christian aged 9
years! We belonged to the Open Brethren, and were known as the Twin Evangelists. My father, a heavy-drinking blastfurnace-man was converted and
eventually became an elder in the brethren. After the war I became the lay
Baptist Pastor at Sipson, Middlesex, teaching in Hayes.' He moved to another pastorate in Hayes in 1951 and to Surbiton in 1955 where he stayed until
1963. 'In 1963 I continued in active ministry at Richmond upon Thames,
but returned to Birkbeck College and in 1966 graduated in English History
and Theology (BA) at evening classes. In 1970, ordained, I became minister
in Kingston upon Thames Baptist Church. I retired from education in 1980
but continued in churches until 1997 when we moved to Westward Ho in
Devon.'*

*He chose this sermon because, having felt such 'dis-satisfaction' in many
areas of life, even in churches, he felt lessons in contentment needed to be
heard.*

*'The sermon lends itself to teaching because of its relevance to modern life
and the culture of materialism, and because it is well illustrated in the teachings of Jesus and in the New Testament letters and because it provides an
opportunity to warn against complacency but, on the other hand, it provides
a formula for a happy life.*

*'The sermon is a vital part of Christian worship. The place of the sermon
is not especially important, but it should be early if it is a challenge to the
prayers which may follow, and later if it is "get up and go" (i.e. demanding
action and personal consecration).'*

*He believes sermons are still relevant because good preaching is expository,
explaining scripture in its historical context and its relevance for today.*

*'I could write a book about my ministry experiences. The most dramatic
were when I led a Baptist delegation to our Baptist friends in Moscow, for*

example, preaching to thousands on Ascension Day, 1987 and in smaller rural congregations. Also, my only TV broadcast on Christmas Day from Kingston (broadcast on Thames TV) in 1987, brought a fascinating mail response.'

His other interests are his grandchildren, sport, especially cricket and football, a love of gardening and walking, especially in the Lake District. His latest book, Major Themes of the Minor Prophets, *sold out. He is also author of* Understanding the Holy Spirit, *with a foreword from John Cole, formerly of the BBC. He has also become involved in bereavement ministry. 'In the two years I have been in Devon, I have been privileged to conduct over 30 funerals.' He says, 'It has given me the greatest pleasure to take part in Preacher of the Year.' This is his third sermon to appear in a* Times *Book of Best Sermons.*

Text: Philippians 11:4 –13.

I have learnt, in whatsoever state I am, to be content. (St Paul)

OF THE MANY GREAT LESSONS which life must teach us none is more important than learning to be content. The lessons are given in the school of experience where we are taught that contentment is the fruit of divine grace. It is a natural wealth. It is an intelligent trust in God, in His promises and His presence.

Contentment is amongst the most persuasive teachings of the New Testament, one of the strongest messages of scripture. It is, moreover, the best antidote to the sin of covetousness. It is in direct conflict with a feature of modern society, the love of money which is described as 'the root of all evil'. It is Socrates who so wisely said, 'The wealthiest man is he who is contented with least.'

Contentment should not be confused with complacency, which is an extreme satisfaction and even smugness, the acceptance of situations and circumstances that can be and should be changed. Contentment is the blissful acceptance of situations within God's will which as we shall see, is not in the abundance of one's material possessions.

However, a cautionary word is appropriate here. It is right to be content with what we have, never with what we are. There is a holy discontent which longs for spiritual growth in grace and in the knowledge of our Lord Jesus Christ. We have not already attained or are already perfect, to use Paul's words again.

We must now take a look at the teachings of Jesus. In his gospel, St Luke tells the story of a man in the crowd who comes forward to ask Jesus to arbitrate between himself and his brother in a family squabble over an inheritance. 'Bid my brother divide the inheritance with me.' Such situations are by no means unknown in today's world. 'Where there's a will, there's a war!', to misquote an old proverb. His brother may well feel that to divide an inheritance would be wrong. He would prefer to keep it intact, believing that to divide is to destroy. Inheritances are not infrequently the cause of much heartache in a family. 'We are spending our kid's inheritance', was the rather unseemly caption in the rear window of a car I saw recently. In his wisdom, the Teacher firmly refused to intervene; rather he issued a stern warning; 'Beware of all covetousness; a man's life does not consist in the abundances of his possessions.' It was an appropriate moment for Jesus to tell another of his powerful parables. The very prosperous man at the heart of the story is engaged in self-satisfied, self-congratulatory reflection. It is an embarrassment of riches! Plenteous harvests pose problems however. The well-known essayist Francis Bacon gives this sharp reminder; 'Prosperity doth best discover vice, adversity doth best discover virtue.' There is nothing immoral in success. Wealth is not inherently evil. Prosperity may be more deserving of congratulation rather than criticism. Neither is there anything wrong in preparing for the future, for thrift, if iced with generosity, is indeed a virtue. So what was wrong with this man's philosophy of life? First of all, his priorities were wrong. The treasure was for himself as he contemplated a life of ease, and of self-indulgence in food and drink. But then, it was his presumption 'I have much goods laid up for many years.' For many years? We may not boast about tomorrow, not knowing what tomorrow may hold for us. It was an alarming word from God; 'You fool! This night, your soul is required of you, the things you have prepared, whose will they be?' A fool in scripture is one who says in his heart, there is no God; there is no greater folly. Such a person may appear to be affluent, but in reality, before God, in abject poverty.

This stirring parable is followed by sublime words of Jesus extracted so skilfully by St Luke from the Great Sermon on the Mount and so fully recorded by St Matthew: 'Don't be anxious about yourself, it is more than food and clothing, the birds are fed, the lilies flower and flourish. Don't be of anxious mind,' said Jesus. 'Seek first the kingdom of God.' 'I do not know what the future holds,' someone so truly said, 'But I know who holds the future.'

We must now take a closer look at the teaching of St Paul. The letter to the Philippians is sometimes described as 'the epistle of joy', yet the apostle, even as he writes, is in prison – in chains! He is facing martyrdom, yet he still rejoices. 'I have learnt, in any and all circumstances, to be content', and he adds, 'I have learnt the secret of facing plenty and hunger, abundance and want. I can do all things through Christ who strengthens me.' Godliness with contentment is a means of gain – we cannot take anything out of this world. The love of money, Paul emphasizes again, is the root of all evil. It is a major cause of backsliding.

The last word is from the writer to the Hebrews (13:5); 'Keep yourself from the love of money. Be content, for He hath said "I will never leave you or forsake you", so that we can confidently say, "The Lord is my keeper, I will not fear."' What better assurances can we have in any and all our circumstances, than the pledge and promise of the Lord's presence, He who is the same yesterday, today and for ever!

The poet Thomas Dekker may have the last word:

> Art thou poor, yet hast thou golden slumbers?
> O sweet content!
> Art thou rich yet is thy mind perplexed?
> O punishment.

Contentment indeed! It is the state of a mind that is filled with the peace of God that passes all understanding.

Note
Quote: Thomas Dekker from 'The Pleasant Comedy of Patient Grisill, 1603' taken from *Poetry of the English-Speaking World* (Heinemann).

If We Get It Wrong

GEOFFREY PARKINSON

Geoffrey Parkinson, 56, from Loughborough, Leicestershire is a retired bank manager who now works as a part-time cashier at Arnold Lodge, Leicester, a secure mental health institution, having previously worked for Thames Valley Police as a Neighbourhood Watch administrator. He has been a reader in the Church of England for 33 years. He and his wife, Pam, have three grown-up children: Stephen, a maths teacher, Rachel, administrator at the Central School of Speech and Drama and Sarah, who was adopted when aged just four months and who is reading Stage Management at Rose Bruford College.

After reading theology at Trinity College, Oxford, gaining a second-class degree, he trained as an RE teacher and taught for three years before joining the banking industry at the age of 25. 'I had been recommended for training for the ministry but the Lord seemed to be calling me away from full-time Christian ministry and I have continued to serve the Lord as a layman.'

His Christian commitment came from being taken to church from a young age and being a church choir member. 'But I really committed my life to the Lord while I was a student at Oxford, and became a Reader and an active leader of young people's groups in churches in Lancashire, Coventry and Billericay, before we moved to St Mary's, Maidenhead some twenty years ago.' The sermon entered for the Preacher of the Year Award 2000 was his farewell sermon at St Mary's, Maidenhead. 'We have susequently moved to Leicestershire where I am now serving my Reader apprenticeship at St Andrew's, Prestwold.'

The subject of his farewell sermon was given to him by the Vicar at three days' notice so he could preach a valedictory sermon to the morning congregation. 'It formed part of a series of sermons on key verses in John's First Epistle. The subject of forgiveness lends itself to preaching because it is the greatest Good News in the Christian Gospel. It was a really happy and triumphant theme on which to depart from St Mary's.'

He believes preaching is relevant to worship but that it must tie in with all the other parts of the service. 'Its content must be something that the congregation can take away with them and apply to their lives day by day. It should be clear and memorable, and the shorter and to the point the better. Preferably it should be towards the end of the service, but I am quite happy with its position in the Church of England's Communion Service after the Gospel.'

His most embarrassing moment in the pulpit was when he was preaching on death. 'An elderly gentleman near the front suddenly passed out and was surrounded by the churchwardens and other members of the congregation. I thought the message must have been altogether too challenging for him and precipitated a life and death crisis. I was pleased to be reassured that he was fully recovered and amazed to find out that he was a visiting American theology professor.'

Outside church, he and Pam are keen supporters of Preston North End. 'I have done a little writing of children's stories, but have had nothing published as yet. I enjoy the theatre and crosswords, and have spent 31 years of married life competing ferociously at Scrabble with Pam, who has the better of our many encounters.'

He has also been active in the community, as a chairman of school governors, leading an ultimately successful fight to keep Altwood Church of England Comprehensive School open. He was elected an Independent Berkshire County Councillor in 1989 and was chairman of Education from 1992–93, and was for five years recently Chairman of the Finance Committee at St Mary's, Maidenhead.

Text: 1 John 2:1.

HEAR WHAT SAINT JOHN SAYS. If anyone sins, we have an advocate with the Father, Jesus Christ the righteous; and he is the propitiation for our sins.

These are the final very familiar comfortable words in the Communion Service whether it is the Book of Common Prayer or the ASB.

John has just reminded his readers that he is writing that they may not sin, but then he says IF anyone does sin then they can be confident that Jesus has sorted it. Our title this morning says IF we get it wrong; well I'm afraid it is not so much IF but WHEN.

When Pam and I first came to St Mary's 19 years ago it was Lent. At the first service we came to after our move the then Vicar announced there would be a Commination Service on the following Thursday. I came to it and really did wonder what we had let ourselves in for because the Commination Service in the Prayer Book is described as the Denouncing of God's Anger and Judgements Against Sinners. Well we have moved on a long way from that very grim service but it did serve to remind those brave souls who attended that we are all sinners and even as Christians we fall short of the mark. A parish newsletter from some other church invited parishioners to a similar communal service of penance and said 'if you don't have any sins, bring a friend who does'. That will strike a chord perhaps because sometimes we think we are all right but we are very well aware of the faults and failings of others but the Bible makes it clear that we have all sinned and fallen short of the glory of God.

But the good news is that Jesus has dealt with all our sin and we have forgiveness through his death. That is why these words from 1 John are such good news. We have an advocate with the Father. The word here translated advocate is the same word *'paracletos'* which is used of the Holy Spirit and translated Comforter. The *paracletos* is one who stands beside us and pleads our case. Jesus pleads for us sinners rather like a solicitor pleading the case for his clients. He speaks up for us. The picture is of the righteous one standing beside us.

But more than that, says John, He is the propitiation for our sins. In the RSV the word is translated 'expiation'. Expiation and Propitiation are not words we regularly use around the breakfast table although you may use them round the Sunday lunch table today. They actually mean Atonement which is only slightly more likely to be used in everyday 21st-century conversation. Very simply, atonement means making 'at one'. Jesus through his death made us at one with God.

The Day of Atonement was the day on which sacrifice was made for the sins of the people and was the only day on which the Jewish High Priest entered the Holy of Holies in the Jewish Temple. He confessed the sins of the people over a goat which was then driven out into the wilderness as a sign of the people's sin being taken away.

When Jesus dies the New Testament writers see him as taking upon himself the sin of mankind. It was this burden of sin which led him to cry 'My God, my God why have you forsaken me' as the sin of mankind cut him off from God. When he cried 'It is finished' it was the work of atonement which was finished. It was as if my sins and your sins were heaped on Jesus and he dealt with them on the Cross, so that you and I could be at one with God and have forgiveness for all our failings. When Jesus died we are told that the curtain in the temple which kept the people away from the Holy of Holies was torn in two, as the barrier of sin had been dealt with by Jesus who had made expiation for the sins of the whole world and given us the opportunity through faith to be at one with God once more.

The Vicar was scheduled to be preaching this morning, but he gave me the opportunity to preach a farewell sermon today in his place as there were no other available slots. I am a substitute preacher. I am preaching in the Vicar's place. Over the years, evangelicals have called the death of Jesus a substitutionary atonement as Jesus died in our place for our sins. Whatever you believe about the substitutionary atonement doctrine, the New Testament writers certainly believed it and rejoiced that Jesus had made the once and for all sacrifice for sin.

From this we can know that through confession of our sins and trust in and obedience to the commands of Jesus, we have forgiveness for our sins. This is the good news for today and for always. When we sin we have an advocate, Jesus Christ the righteous, and he is the propitiation for our sins, and not for ours only but also for the sins of the whole world.

Someone asked Charles Dickens what is the best short story in the English language. His reply was 'The Prodigal Son'. I agree it is the best story in the Bible because it tells us of God's love for us however much we have let him down and gone wrong. We can still come back and confess our sins and be forgiven and be accepted as his child who is loved just as much as ever.

The most memorable talk I have heard in all my years at St Mary's included a modern-day Prodigal parable and I would like to tell it for you again this morning. A well-known politician had a daughter who in her teens went the way of many of that age and went off and did her own thing and got into a number of compromising situations and featured very scandalously in a glossy magazine. Whilst her father took his place in a Conservative Cabinet she had moved up to Scotland and joined the Anti-Capitalist League. Because of her lifestyle and the embarrassment she had caused her parents there had been no contact for a number of years. Then one day she realized that perhaps it was time to be reconciled to her parents but she realized she had caused them so much pain that they might not want to see her. She dared not telephone them so she wrote her father a letter saying she would be travelling down to London by train and would like to meet up with her father again after years of separation. She said she realized he might not want to see her but if he was willing to see her he should put a white handkerchief in the apple tree in the garden which was beside the railway line in Hertfordshire. If she saw a white handkerchief she would make contact with her father and mother. On the day of her train journey the train reached the Hertfordshire border and she began to feel very nervous. She was talking to a fellow passenger and asked him to look out for an apple tree which they would pass after a certain station, after some green railings, and could he see if there was a white handkerchief in the apple tree. When she knew that the train had passed the green railings and should be beyond her parents' garden, she asked her travelling companion if he had seen a handkerchief. 'No', he replied, 'but I did see a tree totally covered in white sheets, tablecloths, tea towels and a man standing on a ladder waving an enormous white flag.'

Jesus will forgive us all our sins if we come to him and ask him to. One of the most memorable sermons I ever preached was in a small Warwickshire village in front of a congregation of about a dozen people. The set reading for the day was John 8:1–11 which is the account of the woman taken in adultery. At this village church they used the New English Bible in which that story is printed in small print at the bottom of the page. My sermon was prepared on the woman taken in adultery – not the easiest subject for a small country church – but the churchwarden after announcing the reading as John 8:1–11 proceeded to read the large print which of course was verses 12 onwards leaving

GEOFFREY PARKINSON

me with a dilemma. Well, I resolved it somehow without telling the churchwarden he had read the wrong passage and read the account of the woman taken in adultery from the pulpit. The point of the incident is that Jesus did not condemn the woman. He simply said 'Let him who is without sin among you cast the first stone', and they all quietly slipped away leaving Jesus alone with the woman. His last words were that he did not condemn her either but she should sin no more. Forgiveness is available to all no matter what they have done.

Even King David was a great sinner. Because of his lust for Bathsheba he arranged for her husband Uriah to be put in the front of the battle so that he would be killed. This evil act and his subsequent remorse and forgiveness was the basis of David's rich understanding of the nature of God's forgiveness which we see in the Psalms. Even St Paul could describe himself as the greatest of all sinners, and he knew that he had been forgiven much which he showed by his ardent love for his Saviour in the years of his ministry.

In his epistles Paul writes that we are justified by faith, which is the basis of our faith. Justification means quite simply 'Just as if I had never sinned.' We do sin but through the love and atonement of Jesus we are treated by God just as if we had never sinned. That is the meaning of our comfortable words – because Jesus has died for us we are forgiven completely if we have faith in Him.

Pam and I once went to see Ken Dodd in Blackpool shortly after we were married. During his act he sang his well-known song, 'Happiness, happiness, the greatest gift that I possess is happiness.' Well, this morning I would change the words to 'Forgiveness, Forgiveness, the greatest gift that I possess is Forgiveness.'

Horace Bushnall put it a little more philosophically when he wrote 'Forgiveness is man's deepest need and highest achievement.'

But there is a big BUT to all of this. We must be forgiving of others if we are to truly experience all the benefits of Jesus' atonement. As the Lord's Prayer reminds us, 'Forgive us our sins as we forgive others their sins.' Jesus tells us that unless we forgive others their sins then God will not forgive us our sins. That was the message of the parable of the king and his servant, where you will remember his servant owed the king 10,000 talents. The king said the servant and his family should be sold into slavery but the servant pleaded for mercy and the king let him off his debt. However the servant was owed a minute amount by a fellow servant who he insisted should be thrown into jail. When the king heard of his servant's unforgiving nature he put him in jail and Jesus warned that unless we forgive those who sin against us, then God will not forgive our sins. The parable was part of the answer to Peter when he asked 'How often shall I forgive my brother?' The first part of Jesus' answer was 70 times 7 which meant always. There is no day off from being forgiving.

Now you may say to me, 'This is wonderful news about forgiveness but I don't really feel forgiven.' Someone asked Martin Luther 'Do you feel you have been forgiven?' And he answered 'No, but I'm *sure* because there's a God in Heaven.' In other words it is not a matter of whether we *feel* forgiven but we *can trust the promise of God*. John in his epistle goes on to say that the proof of our forgiveness is our obedience to the commandments of Jesus – not the state of our feelings, not the state of our faith, but our obedience to the commandments. That is our response to our acceptance of God's promise to forgive. It is his promise which is the basis of our rejoicing this morning.

A Christian doctor in Scotland was very lenient with his poor patients, and when he found that it was difficult for them to pay his fees he wrote in red ink across the record of their indebtedness the one word – 'Forgiven.' This was such a frequent occurrence that his case-book had few pages where the red letters did not appear. After his death his executors thought the doctor's estate would be greatly benefited if some of the 'Forgiven' debts could be collected. After unsuccessful applications to the poor patients, the executors took legal proceedings to recover the amounts. But when the judge examined the casebook and saw the word 'Forgiven' cancelling the entry he said that there was no tribunal in the land that could force payment of the accounts marked 'Forgiven' and he dismissed the case.

Jesus our advocate stands beside us holding the casebook of our Christian lives with the word 'Forgiven' written in red against every past, present and future instance of when we have got it wrong. Our heavenly Father treats us therefore just as if we had never sinned and we share the righteousness of Jesus. Therefore let us show our love and thankfulness in going and seeking to sin no more and obeying His commandments.

Sermon for Trinity Sunday

ANTHONY BIRD

Anthony Bird, a priest in the Church of England and a GP working in Balsall Heath, Birmingham was born in 1931, the son of a parish priest with a considerable reputation as a conscientious preacher. After school and conscription into the army he read classics, 'Greats', and then theology at Oxford. Ordination beckoned and took him to Cuddesdon Theological College, then to a curacy at St Mary's, Stafford, where he learnt two principles of preaching. 'The first from the late Canon Dudley Hodges was about direct communication with one's congregation. He expected his curates to abandon their sermon scripts before entering the pulpit. And from the late Revd Peter Wyld it was integrity of style, and an embargo on clericism, cliché and jargon.'

He was called back to Cuddesdon as chaplain by (the now Bishop) Edward Knapp-Fisher and retained there as Vice-Principal by the late Archbishop Robert Runcie, a model of preaching. In 1964 wholly unforeseen circumstances led him to Birmingham to study medicine and he became a priest-doctor.

'For the past 30 years the interaction of medicine and theology has been the focus of my vocation as a priest. Working for most of that time as a GP in Balsall Heath, an inner-city area of Birmingham, I have concentrated on the personal and organizational consequences of that interaction, linked to regular liturgical involvement in the parish church of St Paul's where my practice is situated and some of its patients worship. On one morning a week I teach (as a volunteer) in a nearby, mainly Muslim, primary school.'

It was during a six-year spell as Principal of The Queen's (ecumenical theological) College, Birmingham in the 1970s that with others he founded the practice where he still works. Designed to promote a vision of 'the human face of medicine' it has given birth to significant NHS innovations like patient access to their medical records, the Nurse Practitioner role, and patient-advocacy. His other occupations include the study of music, sailing and walking, a bit of bridge and, primarily, family and friends.

The subject of the present sermon, 'The Trinity', was chosen for him as he was asked to preach on 18 June, Trinity Sunday.

'No such clarity of theme enlightened me one Sunday in the summer of 1963 when I was to preach at the 9:30 Cuddesdon parish communion. Robert Runcie had detailed me first to conduct the 8 a.m. communion service at Great Milton church, a two-mile walk distant, the incumbent being on hol-

iday. All efforts of composition had failed to produce the merest vestige of a sermon and I was staking all on the beauty of that fine summer walk to inspire. It needed to: the Cuddesdon congregation consisting of college and village was awesomely discerning, and the permitted maximum of seven-and-a-half minutes preaching time would lay any waffle cruelly bare. I arrived at Great Milton church in a Keatsian haze. Desperation was averted by a problem. The verger was prostrate in bed with a hangover, inaccessible along with key, the church locked. "We could go by car to the neighbouring church" was one suggestion from the ten folk now gathered in the churchyard at 7:58. My first inspiration of the day struck: "Perhaps we could use some-one's house?" To hand was the wife of an Eton housemaster. Her large house and drawing room across the road, albeit showing signs of last night's party (probably not the one attended by the verger), lay at our disposal including half a bottle of left-over red wine.

'Thus the Eucarist was celebrated, and it was while I mustered my kit amid an increasing tide of anxiety about my impending assignment, now only a 30-minute walk away, that our hostess said to another woman pre-sent, and clearly from a less privileged quarter of the village: "I've seen you in church many times, but I'm sorry to say I've never spoken to you until now". There it was. Holy Communion. "Gospel for today, they've lost the key at Great Milton" – text of one of the most enjoyable sermons I've ever preached. And the congregation? They really laughed.'

IN BIRMINGHAM SOME YEARS AGO a dozen or so men and women visited the Central Mosque in course of their training to become priests. Leaving their shoes at the entrance they were invited to sit on a carpet where they faced the Imam. His opening works of wel-come to them were: 'You're Christians; so explain the Trinity to me.' No soft landing that: top of the agenda – God matters.

Fortunately no such blast is in store for us here. The challenge of preaching about the Trinity on Trinity Sunday can be avoided. Preach-ers are apt to feel guilty if they evade it; their audiences are not neces-sarily the wiser if they don't. Yet the challenge is there, and in the absence of any Imam the Prayer Book reminds us that 'we worship one God in Trinity and Trinity in Unity. The Father is God, the Son is God and the Holy Spirit is God, and yet they are not three Gods but one God.' And stretching ahead: more than twenty Sundays after Trinity. The Trinity matters. The Christian God matters. It is not just to Mus-lims that we owe an explanation. They at least ask for one. Others, Christians included, have given up on what they regard as abstract and incomprehensible rubbish. Surely once a year we should ask ourselves whether we agree, or even care.

One way of telling whether a ship's course is steady is to glance back at its wake and, if you're lucky, at landmarks still visible astern. Is your track straight as you move through the waves? So, glancing back ourselves as we progress to the Trinity season we see immediately behind us Ascension and Pentecost, St Luke's special territory. This sympathetic doctor and teacher travelled all over the Aegean and Adriatic seas and knew a thing or two about sailing. Fortunately he is at hand to advise us on the best approach to our destination. 'Faced with a fierce headwind like the Imam's interrogation' he counsels us 'you won't make headway sailing directly into it. Tack instead, zigzag, turn the wind to your advantage. Yes, the Trinity is your destination – indeed God matters, but change course to a new bearing, first toward Ascensiontide until you've got one of its main features clearly in view: people matter.'

An attractive approach maybe, more manageable, but will it work? 'People matter.' Isn't that a paradoxical route to take when your goal is the mystery of the living God? But paradox, Luke tells us, is precisely his point, for what did people say when Christ forgave and healed a paralytic man? They said in amazement 'we have seen paradoxical things today'. The translators preferred 'strange things', but 'paradoxical' is what Luke wrote. Paradox: the opposite of what you'd expect – what happened when Christ came on the scene. If you find the Ascension of Christ hard to understand, try the paradox and think descent instead. The disciples did. 'While they beheld he was taken up; and a cloud received him out of their sight. And while they looked steadfastly toward heaven as he went up, two men stood by them in white apparel which also said, "ye men of Galilee why stand ye gazing up into heaven?"' It was pointless to look up; better to get down, so they made their descent from the Mount of Olives to Jerusalem (Luke 5:26, Acts 1:9–12).

What went through their minds on the way down Luke doesn't tell us. At least not directly. But he has told us how previously they had climbed another mountain with Jesus. Then as now there had been fog. 'There came a cloud and overshadowed them: and they feared as they entered the cloud.' Then the voice, 'This is my beloved Son, hear him.' Luke would have us know that what Jesus talked about with Moses and Elijah was the death awaiting him below in Jerusalem. The glory of that ascent was to become apparent in the descent which followed.

'When they were come down from the hill, many people met him. And, behold, a man of the company cried out, saying, Master, I beseech thee, look upon my son: for he is my only child. And, lo, a spirit taketh him, and he suddenly crieth out; and it teareth him that he foameth again, and bruising him hardly departeth from him.' With his physician's brilliant description of the epileptic boy and in the pathos of Christ the only Son, called on to heal another's only child, Luke makes the descent to where people matter. People like the despised taxman, the adulterers, society's lepers, the exile and outcast in every person.

There was no one, Luke is saying, who didn't matter to Christ, witness the crucified thief; witness today those daily crucified by the media. 'Certainly this was a righteous man,' said the centurion who supervised the crucifixions. But by then all righteousness and compassion were snuffed out by a darkness which eclipsed that God-forsaken place, as it still eclipses the places of ultimate descent where people matter for nothing – Milton's bottomless perdition. (Luke 9:37–39; 23:47).

The Ascension makes no sense without descent to the lowest and lowliest areas of human experience. Here, even matters of least significance are found to matter. Here, for example, is an old man disabled in his legs. He walks haltingly with a stick, but can't stand or sit unaided. He is at a huge party for Asian elderly folk, most of them with disabilities of varying degree, mental and physical. His English consists only of a few essential words. Next to him an able-bodied person who can't speak Urdu. Conversation between them – nil. After some time the Asian man prods the person next to him and says 'want piss'. He has to be got to his feet and then later from off the lavatory seat and have his dress adjusted.

Tacking again we now head for Pentecost and Luke's next paradox. To experience this celebration of God's power at work we have to steer a course that brings powerlessness, weakness, paralysis clearly into view. Our own and our church's. Which is what the first disciples had to do. Returning from the Mount of Olives and the Ascension they were under orders to wait, not to rush about being responsible for people however much they mattered. So they waited, vulnerable and powerless like patients, and 'continued with one accord in prayer and supplication' (Acts 1:14). There was much to pray about. Their performance had been pathetic, cowardly. They had seen the power of money, ambition, violence, jealousy, fear mattering more than people to the point of destroying them, and they had been complicit. Then, contrary to any expectation, a new sense of their worth was born with the conviction that Christ was alive. They found themselves powerless to put themselves beyond the power of God's love. They themselves mattered to God: this was living. This was news which had to be shared and spread about.

It's time for our last tack as we make for harbour. Maybe we feel confident enough to face the Imam or anyone else who asks us to explain the Trinity. With thanks to our saintly doctor and navigating instructor we can say 'The answer is paradox. The explanation of the Trinity is that the Trinity cannot be explained. The true God is to be experienced, not defined'.

But we're not quite there; mooring in harbour can go wrong and we must navigate to a safe berth. Steering carefully towards it we recognize the familiar place, for it is where we began. We reach our destination and berth place, the home which is Creator, origin and end.

Harbour, voyage to the deep and distant sea, power of wind and waves: three experiences vital to the one undertaking. But the understanding of these three is only to be had in the single undertaking, as in life and love, as in God.

It was after starting on this sermon that I was required to attend an exhibition aimed (according to its brochure) to promote positive images of Asian older people, particularly those with physical and mental health problems. It was mounted in a huge hall in an unlikely location for a social event of some scale. Factories, warehouses, garages, railway lines all around. Flanking the hall were the usual display stalls presenting the work of various agencies, Day Centres, Housing Assistance, Stroke Support Association, Alzheimer's Society, Sikh religious centres, to name a few. The body of the hall was arranged with tables where two or three hundred elderly Asian men and women were sitting with their carers. A few were dancing to the live band music. The atmosphere was festive; balloons and occasionally singing; and of course food and drink. Speeches followed in each of the main Asian languages and I admired the resonant voice, even if I couldn't understand the words of a star actor from *My Beautiful Laundrette*. The place was vibrant and powerfully conveyed its theme 'Tales of the elderly through their own voices'. It was here that I was called on by my neighbour at the table – 'Want piss'. Eventually I left taking a few brochures for colleagues. Excellent though these documents were, they couldn't match the real flavour of this lively party. Reaching the end of the street while things were still in full swing, I was suddenly amazed. The street is named 'Upper Trinity Street'. It's not far from St Martin's-in-the-Bull Ring, and as I passed this Anglican mosque I wondered how we might welcome a visiting group of Muslims and somehow celebrate the Trinity with them.

Strength to the Weary

STEPHEN HANCE

The Revd Stephen Hance, 34, is Vicar of the Church of the Ascension in Balham Hill, south London. He is married to Jacqui, who works full time bringing up their three children, Natalie, Simeon and Isaac. A banker for two years after leaving school, he then studied for a degree in sociology at Portsmouth Polytechnic and spent a year as a civil servant before training for the Anglican ordained ministry at St John's Theological College in Nottingham. While there he also gained BTh and MA degrees. He then served a curacy for three years at St Jude's, Southsea, was Team Vicar of St Saviour's, Hanley Road in Islington for three years, and has been Vicar of Balham Hill since 1999.

'*I grew up in a Christian family, and asked Jesus into my life as a child aged 5. Between the ages of 15 and 17 I went through a period of examining my faith for myself, and made a re-commitment during that time, which involved a powerful experience of the Holy Spirit. My faith has continued to develop through the experience of theological training and ministry.*'

*He initially sensed God calling him to ordination at the age of 17, and this sense has never left him – he says it is stronger now than ever. '*I love my work, and enjoy the sense that I am doing what I have been created to do.*'*

When he preached the sermon published here, he was following the Lectionary. On other occasions, he does choose preaching themes – usually in series – according to what he perceives to be the present needs of the congregation.

'*I am quite sure that preaching is still relevant, but it is probably harder work in our fast-paced culture. People need to have their attention captured and kept – but good preaching can do that. The Anglican liturgy for Holy Communion, which we still use at some of our services, places the sermon relatively early. Given the choice, I prefer to preach towards the end of the service, with only some sung worship, or prayer, or silence to follow, to allow people to reflect on what they have heard.*'

*The shortest time he has ever had to prepare a sermon was during his time in Islington. '*I had invited the General Secretary of one of the Anglican mission societies to preach, and I was planning to lead the service. Immediately before the service, our visitor was setting up a display of materials about his society, when he fell from the top of a pool table upon which he was standing to balance a display stand. Landing with a thump, he broke his wrist and had to be whisked off to the local hospital, leaving me to preach off-the-cuff a few minutes later.*' Outside religion, his interests are music, cinema, theatre, holidays, family.*

209

Text: Matthew 11:28–30 (Isaiah 40:25–31).

JESUS SAID: 'Come to me, all you who are weary and burdened, and I will give you rest. Take my yoke upon you and learn from me, for I am gentle and humble in heart, and you will find rest for your souls. For my yoke is easy and my burden is light.'

We live in a society where, despite or perhaps because of all the technological advances of our age, many people are more tired than ever before. Some people go through years of their lives feeling constantly exhausted. Many people work harder and longer now than they did a few years ago. Many people commute further than they did. Many more people have to do more than one job just to make ends meet. Pressures on the home and family may be more intense as well, as more families function with just one parent, and increasingly we live away from extended family members who might have helped with childcare and so on. Even children are under more pressure as schools compete to get the best exam results. Even young children do more homework and attend more after-school clubs than ever before. So the pressure is on, and as a result we are increasingly a society which is constantly tired.

Unfortunately the church isn't immune from these pressures. A generation or two back most church members would have attended worship on Sunday and probably done nothing more. That's not true now. Many churches are busier than ever before. Committed, active church members may find themselves out at church meetings maybe two or three evenings in a week, with Sunday on top. For some people church has become another place of work, not a place of renewal and recreation.

And yet Jesus says 'Come to me, all you who are weary and burdened, and I will give you rest.'

Church is supposed to be, amongst other things, a place where we experience the rest that Jesus offers. It is supposed to be a place where we are renewed and refreshed, equipped to serve God in our workplace and our neighbourhood in the week ahead. Yet how can it be like that, when church is also such a hive of activity, when there are so many important and worthwhile things to do, and when it feels sometimes as if we are always being encouraged to do more?

You may be wondering at this point where I am going to end up. Am I going to close down half this church's programme? Am I going to tell you all not to come to too many church meetings, to pull out of the things you are involved in? Well, no; I'm not going to do either of those things – although it may be that there are things we shouldn't be attempting at this point, and it may well be that there are people who should be spending more evenings with their family or their friends or even in prayer or Bible reading rather than coming to so many church activities. What I do want to do is first of all to try and help each of us to make wise decisions about how we spend our own time, and secondly to concentrate on those parts of the church programme which will help us to experience the rest that Jesus offers in our own lives.

How do you spend your free time? By free time I mean the hours that are left when you are not at work, and when you do not *have* to be doing things for your family like taking children to school, doing housework and so on. Some of us are very protective of whatever spare hours we have. We feel we have earned the right to relax, and we don't want to commit ourselves to anything else. Others of us gladly give much of our time to various church activities, perhaps forgetting that we need rest too. In most churches there are some people who seem to be burning themselves out for Jesus perhaps even neglecting their marriage or their children for church activities, whilst others will simply not get involved in anything other than Sunday worship.

The principle which may help us to get this right is the Sabbath. I don't want to get into the debate about how we use Sundays, but the idea of the Sabbath teaches us that there is a time for work, a time for rest, a time for worship, and so on. There needs to be a balance to our lives. For some of us that will mean taking more time to rest, or more time to be at home with our family, or relaxing with friends. For some of us it will mean spending less time doing those things so we can be more involved in the life of the church. The result should be that the work of the church is spread amongst more people, with fewer burned-out Christians about.

But, although this is important, I don't believe it is the most important part of what Jesus says. He doesn't say 'Take it easy, everyone, and then you'll have rest' or 'Share the work out better, and then you'll have rest.' He says, 'Come to me, if you're tired and weary, and I will give you rest.' What should you do if you're tired and weary? Come to Jesus. This is not a passage about time management. It's a passage about a relationship. It's not a self-help principle. It's an invitation.

And this invitation is the central message of the New Testament, the heart of the gospel. Jesus invites us to come to him. Not just to find out more about him, although that is important. Not just to try to be like him, or to obey his teachings, although those things are important too. Not just to do his work. But to come to him. To get to know him. To experience his presence. To be changed by his love. To be empowered by his Spirit. To know him.

Why are there so many exhausted Christians in the church? Because we've turned this upside down. We try to do the work of Jesus, to obey the commands of Jesus, to study the words of Jesus – and of course we need to do those things. But we do those things instead of trying to get to know Jesus. We don't spend time consciously in his presence, worshipping him, letting our thoughts dwell on him, allowing him to speak to us, to change us, to renew and resource us. So we become dry and empty, and God's work quickly becomes a burden to us.

I'm speaking from experience here. It's so easy to become so preoccupied with the Lord's work that we almost lose sight of the Lord himself. At one point in my ministry I felt quite overwhelmed with some of the pressures of the work, and I prayed about this many times, saying to God 'How can you expect me to deal with all of this?' Finally I felt God was showing me something. An intense pressure on the outside of something has to be met by an equal and opposite pressure on the inside. In other words, to cope with increasing demands of ministry from outside, I needed an increased measure of the Holy Spirit on the inside. This sounds straightforward, but it isn't, because when we feel under pressure from outside, we tend to spend less time in prayer, less time reading the Bible, less time worshipping God, less time seeking the presence and the power of the Spirit. Unfortunately this is what happens to many Christians. As their ministry in the church expands over the years, so their relationship with God becomes increasingly fragile. They end up working for God, but not knowing him.

Recently I felt that God was telling me that in order to avoid this happening to me, I need to spend the first part of each day with him in worship and prayer and reading, so I'm trying to do that. I know it won't always happen, but I'm trying to make sure it happens as often as possible. I need to do that, because if I don't stay fresh with God, I can't do his work in the way he wants; I can't hear his voice. Paul Yonggi Cho, who pastors the largest church in the world, spends three to four hours a day in prayer, and he is often asked how he finds time to pray so much when he has so many people to pastor. His reply is that he could not pastor such a large church if he didn't.

Now, I'm not holding this up as an example to all of us – clergy are lucky in that they can plan their own timetable to a certain extent. Others can't. But the principle is the important thing, that we experience the rest that Jesus offers as we come to him, as we spend time with him, as we allow the Holy Spirit to fill us and equip us for the things he wants us to do.

There are lots of great activities in the life of any lively church; but at the heart of the church's life must be those points at which we meet with Jesus, grow to know and love him more, and experience his renewing work. That means worship and fellowship and prayer. I want worship services at this church to be places where we meet with Jesus; not just learn about him, but meet with him, hear from him, be cleansed and renewed by him. The reading we had from Isaiah chapter 40 contains a promise, that 'those who hope in the Lord will renew their strength. They will soar on wings like eagles'. An eagle doesn't have to flap desperately to stay up in the air. Instead he finds out where the wind is blowing, and he lets the wind carry him.

We don't have to keep flapping anxiously to keep going when we accept Jesus' invitation to come to him. Instead we can allow the wind of the Holy Spirit to carry us. That's the way to live and minister in God's strength, not our own. That's the way to experience the rest that Jesus promises to those who come to him.

Harsh Words in the Temple

LAWRIE ADAM

The Revd Lawrie Adam, 62, incumbent of St James' Church, Ashton-under-Lyme, Lancashire is also a highly successful television producer. His wife, Wendy, runs her own theme tearoom and museum in Ashton. They have two daughters, Tracey, a film producer and Fiona, a housewife and mother. In 1983, after 25 years in professional showbusiness he was ordained. In 1987 he pioneered a video production company, called BDTV, for the Church of England. He has been producer, director or scriptwriter on more than 150 TV and video programmes and has also worked as a comedian, theatrical agent and theatre producer. He set up Cranleigh Communications (UK) Ltd in 1995 to make and distribute films globally.

Stars he has worked with include Ken Dodd, Dame Vera Lynn, Sir Harry Secombe and a host of others. He has appeared on Channel 4's 'Big Breakfast' and in New York's Time *magazine this year. He also specializes in making programmes dealing with social problems.*

'I was performing in a Ken Dodd show in 1976 on the Isle of Man and was converted as a result of the "Word" becoming flesh. A non-Christian flew in and a believer flew out,' he says. He describes God as his 'sole agent'. He says, 'He is absolutely brilliant! I am constantly reminded as to what a great privilege it is to work for Him. I have worked in the leafy-green parishes, I am now in an area of violence, vandalism (on my third car in three years!) and depression but there are always great moments when my agent and I witness a triumph.

'I always say that regarding parishes, the cast remains the same, but the scenery changes. Many folk have it seems a skin less than most and can misinterpret something sometimes. I suppose I took this opportunity to explain this and, as I often do, draw on personal experiences which have a certain truthful ring about them. After all I am only following the Master. He would raise his head above the listening crowd and use a visible example. I am always intrigued by this portion of scripture. It reminds us that although we are called the 'salt of the earth' we are never required to be the sugar of the church!'

He believes the sermon should follow the Gradual Hymn and then the Gospel. 'Like a good play, or a good book, or a film, everything has to be timed correctly and the pace is vital. All are part of the whole and should complement each other reaching a high point which is in the communion. There are

important markers along the way and a sermon is one of the main contribu-
tors. It is an opportunity for God, through his priest, to reach out and touch a
soul. However, the priest may never even know!'

Once he used an unusual preaching prop. 'I introduced a ventriloquist doll
and called him Revd Jake McNab. I thought it would be amusing and assist
me to get the point across. He ended up being invited by the Bishop to preach
at Manchester Cathedral, to appear on four network TV programmes and
even invited to New York to take part in a Christmas Special. He very kindly
always asked me to go with him, which was nice.'

When not 'vicaring' he spends his time making video programmes about a
wide range of subjects anywhere in the country. 'I am very interested in our
future generations and sometimes feel we are letting them down. The great-
est thrill for me is to be surrounded by young folk and have the privilege of
being able to make them laugh. I have two schools in my parish and wish I
could have more time to spend with them. My wife and I obtained an old and
disused tailors' shop in 1998. We managed to turn it into a 44-seater Tea-
room and Museum in the middle of Ashton-under-Lyne. My day off is a
Thursday and I am to be found there with my silk waistcoat on acting as a
waiter. We cater for a generation that has been overlooked. They dine from
bone china (circa 1930s), drink 'proper' coffee, excellent tea and listen to
lovely music from a bygone era. Even the wallpaper is original 1940s. We call
it Wendy's Memory Lane Tearooms and Museum. Everyone, whatever their
religion or creed is most welcomed, and God is colour blind.'

Text: Matthew 21:1–13.

IT WAS 1970 and I was producing a summer show for a very important London Management at the Spa Theatre, Bridlington, in Yorkshire. We had been rehearsing very hard. The stars of the show, Joe
(piano) Henderson and The Kay Sisters, had finished their part and
departed. The remainder of the cast then brought the rehearsal to a
close.

Bearing in mind the show was to open the following night I was far
from pleased! As I stood there in the centre aisle of the stalls in this
lovely old theatre, I could easily imagine the place filled with a thousand people. In the front row would be seated the London Management judging whether or not their confidence and trust in me had
been rightly placed, for they had allowed me free reign.

Well, the orchestra finally stopped, and the performers gathered
along the footlights. I noted the anxious little faces preparing for my
comments. I became aware of a gentle hand exerting light pressure on
my arm. It was my wife, Wendy; she was the choreographer. She whis-
pered in my ear, 'Easy now darling.'

I knew I would have to stage some harsh words. They were not trying hard enough. I knew they were well capable of a higher standard.

I walked slowly forward; I knew the silence was deafening. What I said I am now ashamed to say is unrepeatable in this house of God! Yes, I swore and took the Lord's name in vain, finishing with something like 'And if they see this lot they will ******* well crucify me!'

A hush descended upon the plush auditorium. A hush that is all but the sudden sharp intake of breath from behind me. I turned round and came face to face with a clergyman; the vicar from the Anglican church down the road. He was the 'Theatre Chaplain' He stared at me and said, 'Mr Adam that was absolutely awful! I did come here to wish you all luck and to introduce myself but instead I am going home to pray for you!' With that he marched away. I called out after him, ' I love them all really you know'. He didn't reply. But the truth is I really did love this hard-working team and they knew I did. My choice of language was wrong – it was harsh. But to those who knew me knew also that the measure of violence was the measure of the need to sound alarm. Here is an example of how easy it is for harsh words to be misunderstood.

There are many people who think of Our Lord Jesus as permanently meek and mild and who are being quite shocked by the portion of this morning's Gospel where Jesus enters the temple and drives out all who were engaged in buying and selling. Violently overturning the tables of the money-changers and the stools of the dealers selling pigeons. Imagine it . . . Pigeons screeching and fluttering, money flying and rolling everywhere, angry people shouting, frightened folk screaming, and this young man saying sternly to them, 'It is written in the scriptures that God said, "My temple will be called a house of prayer" but you are making it a hideout for thieves!'

The measure of Our Lord's harshness to the Pharisees was the measure of the thickness of their protective armour of hypocrisy against his disturbing truths, and the measure of his concern that they should learn the truth before it was too late.

If you saw your little daughter or granddaughter walking backwards towards an unguarded fire you wouldn't say, 'Oh! Excuse me dear, I hate to interrupt your little game, but there is a fire behind you.' Come off it! You would very likely shout in your loudest voice, 'Look out! Mind that fire!' She would probably cry in fright at your tone, but it would be your love for her that prompted the urgency, and might well have sounded like rough speech.

Jesus, who possessed the gentlest lips in the whole world, lips that said the kindest most loving things to many a sinner, also said the most terrifying things about sin the world has ever heard. In the most tender of all parables, 'The prodigal son', in which the boy is freely forgiven after years of sin and the relationship with his father completely restored, you will read these words, 'For this my son was dead and is alive again. He was lost and is found.' 'Dead'; 'Lost'; these are the words that describe what sin can do to us, unless in God's mercy we are found and restored. We must accept some harsh words sometimes as a measure of loving concern.

I remember once walking my dog along the cliffs at North Shore Blackpool. Suddenly a man shouted harshly at me warning me of a dangerous part that was crumbling. I thank God that he was violent enough to stop me. If a man who can see walks in broad daylight right over a cliff we don't say, 'Oh! Wasn't life cruel to him.' More like, 'Why didn't he look where he was going, the fool, surely he's heard of the law of gravity!'

In the same way surely we have heard of the law of morality, and some of the harsh words warn us with a terrible vehemence to 'look where we are going'. It's always a good idea to take the time periodically to check that you are journeying on a good straight pathway. Are you getting peace of mind from what you are doing? Do you feel that you are on the road that leads to what God desires for you? Stop and look back at the progress you have made. Think of the people known to you whose lives Jesus has changed. Try to imagine your own life without Him in it! Think of some of the things you perhaps first thought of as harsh at the time and try to understand them more clearly now.

Remember Peter the fisherman? Well, he didn't understand very much either. He saw all the harsh events, he heard all the harsh sayings, and in fact one of them was directed at him. But from a cursing, swearing fisherman, he became a saint. I know a certain cursing, swearing, theatrical producer who will never become a saint, but he did become a clergyman . . . a man of God.

Some three years after the Bridlington escapade my wife and I happened to be in Bridlington again. We even paid a visit to the theatre chaplain's church. The service finished, he stood at the door saying goodbye to his departing flock, and then we came. He said 'Goodness me, it's you, well I am surprised.' I told him since seeing him last his prayers had been answered. That I had been called to the ministry and would be starting training. He sank down on a pew and gasped . . . 'Oh! thanks be to God . . . thanks be to God.'

Free At Last
The Winning Sermon for 1999

SHMULEY BOTEACH

Rabbi Shmuley Boteach, Times *Preacher of the Year 2000. Born in 1966, Rabbi Boteach is an internationally-known author, thinker, and the founder and dean of the L'Chaim Society, a high-profile education organization that hosts world leaders lecturing on values-based leadership. Rabbi Boteach founded the organization at Oxford University where he served as rabbi for eleven years becoming 'something of a legend' at the University.*

He is never long out of the headlines. Recently he has been in the news for taking Michael Jackson to synagogue, playing matchmaker to Roseanne's daughters with three Oxford scholars on her TV show, debating Larry Flynt or Jennifer Flowers on the loss of modesty in relationships, persuading Mikhail Gorbachev to light a public Hanukah menorah *and Boy George to lecture to Oxford students about repentance.*

Author of eleven books, including the international best-seller Kosher Sex *and* Dating Secrets of the Ten Commandments, *and the critically acclaimed* Moses of Oxford, *Rabbi Boteach's writings have featured in publications as diverse as* The Times *of London and* Playboy *magazine, which chose* Kosher Sex *as their main book selection for their 45th anniversary edition. His weekly essays have been distributed on the Internet for nearly a decade and are read by a vast following of thousands.*

A frequent guest on television and radio, he has appeared on most major British, American, South African, Australian, and Israeli television and radio shows and was the subject of a full hour documentary on the BBC's prestigious 'Everyman' series. In the United States he has appeared on The Today Show, Good Morning America, The View, Politically Incorrect, Leeza, Larry King Live, The Tonite Show, This Evening with Judith Regan, NBC Evening News, The Fox News Channel, MSNBC, The O'Reily Factor, The Howey Mandell Show, The Roseanne Show, Entertainment Tonight, Extra!, Inside Edition, and The Howard Stern show.

Some of the publications that have profiled Rabbi Boteach include Time *magazine,* Newsweek, The New York Times, The Washington Post, The L.A. Times, The Miami Herald, The New York Post, The New York Daily News, Entertainment Weekly, Maxim, Cosmopolitan, The Times, The Guardian, The Daily Telegraph, The Daily Mail, *and* The Chicago Tribune. *Rabbi Boteach was also the subject of a New York magazine cover story in February 2000.*

An internationally acclaimed speaker, he won the highly prestigious Times

Preacher of the Year Competition in London just days before the millennium, having placed as first runner-up the previous year.

In 1999 he moved his family to New York with his Australian wife Debbie and their six young children. There he opened a new branch of the L'Chaim Society and continues to lecture nationwide. His mission encompasses two main elements. The first is showing the relevance and efficacy of religious ideas in the mainstream culture – to 'show that religion can win arguments in the market-place of ideas.' He pursues this passion mostly through discussion and debate with influential mainstream thinkers like Prof Richard Dawkins, Prof Peter Atkins, Deepak Chopra, Larry Flynt, and Helen Gurley Brown. His second goal is to combat loneliness and to repair the great damage that has been done to the structure of marriage. Himself a child of divorce, and motivated by the fact that 50 per cent of children grow up in similar situations, he aims to battle what he views as 'a modern tragedy unfolding about which no one really seems to care'. He confronts these issues both in his published works and through his role as Matchmaker-in-Chief to Soulmate411.com, a leading online dating service.

'Winning the Times *Preacher of the Year Competition was by far the greatest professional honour of my life,' he says. 'Since the age of 16 I have wanted to be a global exponent of Judaism, and the platform generated with the honour of* Times *Preacher of the Year was indispensable in bringing me closer to that dream. G-d has been kind to me in allowing my relationship writings to reach a wide audience. But what is often overlooked is that those insights are delivered from the perspective of a rabbi. Judaism is inextricably linked in everything I say and do. Winning the competition, therefore, brought to the fore that I am a proponent of the Jewish spiritual tradition who believes that Judaism has untold riches to impart to this generation, and the world is much impoverished in having cast Judaism to its periphery.*

'The Americans made a big deal of my winning the competition. It appeared in all the major American papers, including the USA Today, *and was a big feature on CNN. I guess after having been told for two hundred years that Americans can't even speak English, they played on the fact that an American had beat the Brits at their own game. The fact that I had just lived 11 years in Britain was conveniently overlooked. And whereas in the past I had been invited on to the media mostly to discuss and debate issues pertaining to relationships, winning the competition incited a rash of invitations to debate and discuss the great religious issues of the day – requests that now come in frequently. I appear regularly on one of American Television's foremost debate programmes, CNN's* Larry King Live, *to debate religious issues. Winning the competition further brought many invitations to lecture to Christian groups around the world.*

'I chose the subject of my sermon – how religion has begun confining the spirit rather than liberating it – because of how much I love religion and how pained I am to see it slowly crumble in modern times. So many of us erroneously believe that religion declined due to the advance of science in general, and evolution in particular. Nothing could be further from the truth. Today's generation is secu-

lar out of convenience rather than conviction. Do you really think that modern men and women believe that watching four hours of Reality TV shows a day is better than engaging their hearts and souls in prayers to G-d? Or that reading Cosmo and GQ is more edifying than reading the Bible? Or that spending Saturdays and Sundays in the office is more ennobling that spending it with their children? Of course not. It's just that all the former examples are more exciting than what religion has to offer. It is amazing that religion, which engaged the minds and hearts of men and women for millennia, and which so comforted me after my parents' divorce, is seen as stultifying in today's day and age. Our first priority has got to be to reverse that. For if we don't, what will there be to inspire us? Money? Sex? Rock music?'

When he was thirteen years old, he discovered through a young and passionate mentor just how exciting religion could be. 'With his guidance I experienced religion to be an energy that pulsed through my veins and gave me life. And a sermon should in turn be the channel through which such dynamic energy and life is conducted to a congregation. Or to the world! Let us recall a time when religion brought us all high "up to the mountaintops" rather than shivering cold in the valleys. The silicone valleys, to be sure. Many Jews who go to synagogue twice a year on the High Holy Days do so out of guilt or a desire to preserve the tradition, not because they want to be in a relationship with God.'

He thinks sermons today are no longer as effective as they once were. 'The first reason for this is that we have forgotten their purpose. People use sermons today to teach. On the contrary – that's what lectures are all about. There is only one purpose for a sermon. And that is to uplift the congregation. To impart inspiration. The preacher is he or she who lifts the congregation to unimaginable heights, and then inspires them to make their own effort to stay there, rather than have the effect of the sermon quickly dissipate immediately thereafter. Which leads me to point number two. In order for this to happen, the preacher him or herself must first be moved by the spirit. If he or she is bored, or uninspired by their own words or choice of subject, how can they expect their congregants to even stay awake?'

A RABBI, a Cantor, and the President of a Synagogue are captured by cannibals. Each is given one wish before they become that evening's supper. The Rabbi says, 'All I want is to give one last sermon, just for an hour or two.' The Cantor jumps in, 'I want to sing one last composition, just for two or three hours, maybe days.' The President of the Synagogue turns to the chief cannibal and says, 'Please, shoot me first.'

We stand at the threshold of a new millennium which is of course a religious commemoration. But you would hardly know it. The greatest change to the world over the past thousand years is the death of religion. For ten centuries the world was G-d-intoxicated. Brilliant philosophers devoted themselves to fathoming the mind of G-d. Renaissance masters dedicated themselves to depicting the magnificence of G-d. And gifted composers applied themselves to praising the glory of G-d. And yet here we stand at a competition devoted to the best preachers in the land and how many outside this room really care? In the United States, even this year's Redneck Games, replete with the inspirational Mud-Belly flop and Watermelon-seed Spitting competitions, got televised. Perhaps we should have included a Preacher's swimsuit competition to excite greater interest. Or a Preacher Olympics with the 'Javelin Throw at the Infidel' as the main event.

Whereas our ancestors struggled to keep the faith amid poverty and persecution, we today struggle simply to stave off slumber in the Synagogue. I personally have developed a new pill called 'Preachagra' which keeps congregants upright through the sermon. How did we ever sink so low? Ladies and gentlemen, religion fell not because it was refuted, but because it became irrelevant, boring, oppressive, insipid. What every person wants – the greatest human need – is to feel intensely alive. We want to be inspired, unfettered, energetic, infinite. And in the absence of a meaningful spiritual high, the world has opted for superficial substitutes. Young people dance at nightclubs to feel exhilaration. They run to Wall Street to find excitement. They pursue the opposite sex to experience the thrill of the chase. And they cheer their favourite sports team to rise with the triumph of victory. That's why the Spice Girls and Manchester United arguably carry more influence among today's teenagers than all the world's clergy combined.

It wasn't always like this. Once upon a time, long, long, ago, mankind discovered the secret of freedom and ecstasy. Religion took off in the world by teaching men and women how to liberate the spirit. Ancient man, desperate and alone, labouring under the toil of hopelessness and helplessness, cried out to attach himself to something higher. He relied on religion to rescue him from a stultifying earth-centredness. Belief in G-d opened to man the infinite expanse of the cosmos. In so doing, religion made men and women feel intensely alive and gave them wings with which to soar.

To those burdened with bigotry and bias, religion roared that all men were created equal. To those hemmed in by the horrors of hatred, religion revealed the blessings of brotherhood. To troubled souls trapped in transgression, stymied by sin, fearing that their failings would condemn their futures, religion promised that penitence would purge them of their past.

A few years back a young and anguished husband came to see me. His newly-wed bride exposed to him that before their wedding she had had an abortion after a long sexual relationship with another man. Although she begged his forgiveness, the husband moved out of the house. 'The thought of her having become pregnant by another man is too painful. I just can't shake it.' I told him, 'Fool, that woman who had the abortion is not your wife. Your wife is someone else. She has repented of her past and in so doing has been created anew. Now go home to your bride and let your love for each other set your spirits free.'

Four millennia ago under the starlit heavens of Mesopotamia, G-d gave

Abraham the first-ever religious commandment: *'Lech Lecho'* Go out, break free. *'Me'artzecho'* from your community, representing peer-pressure and the desire to be popular. Pursue your convictions whatever the consequence. *'Mimoladetecha'* from your birthplace. Free yourself of your natural inborn, limitations – lethargy, laziness, the part of you that says, 'I can't.' *'Umibeis avicha'* your father's household. Unshackle yourself from the accumulated prejudices of generations. Abraham became not merely the father of religion, but the first free man that ever lived. Later, his children are liberated from the slavery of Egypt where they built pyramids, glorified temples of death. Religion liberates us from the slavery of working ourselves to death. A life of death where reading a stock report comes before reading our children a bedtime story; where holding the remote comes before hugging our wives; where surfing the Internet for content takes precedence over searching our hearts for meaning; a life where shopping on Sunday comes before resting on the Sabbath. A life with sporadic sparks and never an eternal flame.

A man who wanted to be a better person recited the following prayer: 'Dear G-d, so far today I've done all right. I haven't gossiped, and I haven't lost my temper. I haven't been grumpy, nasty or selfish, and I'm really glad of that! But in a few minutes, I'm going to get out of bed, and from then on, I'm probably going to need a lot of help. Thank you! Amen.' We pride ourselves today on our having supplanted G-d with our techno-wizardry. We have been released from the shackles of religion and entered the modern age. But what we have really is nothing but an illusion of freedom. Wherein lies our freedom today? Is the freedom to be on call to our cellphones 24 hours a day? Or is it the freedom to starve ourselves and become anorexic or bulimic just in order to walk into a bar and get looked over rather than overlooked? Or is it perhaps the freedom to sink ever deeper into our couches as we watch yet another mind-numbing sitcom or celebrity interview? Or is the freedom to be in servitude to the consumer culture where our principal passion becomes shopping and impulse purchases?

In previous generations people were on guard so as not to sell their souls to the devil. Friends, I'm here to tell you today that we thank G-d, have nothing to fear in that regard. Who among us has a soul left to sell anyway? All colour has been stripped from our spirit. Any individuality we once possessed has been supplanted by cookie-cutter conformity, as we receive our opinions and biases from the editorials we read in the morning papers and our great joy in life is reading of celebrity gossip. Other people's lives have become so much more interesting to us than our own. To paraphrase Abraham Lincoln, we all start out as G-d's original, but nearly all of us have ended up as man-made copies. It is no wonder then that our lives are weighed down by a laborious listlessness. And to counter that apathy and numbness, and guarantee that fire and passion will always pervade our lives, G-d gave us religion to set our lives aflame and take us up the mountain.

Man is the candle who is meant to be impassioned with G-d's heat, providing warmth to his fellow man. The Jews discover G-d as a devouring flame on the top of Mt Sinai. Moses discovers G-d in a burning bush. But where is that fire today? What caused religion to leave the mountain and enter the valleys? The answer, to our great sadness, is that what we are bequeathing our children today is a faith without G-d; rituals without spirit; a lifeless corpse rather than a living fountain. Religion has one purpose only: to serve as the ladder by which man ascends to G-d. But we have become more interested in Church attendance than heavenly ascendance. More interested in affiliation and membership than redemption and divine relationship. More interested in fighting iniquity than inspiring virtue. Rather than emancipating the spirit, organized religion has nailed it to a cross.

Last year a married, middle-aged woman came to me crying. 'I am the loneliest woman on earth.' Her husband objected. 'Look at how much money I spend on her,' and he showed me his credit card statements. 'I take her out to dinner and buy her so many gifts.' His wife shot him an ice-cold stare. 'You just don't get it. You do all those things not because you love me, but because you want to be a good husband.' We today all want to be religious rather than be in a relationship with G-d. We have become like the student who wants to get a degree but is indifferent to the acquisition of knowledge. Abraham Heschel said, 'When faith is completely replaced by creed, worship by discipline, love by habit. When religion speaks only in the name of authority rather than with the voice of compassion – its message becomes meaningless.'

And it was to forewarn against this danger – the possibility that religion itself should become a prison – that G-d came to Abraham in his old age and gave him the greatest test of all. 'Take your son Isaac and bring him as a sacrifice upon the mountain that I will show you.' What was the meaning behind this cruel commandment? Friends, the key to the story is the following critical point. Isaac wasn't Isaac. Isaac represented religion, the continuity of Abraham's faith and tradition. If Isaac were to die, religion would die with him. Everyone else was pagan. In this, the greatest of all tests, G-d was saying to Abraham: 'Take care that your religion, designed to be your liberation, does not end up your straightjacket!' G-d commanded Abraham to kill off Isaac, who represented his faith, to teach him that there will be times when the word of G-d will be in direct conflict with organized religion, and it is the word of G-d which must prevail. When religion commands you to murder people who are not of your faith, it is the religion itself which must be put to death. When religion makes you aflame with hatred, its fire must be extinguished. And when religion lifts you atop the 'holier than thou' mountain, sacrifice it upon G-d's holy mountain.

This mountain where Abraham was commanded to bring Isaac was the same mountain, Mt Moriah, which housed G-d's Temple in Jerusalem. The ancient Rabbis tell us why it was chosen. Centuries earlier two brothers lived there, one married with children, the other single. Together they owned a wheat field and each day they would gather up and divide the wheat. The married brother arrived home and thought, 'Is it fair that I take half of the produce when I have a wife and children to look after me and my brother has nothing? I will take part of my portion and give it to secretly to my brother.' Across the field the single brother made a similar calculation. 'Is it fair that I take half the wheat when I have only one mouth to feed?' That night, they both stole across the field and deposited a portion of their shares to the other. In the morning they were startled to discover that their portions had not been diminished. The following night they both tried again and awoke even more puzzled. Finally, on the third night, as the moon and the stars shone brightly, they set out to accomplish their mission. In the distance, each brother saw the other approaching, clutching a pile of wheat. They immediately understood what had been happening and fell into each other's arms and cried until the morning. Looking down at the love of these two brothers from the heavens, the Almighty said, 'On this mountain I shall build my Holy Temple.'

In this coming millennium, ladies and gentlemen, let us go up together to the mountain of the Lord and rebuild G-d's home. I am a Jew to my very bones and my Judaism is my life. I trust that the same can be said of the faith of my Christian brethren. But my Judaism is only important in so far as it teaches me to love Almighty G-d 'with all my heart, with all my soul, and with all my might'. And the only true test of my love for G-d is the degree to which I love his children. The ancient Jewish mystics taught that G-d is in hiding in our world. The only way to find Him is to connect with His image in this world, our human brothers and sisters.

When my wife gave birth to our second child in Oxford in the middle of the night, I waited in the hospital until five in the morning and then went to buy a newspaper. Outside the newsagents, a group of four ruffians were standing trying to nick *The Sunday Times*. One of them asked me what I was doing there so early. Frightened, but too tired to run or hide, I said, 'My wife just gave birth to a baby girl.' Then the biggest among them approached, threw his arms around me and said, 'That's amazing man. You just brought more G-d into the world.' And he put me on his shoulders and started to dance. Soon we were all dancing and singing with wild abandon like a bunch of lunatics in the soft morning light, not caring what anyone thought. We danced like King David when he brought G-d's holy ark into Jerusalem. And as I boogied over the birth of my child with total strangers, I suddenly felt moved by the spirit. Raising my hands high into the air I shouted the words of the old African-American spiritual, 'Free at last, free at last. Thank G-d Almighty, I'm free at last.'

The Judges

Shmuley Boteach
Last year's winner. See the final sermon in this collection (page 217).

Michael Saward
Canon Michael Saward, who retired as Canon Treasurer of St Paul's in 2000 after nearly nine years at Wren's outstanding cathedral, is one of the most prolific sermon writers and preachers of his generation. Priested in 1957, he served curacies in Croydon and Edgware before going to Liverpool to work as the secretary of the city's Council of Churches for two years. He then picked up some of his excellent communications skills as the Church of England's radio and television officer for five years before becoming Vicar of St Matthew's Fulham and then of Ealing, where he established a reputation as one of the Church's leading evangelicals. He has served as a member of the General Synod, as a Church Commissioner and on the committees of numerous trusts and charities. Besides sermons he also a prizewinning hymn writer and has edited numerous hymn books. His best-known hymn, 'Christ Triumphant', was recently described as 'surely one of the great hymns of our time'. He chaired the panel of judges for the St Paul's Millennium Hymn Competition. His many books include *And So to Bed?* and *Evangelicals on the Move* and his autobiography *A Faint Streak of Humility*. His views on the sermon today are spelled out in the foreword to this book.

Kieran Conry
For the past six years Monsignor Kieran Conry has been director of the Catholic Media Office, having been ordained as a Catholic priest in 1975. The first four years of his ministry were spent teaching in north Staffordshire; thereafter he was sent down to London to serve as Secretary to the Apostolic Nuncio, the Pope's representative to England and Wales. He returned to his own archdiocese in Birmingham, and then to the Cathedral parish at the city's heart. Now he lives in the parish house of St Thomas à Becket in Wandsworth, south-west London.

Kieran is realistic about the current status of the sermon, recognizing that the power of the spoken word as a living thing can be threatened by cultural forces such as the Internet. But he is hopeful that a widespread interest in communication may lead to a greater involvement in religious affairs, and acknowledges the importance of electronic media as useful tools.

Margaret Brearley

Dr Margaret Brearley, an Anglican, is married to Stephen, a general and vascular consultant surgeon. They have two sons. After studying at Oxford, Münster and Cambridge, she became a research academic in the German Department of Birmingham University, lecturing in mediaeval, Renaissance and Reformation literature and ideas, during which time she set up a day-centre for the mentally ill. Dr Brearley took early retirement after thirteen years in order to found and direct the West Midlands Israel Information Centre, based in Singer's Hall Synagogue. In 1987 she became Senior Fellow at the Centre for Judiasm and Jewish-Christian Relations at the Selly Oak Colleges, and from 1992 to 1996 was part-time Research Fellow in Christian-Jewish relations at the Institute of Jewish Affairs in London. She has recently adopted a new role, acting as Special Advisor on the Holocaust to the Archbishops' Council of the Church of England. She has lectured widely in Britain, Germany, Finland, Israel and the USA, and has published many articles.

Jonathan Romain

Rabbi, writer and broadcaster, Jonathan was born in 1954 and studied for the rabbinate at Leo Baeck College, having taken his first degree at UCL. He is currently the Director of the Jewish Information and Media Service, a member of the National Board of the Council of Christians and Jews, and a trustee of the Family Policy Studies Centre. He is married with four sons. His forthcoming book, *Your God shall be my God; religious conversion in Britain today*, develops a longstanding interest in questions of mixed or altered faith to point to a hidden revolution in the forms of contemporary worship – where the decline in church attendance conceals a radical increase in the numbers of those whose faith converts or changes.

Jonathan sees preachers as uniquely placed to counter the increasing isolation of modern society, providing in the church or the synagogue a rare opportunity for communities to gather together. This demands sermons that respond to these changing lifestyles but root themselves in tradition, 'where the key question to ask is; what one line will people take away from the sermon – and will it be worthwhile?'

Andrew Sails

The Revd Andrew Sails, 51, is chair of the panel this year. He went to Nottingham High School, Sussex and Cambridge Universities before entering the Methodist ministry in 1972. He worked for fifteen years as a University Chaplain in London, Brighton, Liverpool and Bristol. He then left the ministry to work for the NHS, eventually as Head of Strategic Programmes for the national NHS Training Division. In 1996 he returned to the Methodist ministry, where he is now minister in pastoral charge of the Central Hall and three other Methodist churches in the centre of Walsall. Whilst there, he has overseen a major building programme and development of the work at the Central Hall, which was chosen as the venue for the 2000 Preacher of the Year Final. Andrew is a great advocate of the preaching ministry, and was placed second in the final of the 1999 Preacher of the Year competition. He is married to Liz, and has two children, Dan and Katie, by his first marriage.

William Beaver

The Revd Dr William Beaver is the first Director of Communications of the Archbishops' Council of the Church of England. He is also holds that position for the Church Commissioners and the Pensions Board. Prior to this, he held the senior communications posts at the National Westminster Bank, the Industrial Society, Barnardo's and Pergammon AGB International Research.

Dr Beaver prepared for his doctorate and Holy Orders at Oxford while directing the University's Development Records Project for the Bodleian Library. Before Oxford, Dr Beaver was a regular serving Army officer. Dr Beaver's first curacy (lasting a mere fifteen years) was in Brixton at St John the Divine, Kennington. He then became priest-in-charge of St Andrew's, Avonmouth and is currently junior curate at St Mary Redcliffe, Bristol. He has served as a judge for *The Times* Preacher of the Year competition for three years.

Married to the Director of Health (Finance) of the Welsh Assembly, Dr Beaver is the Vice-chair of governors of the only five-form entry state girls' school in Lambeth, South London. His two young sons claim to know him by sight.